THE CORRESPONDENCE
OF
JOHN OWEN

THE CORRESPONDENCE OF JOHN OWEN (1616-1683)

With an account of his life and work

Edited by

PETER TOON

*Lecturer in Divinity,
Edge Hill College, Ormskirk, Lancs.*

Foreword by

Rev. Dr. Geoffrey F. Nuttall, M.A.

*Lecturer in Church History,
New College, London*

WIPF & STOCK · Eugene, Oregon

Wipf and Stock Publishers
199 W 8th Ave, Suite 3
Eugene, OR 97401

The Correspondence of John Owen (1616-1683)
With an account of his life and work
By Toon, Peter and Nuttall, Geoffrey F.
Copyright©1970 James Clarke & Co.
ISBN 13: 978-1-5326-4310-1
Publication date 11/10/2017
Previously published by James Clarke & Co., 1970

Preface

It was thirty years after the death of Dr John Owen that the first (anonymous) biography appeared. Though written by one 'who had the honour to know this eminent person well',[1] the little book of fifty-six pages had little information in its pages about Owen's life. Most of its pages described the contents of his books. A year later another short biography appeared written by John Asty who was given information about his subject by Sir John Hartopp who had known Owen personally.[2] Yet, as several writers have pointed out, this second biography contained less pages than books written by Owen. Furthermore Sir John had only known Owen from about the year 1665 and thus knew little about the years 1616 to 1665. The first serious attempt to provide a comprehensive biography was by William Orme in 1820.[3] A second improved edition came out in 1826 as Volume I of the Russell edition of *The Works of John Owen*. Orme performed a valiant task and collected much additional information about his hero. Yet, although he was willing to criticise certain scholastic tendencies in Owen's theological tomes, he was at pains to minimise Owen's involvement in the political affairs of the Commonwealth period. It was chiefly from the work of Orme that Andrew Thomson wrote his brief 'Life of Dr. Owen' found in *The Works of John Owen* (ed. W. H. Goold) in 1850, and from the same basic source James Moffatt wrote his brief biographies of Owen. One is found in *The Golden Book of John Owen* (1904) and the other in *The Life of Dr Owen* (1911) in the Congregational Worthies Series.

Although several important biographies of Richard Baxter have appeared in the last fifty years,[4] not one has appeared of John Owen. Why is this? We may make two suggestions. First, there is a scarcity of information about Owen. Whilst the student of Baxter has the famous *Reliquiæ* and many manuscript letters to peruse, the student of Owen has to rely on Asty and Orme and then work hard for every new piece of information. Secondly, it is exceedingly difficult to get to know John Owen as a man, a father, a College principal, or a pastor. One cannot, as it were, get beneath the views of the great theologian to the human being himself.

[1]*The Life of the late Reverend and Learned John Owen, D.D.*, 1720.
[2]This appeared in a folio volume entitled, *A Complete Collection of the Sermons of John Owen*, 1721.
[3]Orme, *Memoirs of the Life, Writings, and Religious Connections of John Owen.*
[4]e.g. by G. F. Nuttall and F. J. Powicke.

PREFACE

What follows is not meant to be a biography of John Owen. It is basically an edition of his extant correspondence set in a biographical framework. As only one incomplete letter remains for the first 35 years of his life I have sought in Part I to give a fairly full account of his life, work and thought in those years; but, in Parts II and III where there are many letters, I have given only a brief account of his life and supplied brief explanatory notes to the letters. It is my intention to produce in the near future a translation of Owen's University Orations with explanatory notes.

Ideally the Correspondence should have been printed on its own. Yet, as no biography of Owen is currently available, I thought that ordinary readers would be able to understand the letters better if they were given a short account of his Life and Work—especially of the formative years, 1616 to 1651.

When I began work on Owen at Durham in August 1967 I knew of only the nine letters which are mentioned in Vol. I of his *Works* (ed. Goold). That I have over the last two years traced about a hundred is due to the generous help of Dr Geoffrey F. Nuttall, the staff of the Western Manuscripts Department of the Bodleian Library and of the Public Record Office, London. S. M. Houghton, P. T. Hornsby and H. R. P. McDermott also helped me and so did my wife.

Permission to print material from Christ Church archives was kindly given by the Dean and Chapter, and the Keeper of the University Archives, W. L. Pantin, gave permission to make extensive use of the Register of Convocation.

Edge Hill College,
Ormskirk, Lancs.
   August 1969
                                                    Peter Toon.

Foreword

EVERY student of religion in mid-seventeenth-century England is familiar with the name of John Owen. He has his place in any serious study, whether of theology or of politics, particularly, though not only, during the Interregnum. Some of his numerous and voluminous works have recently been reprinted. His life and thought have been the subject of more than one academic thesis. Despite this, the man himself remains strangely elusive. As James Moffatt puts it in *The Golden Book of John Owen* (1904)—still the most penetrating account of Owen—his mind "was essentially abstract"; "deficient in imaginative power", "he failed to allow for the wind". His "dry, stiff prose" is often "wooden" and "wire-drawn", his contribution generally "solid but stolid". I have often wondered whether one might not come closer to him through his letters but these, so far as previously published, amount to no more than a round dozen.

Mr. Toon thus deserves very warm thanks for his labour in, for the first time, collecting and editing Owen's letters. Alongside many other interests, he has for a number of years given himself with remarkable devotion to research on Owen. For Owen's letters he has looked far and wide, not only in a variety of published works, but in the manuscript collections of libraries in this country and beyond. This book is the result. I take peculiar pleasure in commending it in that the library of New College, London, has provided him with material. In some sense New College is Owen's residual legatee. We have sermons as well as letters by him among our manuscripts. We have a very considerable collection of his published writings, ranging from a rubricated and sumptuously bound copy of his *Hebrews*, which is thought to have been a presentation copy (probably to Sir John Hartopp), to those often anonymous and slight but weighty pieces contributed by him to the post-Restoration debate over relations between Church and State. We also have a portrait of Owen which at one time was in the possession of the D'Oyley family, into which he married. According to experts, however, this is less a likeness than an imaginary reconstruction.

For a true portrait, therefore, we come back to Owen's letters. These also throw light at various points on the multifarious concerns which give his life its outward importance and fascination. He was Vice-Chancellor of the University of Oxford, and active in Oxford, yet he stood close to the Lord Protector in the Councils of the Commonwealth, and would have represented the University in Parliament, had not his episcopal orders, though now repudiated, debarred him. A cool scholar, "an Aristotle among Puritans" as Stoughton calls him, he yet ranked ecclesiastically as well as politically with the Independents, stayed unshakeable in his detestation of read prayer as "false worship", and held the notion that *things* could be "dedicated" to be "the greatest ruin that ever befell religion in this world". A leader of the theologians who drew up the Savoy *Declaration* in 1658 and one who himself claimed to be the first to represent "the whole oeconomy of the Holy Spirit", he yet "would most gladly relinquish" all his learning in exchange for Bunyan the tinker's "abilities for preaching", and acclaimed "the most superstitious love to Christ" as "better than none at all". Owen is clearly a real *person*, and one worth coming to grips with. Mr. Toon's book will help us to do this.

New College, London.   GEOFFREY F. NUTTALL

Contents

PART I: 1616-1651

I	THE EARLY YEARS	3
II	AN ESSEX MINISTER	14
III	CHAPLAIN TO OLIVER CROMWELL	32

PART II: ATLAS OF INDEPENDENCY 1651–1660

IV	INTRODUCTORY	45
V	CORRESPONDENCE	50

PART III: PATRIARCH OF INDEPENDENCY 1660–1683

VI	INTRODUCTORY	125
VII	CORRESPONDENCE	129

APPENDICES

I	The Works of Dr John Owen	175
II	Books which contain 'Prefaces', 'Epistles to the Reader' or 'Commendations' by Dr John Owen	178
III	Proposal for Indulgence	180
IV	The Will of Dr John Owen	181
	Printed and Manuscript Sources	187
	Index of Correspondents	189

List of Correspondence

1.	From the Commissioners in Ireland	2 July	1651	50
2.	From Lewis Du Moulin	Sept.	1652	51
3.	From Oliver Cromwell	16 Oct.	1652	52
4.	From Oliver Cromwell	28 Oct.	1652	54
5.	From Oliver Cromwell		1652	54
6.	To the Master of Balliol College	22 Nov.	1652	55
7.	To the Parliament		1652	56
8.	From the Committee for Public Revenue	14 Dec.	1652	58
9.	From the Commissioners in Ireland	31 Aug.	1653	59
10.	To the City of London	13 Sept.	1653	59
11.	From Baron Herbert of Cherbury	23 July	1653	61
12.	From Oliver Cromwell	14 Oct.	1653	62
13.	From Oliver Cromwell	24 Oct.	1653	62
14.	From the Visitors of Oxford University	8 Nov.	1653	63
15.	From Oliver Cromwell		1653	64
16.	To the Lord Protector	Dec.	1653	64
17.	From the Lord Protector	28 Dec.	1653	65
18.	To the Congregational Churches	9 Jan.	1654	66
19.	To the Evangelical Churches of Europe	[Mar. 1654]		68
20.	From Charnell Petty	10 June	1654	70
21.	From Henry Lawrence		1654	71
22.	To the Lord Protector	9 Aug.	1654	72
23.	From Edward Lowe	Sept.	1654	73
24.	From the Lord Protector	31 Oct.	1654	74
25.	To Henry Wilkinson		1654	74
26.	To the Parliament	18 Nov.	1654	75
27.	To Bulstrode Whitelock	26 Nov.	1654	76
28.	To Sir Thomas Widdrington	26 Nov.	1654	77
29.	To the Lord Protector	Dec.	1654	78
30.	From Philip Henry		1655	79
31.	From George Gale and Edward Farrar	22 Feb.	1655	81
32.	To John Thurloe	20 Mar.	1655	82
33.	From Thomas Down	30 Mar.	1655	83
34.	To John Thurloe	29 May	1655	84
35.	From the Lord Protector	22 Aug.	1655	84

LIST OF CORRESPONDENCE

36.	To the Lord Protector	2 Oct.	1655	85
37.	From John Wallis	10 Oct.	1655	86
38.	From Henry Lawrence	16 Nov.	1655	88
39.	From Henry Lawrence	20 Nov.	1655	88
40.	From Robert Wickens		1655	89
41.	From Thomas Gilbert		1655	91
42.	From the Lord Protector	4 Mar.	1656	92
43.	From the Lord Protector	25 Mar.	1656	92
44.	From Francis Martyn	17 July	1656	93
45.	From the Lord Protector		1656	94
46.	To Nathaniel Fiennes	9 Feb.	1657	94
47.	From John Beverley	24 Feb.	1657	96
48.	To George Kendall		1657	98
49.	From the Lord Protector	3 July	1657	98
50.	From Henry Lawrence	16 July	1657	99
51.	From Richard Cromwell	29 July	1657	100
52.	To Henry Cromwell	9 Sept.	1657	100
53.	From Richard Cromwell	5 Oct.	1657	101
54.	To John Maidstone	Jan.	1658	102
55.	To Lady Elizabeth Puleston	26 Jan.	1658	103
56.	From Lady Elizabeth Puleston	Aug.	1658	103
57.	From Richard Salwey	24 Sept.	1658	104
58.	To General Monck	31 Oct.	1659	105
59.	To General Monck	19 Nov.	1659	106
60.	From General Monck	23 Nov.	1659	109
61.	From General Monck	29 Nov.	1659	110
62.	To General Monck	13 Dec.	1659	112
63.	From General Monck	22 Dec.	1659	114
64.	From Thomas Truthsbye		1660	116
65.	Legal documents and correspondence from 'Christ Church Chapter Book'	1651 to 1657		118
66.	Legal documents and correspondence from the 'Register of Convocation'	1651 to 1657		119
67.	From Unton Croke	11 Aug.	1653	121
68.	To John Thornton		1662	129
69.	To John Thornton		[1663]	130
70.	To John Thornton		[1663]	132
71.	From the General Court of Massachusetts	20 Oct.	1663	135
72.	To Richard Baxter	25 Jan.	1669	136
73.	From Richard Baxter	16 Feb.	1669	138
74.	To the Governor of Massachusetts	25 Mar.	1669	145

75.	To the Independent Church at Hitchin	18 June 1669	146
76.	To Charles Nichols	10 Nov. [1670]	148
77.	From the Magistrates and Ministers of Massachusetts	21 Aug. 1671	149
78.	To the Magistrates and Ministers of Massachusetts	5 Feb. 1672	151
79.	To John Eliot	[1672]	153
80.	To Lord Wharton	[1673]	155
81.	To Lord Wharton	11 May [1673]	155
82.	To Lord Wharton	[1673]	156
83.	To Lady Elizabeth Hartopp	[May 1674]	157
84.	To Sir John Hartopp	3 July [1674]	158
85.	To Charles Fleetwood	8 July [1674]	159
86.	To Sir John Hartopp	21 Aug. [1674]	160
87.	To Sir John Hartopp	2 Sept. [1674]	160
88.	To Robert Asty	16 Mar. [1675]	161
89.	To Robert Asty	2 Jan. 1679	162
90.	To Robert Asty	25 April 1679	163
91.	To an unknown recipient	[1679]	164
92.	To Monsieur Peter Du Moulin	[1679]	165
93.	To Mrs Polhill	[1680]	168
94.	To the Church meeting in Leadenhall Street	[1680]	170
95.	To Thomas Whitaker	29 Oct. [1681]	172
96.	To Charles Fleetwood	6 Aug. 1682	172
97.	From Edmund King	26 Jan. 1683	173
98.	To Charles Fleetwood	22 Aug. 1683	173

Abbreviations

Abbott	W. C. Abbott, *The Writings and Speeches of Oliver Cromwell*, 4 vols., Cambridge, Mass., 1937–47.
Asty	John Asty, 'Memoir of Dr Owen' in *A Complete Collection of the Sermons of John Owen*, 1721.
C.J.	*The Journals of the House of Commons*.
C.R.	*Calamy Revised* (ed. A. G. Matthews), Oxford, 1934.
C.S.P.D.	*Calendar of State Papers* (Domestic).
D.N.B.	*Dictionary of National Biography*.
L.J.	*The Journals of the House of Lords*.
Reg. Convoc.	'Register of Convocation, 1647–1659'. (In the Bodleian Library.)
Register.	*The Register of the Visitors of the University of Oxford from A.D. 1647 to A.D. 1658* (ed. M. Burrows), 1881.
Thomason	*Catalogue of the Pamphlets, Books, Newspapers Collected by George Thomason, 1640–1661*, 2 vols., 1908.
Wood	*The Life and Times of Anthony Wood* (ed. A. Clark), vol. I, 1891.
Works	*The Works of John Owen* (ed. William H. Goold), 1850–53.

PART I
1616–1651

CHAPTER I

The Early Years

JOHN OWEN was born in England but his ancestors and some of his relatives lived in Wales. His father, Henry Owen, was born about 1586 in Merionethshire, being a descendant of 'baron' Lewis Owen who died in 1555.[1] Anthony Wood[2] informs us that Henry Owen was educated at Oxford and then taught in a school at Stokenchurch[3] in the parish of Aston Rowant. Some time after the death in March 1615 of Walter Chaundler,[4] who was curate of Stadham (now Stadhampton) with Chislehampton near Oxford, he was presented to the vicarage by the D'Oyley family who owned the local manor house.[5]

Henry Owen was married before he moved to Stadhampton. A son, William, was born to his wife in 1612, another son, John, in 1616, and Philemon in 1622.[6] There were also other children—a son, Henry, and at least one girl.[7] William was educated at Queen's College, Oxford, and ordained as a minister of the Church of England. He was at Ewelme, near Oxford, for several years, where he probably acted as curate and taught in the parish school before he moved in 1648 to

[1] Cf. *Dictionary of Welsh Biography* (1959), s.v. John Owen.
[2] Wood, *Athenae Oxonienses* (ed. P. Bliss), Vol. IV, col. 97.
[3] No records exist describing a school there in the early part of the seventeenth century but in 1675 a school was endowed by Bartholomew Tipping for 'instructing twelve boys in reading, writing, and casting of accounts' which probably took over the work of a school that had previously existed. I am grateful to Miss Mary Towerton, J.P., of Stokenchurch, for this information.
[4] According to the parish registers (in the Bodleian Library) he was buried 7 March 1614/15. In 1618 'Peter Wilmott did build the Tomb upon Mr Chaundler grave at the Chancell End, at his own Charge, in love that he bore to Mr Chaundler'. In view of this it seems unlikely that Henry Owen was at Stadhampton before 1618.
[5] For the D'Oyley family see, William D'Oyley Bayley, *A Biographical, Historical, Genealogical, and Heraldic Account of the House of D'Oyley*, 1845.
[6] These dates of birth are from *Alumni Oxonienses*. There are no records of the baptisms of any Owen children in the Stadhampton registers, neither are there any in the Aston Rowant registers. *Biographia Britannica* states that John Owen was born at Hadham near Watlington but there is no such place. S. Lewis, *Topographical Dictionary*, states that he was born both at Stadhampton and at Much Hadham in Hertfordshire! But the parish registers of both Much and Little Hadham contain no reference to any members of the Owen family. Probably the children were baptised in the home and thus no record was made in any parish register.
[7] A John Singleton is said to be a nephew of John Owen (cf. *C.R.*, p. 443), so presumably there was a Miss Owen who married a Mr Singleton.

Remenham in Berkshire, where he died in 1660.[8] Philemon matriculated on 14 December 1638 in All Souls College, Oxford, but never seems to have graduated. He fought in the parliamentary army which went to Ireland in 1649 and was killed there.[9] Henry also joined the parliamentary army which went to Ireland and was a Major in Sir John Reynolds' regiment until 1657 when he became a Major in the Lord Protector's regiment.[10] He supported the move to make Cromwell a king and represented Ireland in the Protector's Parliaments. After 1660 he seems to have lived in lodgings in Gray's Inn and to have kept in touch with his (by that time) famous brother, John.[11]

(a) *Education* 1628 to 1637

The routine of the vicarage at Stadhampton was moulded by Puritan principles. Regular daily worship, strict observance of the Lord's Day, a dislike of Popery and all popish ceremonies in worship, the need for a personal inward religion, and a deep regard for the Bible as God's only authoritative Word to mankind, were instilled into the children. The only reference that John Owen makes to his father reveals that though he was a beneficed clergyman of the Church of England Henry Owen did not keep to the canonical and liturgical requirement of the Elizabethan Settlement of Religion. 'I was bred up from my infancy', wrote John in 1657, 'under the care of my father, who was a nonconformist all his days, and a painful labourer in the vineyard of the Lord.'[12]

With his brother William, John was sent to the grammar school kept by Edward Sylvester in a private house in the parish of All Saints, Oxford,[13] in order to be prepared for entrance into the University. The fees for the two boys, both at this period and later when they were in Queen's College, were paid by an uncle, probably a brother of their father, who lived in Wales.

Queen's College (originally Quene Hall) was founded in 1340/1 by Robert de Eglesfield, chaplain to Queen Philippa, who herself assisted in its foundation. In the 1360s and 1370s it had sheltered John Wyclif, the Bible translator, within its walls. When John and William Owen entered its gates the Provost of the College was Christopher Potter.

[8]The House of Lords authorised William to go to Remenham on 28 September 1648. *L.J.*, Vol. X, p 516. There is a reference to his death in 1660 in MS. Archd. pprs. Berks. d. 8, fol. 205 in the Bodleian.

[9]*C.J.*, Vol. VII, p. 39, refers to an Elizabeth Owen, widow of Captain Philemon Owen, who died 'in the service' in Ireland.

[10]Cf. C. Firth and G. Davies, *The Regimental History of Cromwell's Army*, Oxford, 1940, p. 594.

[11]*C.S.P.D.* (1682), p. 106.

[12]*Works*, Vol. XIII, p. 224.

[13]Cf. A. Wood, *Fasti Oxonienses* (ed. P. Bliss), Vol. II, p. 34, for details of Sylvester.

From the diary kept by Thomas Crosfield,[14] who was a Fellow at Queen's in this period, we are able to catch a glimpse of student life. On many mornings there was a Latin sermon in the chapel at 6 a.m. followed by breakfast. Lectures, tutorials, and disputations (exercises in logical argument) took up the hours before dinner at 10 a.m. After dinner there was time for sports before more disputations and lectures were held. After chapel in the afternoon the evenings were spent in private study. The Michaelmas term began on 9 October with a parade of the whole College, led by the Provost, up the High Street to St Mary's to hear a Latin sermon. On the following morning there was a celebration of Holy Communion, attendance at which was compulsory, in the College chapel, after which the courses in the various faculties began. Perhaps the happiest day in College life was Founder's Day, 15 August (the *obiit* of Queen Philippa). Former Fellows returned to Oxford to gaudy, to drink from the founder's loving-cup, and to keep up their merriment for several days. Another great social occasion for the College as well as the University was the annual Oxford Act or *Comitia*, held on the Monday immediately following 7 July. The ceremonies, which began on the Saturday and ended on the Tuesday, signified the close of the academic year. They included disputations, processions, the conferring of degrees, a speech by the Vice-Chancellor as well as the time-honoured custom of *Terrae Filius* (the elected wag of the students who was allowed the greatest licence to dress up and say what he liked).

John entered Queen's at the tender age of twelve years but was not allowed to matriculate until 4 November 1631 when he was fifteen. He became Bachelor of Arts on 11 June 1632, the same day on which his brother William also graduated. To secure the B.A. degree John and William, with all other students, were required to be in residence for sixteen terms or four years,[15] to attend specified lectures in College or in the Schools of the University, and to perform prescribed academic exercises. Lectures were on such subjects as grammar, rhetoric, dialectic, logic, arithmetic, Greek and music. Several terms were given to each subject. The academic exercises were scholastic disputations or formal organised debates. They had developed in the medieval universities as a means of resolving questions left in doubt by the best authorities and as a way of reconciling conflicting opinions or conclusions. After a controversial point from logic, grammar or philosophy had been cast into the form of a question the debate proceeded in three stages. A participant (called the respondent) offered an answer

[14]*The Diary of Thomas Crosfield* (ed. F. S. Boas), 1935.
[15]The year had four terms: mid-October to mid-December, mid-January to the eve of Palm Sunday, the tenth day after Easter to the Thursday before Whitsuntide, and the Wednesday after Trinity Sunday to the Saturday before the Act.

to or an interpretation of the question. Next, several opponents stated contradictory propositions attacking flaws in the respondent's reasoning. Finally came the determination. The moderator who presided over the proceedings summed up the arguments on each side, called attention to aspects of the question that had not been covered, bestowed praise or blame as due, and gave his decision. During the first two years of the course, John and William were probably only required to respond twice at the Lenten disputations before the determining Bachelors. Apart from the academic exercises John also found time for physical exercises and was fond of ringing bells, leaping, and throwing the bar.

Bachelorship did not signify the completion of a course of study but only of the attainment of a standing or status sufficient to qualify a student to pursue higher studies for the Mastership, which was considered to be a degree in the full sense of the word. John was fortunate in having Thomas Barlow,[16] a distinguished Aristotelian scholar, as his tutor for the M.A. course, which included Greek, geometry, astronomy, natural philosophy, metaphysics, moral philosophy, and Hebrew. From his tutor he imbibed 'a full draught of Oxford learning at a time when the streams of controversy were in tumultous conflict'.[17] And as Mark Curtis has shown 'the work of College tutors was definitely in the seventeenth century the most important influence on a scholar's education'.[18] As a perusal of the books he wrote later shows, John Owen never forgot his training in Aristotelian logic and method. Unlike some of his Puritan contemporaries at Cambridge, he never seems to have been introduced to the Ramist critique of Aristotelianism. So great was his zeal for knowledge that often he only allowed himself four hours sleep each day; this ill-advised extra study impaired his health and he regretted it later in life. His interests were not confined to the compulsory subjects for the M.A. He took music lessons with Dr Thomas Wilson and learned to play the flute. Twenty years later, when he was Vice-Chancellor, he appointed Thomas Wilson professor of music.

On 27 April 1635 both John and William received the degree of M.A. Since their father intended both his sons for the ministry of the Church they were ordained by Bishop Bancroft of Oxford.[19] Still in receipt of an allowance from his uncle, John began the seven-year course of theological study for the Bachelor of Divinity degree. This

[16] For details of his career see *D.N.B.*
[17] *Register*, p. xxix.
[18] M. H. Curtis, *Oxford and Cambridge in Transition*, Oxford, 1959, p. 107.
[19] I was unable to trace any records of ordinations in the Diocese of Oxford in the 1630s. Therefore we do not know the exact date of ordination to the diaconate and whether or not they were made priest.

gave him an opportunity to read widely in both English and Continental authors and come to grips with the whole controversy between Roman Catholics and Protestants, as well as with the controversies over grace and predestination which had rocked the Protestant churches throughout Europe.

In the 1630s Queen's College could hardly be called a Puritan College.[20] From the days of Queen Elizabeth the theology taught there had been Calvinistic in tone. Barlow himself was certainly of this mould but he also believed in diocesan episcopacy and wanted the Church of England to remain faithful to the Book of Common Prayer. Many of the senior members of the College were of like mind although some, like the Provost, favoured Arminian views. In obedience to the wishes of Archbishop Laud, the new Chancellor of the University, Provost Potter revived in the College chapel, after 1633, practices which his predecessors had abhorred as papistical! He required staff and students to bow to the holy table and at the mention of the name 'Jesus', to wear surplices, and to stand for the reading of the Creed and Gospel. Sometimes he even burned incense. He pleased the Chancellor by beautifying the chapel at a cost of £2,800 which had been saved in the College chest since 1603. A few years later he was able to send £800 from the College and £400 from his own resources to King Charles to help the royalist cause in the civil war. It is worthy also of note that in 1642 all the Fellows of Queen's were royalists: to this day the College prays for 'King Charles the Martyr' as a benefactor.

After the new statutes for the University were ratified in 1636 the influence of Laud was supreme.[21] Zealous Puritans could only remain if they were ready to compromise their principles by using the Book of Common Prayer and by taking part in 'ceremonies'. Some University men left to settle in New England, joining parish ministers and lecturers who were feeling the pressure of the Laudian administration. John Owen's departure from Oxford in 1637 was certainly caused by his inability to conform to the Laudian requirements as put into force by the Provost of Queen's. Being an ordained clergyman, he was required to say Matins and Evensong and take part in the celebration of Holy Communion in the chapel with all the 'popish dress' and ceremony this involved. The 'nonconformist' blood of his father flowed in the veins of the son and sadly, but with a clear conscience, he left the University when a brilliant academic career lay before him. It was 'an opposition to Episcopacy and ceremonies' that made him leave,

---

[20] A recent history of Queen's College is R. H. Hodgkin, *Six Centuries of an Oxford College*, Oxford, 1949.

[21] Cf. C. E. Mallet, *A History of the University of Oxford*, 1924, Vol. II, pp. 303ff.

he told Daniel Cawdry twenty years later.[22] In a sermon to Parliament nine years later he had some strong words to say about the Laudian innovations:

> Now, such were the innovations of the late hierarchists. In worship, their paintings, crossings, crucifixes, bowings, cringings, altars, tapers, wafers, organs, anthems, litany, rails, images, copes, vestments—what were they but Roman varnish, an Italian dress for our devotion, to draw on conformity with that enemy of the Lord Jesus? In doctrine, the divinity of Episcopacy, auricular confession, free-will, predestination on faith, yea, works foreseen, 'limbus patrum', justification by works, falling from grace, authority of a church, which none knew what it was, canonical obedience, holiness of churches, and the like innumerable—what were they but helps to Sancta Clara, to make all our articles of religion speak good Roman Catholic? How did their old father of Rome refresh his spirit, to see such chariots as those provided to bring England again unto him.[23]

Whether he felt as bitter in 1637 as he did in 1646 we are unable to tell. Yet as young men of twenty years of age are very prone to become over-zealous for a cause they support, it is very probable that he did. But he little realised as he left his rooms in Queen's that in fifteen years' time he would be occupying the large and important rooms of the Dean of Christ Church not many hundred yards away.

(b) *Chaplain and Tutor, 1637 to 1642*

John Owen did not go far away from Oxford or Stadhampton. He accepted an invitation to become chaplain to Sir Robert Dormer and tutor to his eldest son at the manor house in the hamlet of Ascot in the parish of Great Milton.[24] The Dormer family also owned property in Stadhampton and in 1633 Sir Robert had been given permission to erect a pew near the pulpit in the parish church there.[25] Thus Henry Owen and Sir Robert knew each other and John's appointment to the chaplaincy probably grew out of this relationship. Attached to the manor house in Ascot was a private chapel built about A.D. 1200. It was in this chapel that, according to Anthony Wood,[26] Owen did 'all things requisite to his office according to the Church of England'. Possibly all that this statement means is that he said Matins and

---

[22]*Works*, Vol. XIII, p. 223.
[23]*Works*, Vol. VIII, p. 28.
[24]*Victoria County History of Oxfordshire*, Vol. VII, pp. 117ff.
[25]ibid, p. 90.
[26]*Ath. Oxon.*, Vol. IV, col. 97.

Evensong each day, since the family would probably have taken Holy Communion in the parish church.

About the same time that Henry Owen moved from the vicarage in Stadhampton to the parish of Harpsden in Berkshire,[27] John moved to Hurley, which was only five miles away. It is tempting to see some connection between these moves but the lack of documentary evidence makes it impossible to draw any reliable conclusions. John became chaplain to Lord John Lovelace who lived in the mansion house which went by the name of 'Ladye Place'.[28] Originally a priory, the house was bought by the Lovelace family in 1545. After about two years in the service of Lord Lovelace a crisis loomed between the king and Parliament and people began to decide which party they supported. Lord Lovelace declared himself a supporter of Charles I whilst his chaplain sympathised with Parliament. So when civil war broke out, the young clergyman had to leave the quiet life of Hurley and move to London where he had relatives. Perhaps it was with them that he took lodgings. News of his decision to support the Parliament against the king came as a shock to his Welsh uncle who immediately cancelled his allowance and disinherited him.

From 1629 to 1640, the period often referred to as the 'eleven years' tyranny', Charles I had ruled without calling a Parliament, but, to raise money for further war against the Scots he had to recall Parliament. The new assembly was in no mood to be bullied by the king, and the 'Short Parliament', as it is usually called, was dissolved by Charles only three weeks after it had begun to sit. A few months later, with the Scottish army occupying the North of England, Charles had no alternative but to throw himself on the mercy of elected representatives of the nation. On 3 November 1640 the 'Long Parliament' met in a black mood, determined not only on reform of national government, but also on keeping the king in his place. It was not long before the Earl of Strafford, Charles's faithful servant, was executed and the unpopular Archbishop Laud put in the Tower of London. The king had to agree that Parliament could not be dissolved against its own will. A majority of the M.P.s made it clear that they wished to abolish English bishoprics and their hatred of Roman Catholicism and any-

---

[27]Henry Owen died in 1649. A brass plate commemorating him is over the entrance to the vestry of St Margaret's Church, Harpsden-cum-Bolney. The parish registers make no mention of Henry Owen but on 28 May 1650 the marriage of Mrs Hester Owen and Mr John Hartcliffe, is recorded. Hartcliffe was the minister of Harpsden at that time. Cf. *C.R.* On 8 September 1674 Mary Owen, the daughter of William Owen, married Bartholomew Hall of Harpsden. The present Principal of Brasenose College, Oxford, Sir Noel Hall, and the retired Bishop of Hong Kong, Ronald Hall, are direct descendants of Bartholomew and Mary Hall.

[28] *Victoria County History of Berkshire*, Vol. III, p. 155.

thing that savoured of it was deepened by news of 'the great massacre' of Protestants in Ireland. The tension between Charles and Parliament grew in intensity. In June 1642 the two Houses of Parliament dispatched to the king who was in York their proposals for a settlement. In the 'Nineteen Propositions' they set out a new constitution under which Parliament would become the supreme power in the land: no Privy Councillors or Ministers of State were to be appointed except with its approval: judges were to hold office only during good behaviour: the army was to come under parliamentary control and the future of the Church of England was to be determined by Parliament. In effect the 'Nineteen Propositions' were an ultimatum by men who appeared ready for war. The king rejected them and war broke out.

(c) *In London and Kent*, 1642–3

It would seem that although John Owen was committed by 1637 to the Puritan way of life and worship, he did not before late 1642 have that peace of heart and mind for which Puritan pastors bade their people search. A Puritan casuist would probably have diagnosed that while he was certainly one of God's elect and regenerate, he did not possess the assurance of salvation; the Spirit of God had not yet witnessed to his spirit that he was a child of God (Romans 8:16). Happily Owen found what his soul desired in St Mary's Church, Aldermanbury. He went with his cousin to hear the famous Presbyterian preacher, Edmund Calamy, who was parish minister there. On arrival they were told that Calamy was unable to preach. His cousin wanted to leave and hurry to nearby St Michael's to hear Arthur Jackson, but John Owen decided that he wanted to remain. The preacher turned out to be an obscure country minister whose name he was never able to ascertain. Yet the preacher's message from Matthew 8:26, 'Why are ye fearful, O ye of little faith?', was so well suited to his need that the assurance of salvation he now received enabled him, in the words of St Paul, 'to rejoice in hope of the glory of God.'

It is quite possible that his spiritual problems were the outcome of his theological reading. The clash between the orthodox Calvinists and the Arminians in Holland both before and after the Synod of Dort (1618), with its repercussions in England, and, more importantly for Owen's experience, the growth of Arminian doctrines in England under the 'eleven years' tyranny' of Charles I and Archbishop Laud, must have caused him and all thoughtful young men to seek to understand the issues at stake in the Arminian controversy. Therefore it is no surprise to learn that his first book dealt with aspects of this controversy. The abundance of references and quotations he supplied in the book from the divines who were involved in the debates in Holland from 1612 to 1640 shows his wide reading. His manuscript must have been well on the way to completion by the time he left Hurley in late 1642, since permission to publish it was given by the Committee of the House of Commons, which dealt with the publication of books, on 2 March, 1643.[29] The title was *A Display of Arminianism: being a discovery of the old Pelagian idol, free-will, with the new goddess contingency, advancing themselves into the throne of God in heaven, to the prejudice of his grace, providence, and supreme dominion over the children of men.* He dedicated it 'to the right honourable, the Lords and Gentlemen of the Committee for Religion'. This Committee was set up in March 1640 by the House of Lords to examine innovations in doctrine introduced into the Church of England. His purpose in desiring to have the work published may be seen in the following quotation from the 'Epistle to the Christian Reader':

> The fates of our church having of late devolved the government thereof into the hands of men tainted with this poison [Arminianism] became backed with the powerful arguments of praise and preferment, and quickly prevailed to beat poor naked Truth into a corner. It is high time, then, for all the lovers of the old way to oppose this innovation, prevailing by such unworthy means, before our breach grows great like the sea, and there be none to heal it. My intention in this weak endeavour (which is but the undigested issue of a few broken hours, too many causes, in these furious malignant days, continually interrupting the course of my studies), is but to stir up such who, having more leisure and greater abilities, will not as yet move a finger to help to vindicate oppressed truth.

In fact, no one defended the doctrine of orthodox Calvinism in the next forty years with more zeal and ability than did John Owen himself.

The book deals in particular with only two of the five major areas of disagreement between orthodox Calvinists and the Remonstrants or Arminians, those of divine predestination and the limits of human free-will. Owen quoted copiously from the works of the Dutch Remonstrants (e.g. Episcopius) as well as from Arminius in order to show the resemblance of their doctrines to those of Pelagius, whom Augustine of Hippo had opposed in the fifth century, and to show how their interpretation did not convey the true sense of Scripture. This

---

[29] Thomason dated his copy 19 April 1643, so it was presumably published in mid-April.

first adventure into print by John Owen revealed that he was a gifted scholar and that his doctrines of God and His salvation for sinful men were in essence identical with those agreed upon by the great Synod of Dort. He adhered resolutely to this theology for the rest of his life and defended it unceasingly. If then the years from 1637 to 1642 were spent in coming to conclusions as to what was the 'correct' teaching about God's grace to men, we shall see that the next three or four years were to be spent in arriving at a conclusion concerning the doctrine of the Church.

Only one minor item of information has survived concerning Owen's activities in London in the winter of 1642/3. On 24 March 1643 several citizens of London petitioned the House of Lords about a certain John Barnes (or Baynes), a goldsmith who worked in the Strand, and who was in debt to them. He had been in prison but was released on the information that he was Lord Morley's servant. The petitioners asked the Lords to rearrest him and to ensure he paid his debts. To make their case stronger they enclosed information about Barnes that was not to his advantage, especially since Parliament was at war with the king. Part of this information was an affidavit by John Owen in which he stated that the man was 'a recusant convict, a Sabbath-breaker, and one that had lately been with the cavaliers at Oxford'.[30] The use of the word 'lately' seems to mean 'within the last few weeks'. If so this suggests that Owen had been back to Oxfordshire, perhaps to visit his family.

In November and December 1642, before he signed the affidavit, John Owen stayed at Scot's Hall in the parish of Smeeth, near Ashford in Kent. His host was Sir Edward Scott. During his stay the county was in great danger because of the possibility (in Owen's words) of 'the invasion of a potent enemy prevailing in the neighbour county' of Sussex.[31] Presumably 'the potent enemy' was the Earl of Thanet who made efforts to march through Sussex into Kent to support an uprising there led by Sir William Brockman. Again in the summer of 1643 he was at Smeeth when, to use his own words again, the county was 'in great danger to be ruined by the horrid insurrection of a rude, godless, multitude'. This was the Kentish Rebellion of July 1643.[32] Perhaps Owen was invited to the house because of his friendship with

---

[30] *Fifth Report of the Royal Commission on Historical Manuscripts*, 1876, p. 78, and cf. *L.J.* Vol. V., p. 668.

[31] This and the following quotations are from the dedicatory letter to Sir Edward Scott printed in Owen's second book, *The Duty of Pastors* (1644), in *Works*, Vol. XIII.

[32] The political situation in Kent in this period is described by A. M. Everitt, *The Community of Kent and the Great Rebellion, 1640–1660*, Leicester University Press, 1966, pp. 186 ff.

C[harles] Westrow, Lady Scott's son by her first marriage.³³ Of this young man Owen held the highest opinion: 'His judgement to discern the differences of these times, and his valour in prosecuting what he is resolved to be just and lawful, place him among the number of those very few to whom it is given to know aright the causes of things, and vigorously to execute holy and laudable designs'. Another resident at Scot's Hall at this time was Thomas Rooke, a kinsman of Sir Edward's, who was the treasurer in Shepway for the collection organised by the County Committee.³⁴ Since John Owen married a Miss Mary Rooke in 1644 this meeting with Thomas Rooke may have been a source of introduction to the young lady.

---

³³ Owen was a student at Queen's College at the same time as Thomas Westrow who became M.P. for Hythe in 1645. Presumably Charles and Thomas were brothers but it may well be that the letter 'C' is a printer's mistake and it should be a 'T' which would mean that it refers to Thomas.

³⁴ Cf. Everitt, op. cit., pp. 155–6.

CHAPTER II

An Essex Minister

(a) *At Fordham*

John Owen's first pastoral charge was at Fordham, a village five miles to the west of Colchester, Essex, at the parish church of All Saints. John Alsop,[1] the rector since 1633, had been a chaplain to Archbishop Laud after whose death in 1645 he fled to France. Between the time of the disgrace of Laud and his death, Alsop was absent from the living. Desertion of a cure by a royalist minister was the most ordinary form of what the Parliament was pleased to style 'delinquency' and delinquency was the most ordinary reason given for the sequestration of a living. John Alsop was sequestered in 1643 by the Committee for Plundered Ministers, and John Owen, whose book *The Display of Arminianism* had won him the favour of the House of Lords, was sent to Fordham as parish minister in Alsop's place. The official patrons of the parsonage were Sir John Lucas and Mr William Abell; the tithes amounted to £100 and the glebe £16.[2] A note at the top of a page in the parish registers reads: 'John Owen, Pastor, Anno Dom. July 16: 1643'.[3] This is probably the day on which he was authorised to begin his ministry at Fordham. Immediately after agreeing to go to Essex he was offered a living by his friend, Sir Edward Scott, but he had to decline it.[4] Soon after his arrival in Fordham he was married to a Miss Mary Rooke. It appears that she was the daughter of William Rooke, a clothier whose business had been in nearby Coggeshall. In his will which was proved in 1622 he made provision for the education of his very young daughter, Mary.[5] Thus in 1643 Mary would have been an accomplished young lady of about twenty-five years, whilst Owen was just two years older. The baptism of their first child is recorded in the parish registers: 'John the sonne of John Owen pastor of the church at Much Fordham and Mary his wife was baptized. December 20th 1644'.

[1] Cf. *Walker Revised* (ed. A. G. Matthews), Oxford, 1948, p. 145 for Alsop.
[2] Cf. H. Smith, *The Ecclesiastical History of Essex*, Colchester, 1930, p. 310, where there is a transcript of the returns of the Parochial Inquisition of September 1650.
[3] The Rev. Hugh Barber, rector of Fordham, kindly sent me photocopies of pages from the parish registers.
[4] He mentions this in his Epistle to Sir Edward Scott in *The Duty of Pastors*.
[5] Essex Record Office D/ACW. 9/99. Mrs Dorothy Greenald kindly made a transcript for me.

Unfortunately we have no information about life in the parsonage or the religious climate in the small village. From an Epistle 'To my loving neighbours and Christian friends' written in his study in September 1645 we learn that Owen went from house to house teaching both young and old and composed two catechisms for this task.[6] Also he preached regularly in the parish church about 'the Person and Offices of Christ'. There was an outbreak of the plague at Colchester in August 1644 and if this reached Fordham he would have been busily engaged ministering to the sick and dying. Very early in his days in the village, perhaps even before his marriage, he wrote a short treatise based upon 'an hour's country discourse' which he had delivered. Its title reads *The Duty of Pastors and People distinguished, or, a brief discourse touching the administration of things commanded in religion: especially concerning the means to be used by the people of God (distinct from church officers) for the increasing of divine knowledge in themselves and others*. It was published in May 1644.[7] In its pages he tells the reader that his judgement in regard to church polity is 'presbyterial or synodical, in opposition to prelatical or diocesan on the one side, and that which is commonly called independent or congregational on the other'. This does not mean that he was committed to the Scottish 'divine right' theory of Presbyterianism. Like many Puritans he was opposed to diocesan episcopacy but feared 'congregational democracy'; he was willing to have any system that came somewhere between these two and which escaped the 'evils' of both extremes.

We have but one small piece of information concerning his involvement in Church affairs in the Colchester area. By an ordinance of January 1644 the Earl of Manchester was empowered to appoint one or more committees in Essex, Norfolk, Suffolk and other counties for the purpose of investigating complaints against ministers of religion. The Essex Committee was made up of nine men, two of whom were Sir Thomas Honeywood and Sir Henry Mildmay, who became friends of Owen. On 3 April 1644 depositions were taken out under this ordinance against Samuel Cock, the rector of St Giles and Master of St Mary's Hospital, Colchester. Three witness swore before the committee that he was unfit for the ministry and they desired 'that he be tried by some judicious divines, *videlicet*, Mr Owen of Fordham nigh Colchester, and Mr Ellis of St Peter's in Colchester'.[8]

[6] The Epistle is in the published Catechisms. *Works*, Vol. I, p. 465.

[7] Thomason dated his copy 21 May 1644 but in 1657 Owen said it was published in 1643. See *Works*, Vol. XIII, p. 222.

[8] Cole MSS., xxxiii, 71-2, cited by T. W. Davids, *Annals of Evangelical Nonconformity in Essex*, 1863, p. 324. For Cock see Matthews, *Walker Revised*, p. 148.

Thus at this early stage in his career Owen was known as a competent divine.

The last entry in the parish registers for the period of John Owen's ministry is the record of a baptism performed on 28 December 1645. A report, which seemed authentic, was circulated that John Alsop was dead. Therefore John Owen prepared to move since the patrons could now exercise their right to nominate a successor to Alsop. Hearing of the situation the Committee for Plundered Ministers made the following order on 14 March 1646, 'Ordered that an ordinance be drawne and executed to the House, for the settling of Mr John Owen, minister of the Word, in the Church of St Botolphs in Colchester, void by death; in the gift of Sir Henry Audley, Delinquent; and that he shall officiate the said cure in the mean time and have and enjoy the profits of the said cure'.[9] There is no record in the *Journals* of the matter being brought before the House of Lords. If it was framed the arrangement must have been a temporary one, for in June 1646 there is another entry in the minutes of the Committee to the effect that, upon the 'joint petition of the church-wardens of the parishes of Buttolphes and All Saintes, it is ordered that, in regard the said churches are worth but £50 per annum . . . these churches are wholly unprovided for, the said benefices and churches shall be united'.

The people of Coggeshall, a town to the south-west of Fordham, perhaps through Mrs Mary Owen and her relatives, had heard good reports of the abilities of the young minister at Fordham and so they made it known to the patron of their living, the 'good' Earl of Warwick, that they wished John Owen to become minister at St Peter's in succession to Obadiah Sedgwick who was moving to St Paul's, Covent Garden. It was perhaps a good thing that Owen did decide to go to Coggeshall since the parish church of St Botolph was destroyed during the siege of Colchester in 1648.

(b) *At Coggeshall*

It is not possible to ascertain the exact date when John Owen began his ministry at Coggeshall. The official order of institution by the House of Lords was not given until 18 August 1646,[10] but he was certainly preaching at St Peter's before then. On the title-page of a sermon published in May he is described as being 'a minister of the

[9] 'Minutes of the Committee', B.M. Additional Manuscripts, 15670, f. 77. Though this committee was originally instituted to provide benefices for the Puritan clergy turned out from their livings by royalist forces, ultimately it acquired a practical supervision over the financial side of ecclesiastical affairs. The proceedings of the committee may be read in the British Museum, additional Manuscripts 15669, 15670, and 15671, and also in the Bodleian.

[10] *L.J.*, Vol. VIII, p. 46.

Gospel at Coggeshall'.[11] The following quotation from the minutes of the Committee for Plundered Ministers for May 1646 not only shows that he was resident there in May but also reveals some of the confusion at Fordham caused by the report of the death of John Alsop:[12]

> Whereas the Rectorie of the parish church of Much Fordham was, by order of this Committee, sequestered from Mr Alsopp to the use of Mr Owen, who, upon report that the said Mr Alsopp was deceased, hath accepted of the presentation of the Church of Coggeshall in the said countie, and is minister thereof; and in regard that it is not determined of the said Mr Alsopp his death, and it is considered that he is yet living, the Committee did, by the order of the 20th May instant, upon petition of divers of the said parish for the settling of Mr Richard Pulley in the said Mr Owen his stead, order the said Mr Owen to have notice thereof, to the end that the said Committee might be satisfied whether he had left the same; who appearing this day, this Committee has left him to his election to return to the said Chappell of Fordham or continue at Coggeshall. It is therefore ordered that the Rectorie and the profits thereof shall from henceforth stand sequestered to the use of the said Richard Pulley, who is required to officiate the cure of the said Church as rector till further order taken in the premises.[13]

Owen had moved to Coggeshall and there he intended to remain.

The sermon mentioned above was preached before the House of Commons on the day of the monthly fast for April 1646. On 23 February 1643 the Long Parliament began to hold regular fast days. Henceforward, on the last Wednesday of every month, a day of fasting, prayer and hearing of the Word of God was ordered to be observed not only by Parliament but also by the country as a whole. There was a political as well as religious purpose in holding these monthly fasts and, as Professor H. R. Trevor-Roper has clearly shown,[14] the sermons preached before the House of Commons on the fast days were often 'a means of co-ordination and propaganda' for the leaders of Parliament to which Charles had no parallel. These monthly fasts continued for seven years. When one was over the next was prepared. Each House separately chose and invited the two preachers. The day after

---

[11] Entitled *A Vision of Unchangeable Mercy*, in *Works*, Vol. VIII.

[12] It should also be noted that Sedgwick was settled at Covent Garden by May 1646. Cf. *D.N.B.*, s.v. Obadiah Sedgwick.

[13] Add. MSS. 15670, f. 221. Pulley was the son of Richard Pulley of Leighs by his first wife, Dorothy. Since his father acted for the county committee for sequestrations his appointment may have been due to his father's influence.

[14] Trevor-Roper, 'The Fast Sermons of the Long Parliament', in *Religion, the Reformation and Social Change* (1967).

C

the fast, or within a few days, votes of thanks were passed and the preachers were usually requested to print their sermons. Additional days of humiliation or thanksgiving were held as occasion demanded.

The first occasion that Owen preached at a monthly fast was Wednesday, 29 April 1646. His name was suggested on 25 March by Sir Peter Wentworth and Thomas Westrow; the vote of thanks after the sermon was proposed by Robert Jenner and Sir Peter Wentworth.[15] The sermon was preached in St Margaret's Church, Westminster, but, in good Puritan style, the *Journal* of the House of Commons simply speaks of 'Margaretts Church'![16] It was published as *A Vision of Unchangeable Free Mercy in sending the means of Grace to undeserving sinners*. His fellow preacher was James Nalton whose sermon was published under the title *Delay of Reformation provoking God's further indignation*. Owen sought to show that whatever happens on earth, especially in events and matters connected with the propagation of the Gospel, is controlled by the will and counsel of God. The sermon was from Acts of the Apostles 16:9, 'A vision appeared to Paul in the night; there stood a man of Macedonia, and prayed him, saying, "Come over into Macedonia and help us".' From the words 'come over and help us' he deduced that the people who are in the greatest need are those who do not have the richness of the Gospel message proclaimed unto them; and, he pointed out, there were many people in England who had no preacher of the Gospel in their parish. The sermon closes with an eloquent appeal for the Gospel to be taken to the parts of the nation ravaged by war and destitute of a godly ministry.

> Doth not Wales cry, and the North cry, yea and the West cry, Come and help us?—we are yet in a worse bondage than any by your means we have been delivered from;—if you leave us thus, all your protection will but yield us a more free and jovial passage to the chambers of death . . . O that you would labour to let all the parts of the kingdom taste of the sweetness of your successes, in carrying to them the gospel of the Lord Jesus; that the doctrine of the gospel might make way for the discipline of the gospel, without which it will be a very skeleton.[17]

Attached to the sermon were two essays, 'A Short Defensative about Church Government' and 'A Country Essay for the Practice of Church

---

[15] For a study of the members of the Long Parliament see D. Brunton and D. H. Pennington, *Members of the Long Parliament*, 1954. Wentworth was member for Tamworth, Westrow for Hythe, and Jenner for Cricklade.

[16] For a history of this church see H. F. Westlake, *St. Margaret's Westminster, the Church of the House of Commons*, 1914.

[17] In *Works*, Vol. VIII, pp. 40–41.

Government'. In the former he supplied four reasons why he had not been a subscriber to recent petitions about Church government submitted to Parliament.[18] The latter, he explained, had been written for a 'worthy friend' several years previously and had been circulating in manuscript form in Essex. It purpose was reconciliatory and he hoped that it would help to bring some measure of peace to the churches since great arguments were going on in Essex and London, where the Assembly of divines was discussing these points.

Though firmly established in the orthodox Calvinist theological tradition, John Owen was obviously rather confused between 1644 and 1646 by the opposing views held by orthodox Calvinists on the doctrine of the Church. His first inclination seems to have been to take a mediating position between the 'Congregational way' and the 'Presbyterian way'. Soon after the publication of *The Duty of Pastors and People distinguished* (1644), in which he described himself a Presbyterian and opposed to the democratical confusion he believed the Congregational way bred, he began a careful examination of these opposing views. Twelve years later he described his experience:

> I set myself to inquire into the controversies then warmly agitated in these nations. Of the Congregational way I was not acquainted with any one person, minister or other; nor had I, to my knowledge, seen any more than one in my life. My acquaintance lay wholly with ministers and people of the Presbyterian way. But sundry books being published on either side, I perused and compared them with the Scripture and one another, according as I received ability from God. After a general view of them, as was my manner in other controversies I fixed on one to take under peculiar consideration and examination, which seemed most methodically and strongly to maintain that which was contrary, as I thought, to my present persuasion. This was Mr Cotton's book of the Keys. The examination and confutation hereof, merely for my own particular satisfaction, with what diligence and sincerity I was able, I engaged in. What progress I made in that undertaking I can manifest unto any by the discourses on the subject and animadversions on that book, yet abiding by me. In the pursuit and management of this work, quite beside and contrary to my expectation, at a time and season wherein I could expect nothing on that account but ruin in the world, without the knowledge or advice of, or conference

---

[18] One such petition was presented in May 1646 to the House of Lords—*L.J.*, Vol. VIII, p. 338—by ministers in Essex and Suffolk for the setting up of a Presbyterian system in the counties. No doubt copies of this petition were circulating in Essex both before and after Owen preached before the Commons.

with, any one person of that judgement, I was prevailed on to receive that and those principles which I had thought to have set myself in an opposition unto.[19]

Thus very soon after, or, more probably, even before arriving in Coggeshall, John Owen became a Congregationalist in regard to Church polity. He came to believe that the local church has authority from Christ to act in His name without any interference from any one outside the church membership. Putting his new views into practice he organised a church of the Congregational way within the parish system. Unfortunately we have no details of this church but we do know that it has continued throughout the years until the present time.[20]

After Parliament decided that the Presbyterian system was to be set up throughout Essex, Owen was present at a meeting in Colchester on 31 March 1648 to discuss how this could be done.[21] Ralph Josselin, the minister at Earles Colne, was also present and has left a short account of Owen's attitude:

> Rid to Colchester; met Mr Newcomen, & divers other Ministers; wee had much discourse concerning falling into practice, and in the first place, seeing that elders are to bee chosen, by whom it shall be done; the parliament proposeth by the people that have taken the covenant: others, as Mr Owen, conceived this too broad, & would have first a separation to bee made in our parishes, and that by the minister, and those godly that joyne unto him, and then proceed to choosing.[22]

This entry clearly reveals the difference between the views of those of the Presbyterian way and those of the Congregational way.[23] The former wanted to reform the whole parish and treat all who claimed

---

[19] *Works*, Vol. XIII, p. 223. p. 223. John Cotton's book was *The Keyes of the Kingdom of Heaven* (1644). For Cotton see Supplement to *D.N.B.*

[20] Cf. J. A. Dods, 'The Story of Congregationalism in Coggeshall', *Transactions of the Congregational Historical Society*, Vol. V, pp. 40 ff. The *Congregational Year Book* for 1967 states that the church now has sixty members.

[21] Cf. *The Division of the County of Essex into several Classes* . . . (1648). Owen's name does not appear by the name of the Coggeshall church but the names of two elders, Robert Crane and William Tanner, are given.

[22] *The Diary of Ralph Josselin* (ed. E. Hockliffe), 1908, p. 48. Matthew Newcomen was a lecturer at Dedham.

[23] For a recent account of Presbyterians see G. G. Bolam, J. Goring, H. L. Short and R. Thomas, *The English Presbyterians*, 1968; for an exposition of the Congregational way see G. F. Nuttall, *Visible Saints*, Oxford, 1957.

to be Christians as church members whereas the latter wanted to form a church of regenerate saints out of the people who attended the parish services. Owen only wanted elders who were regenerate and godly.

In his first year at Coggeshall, Owen produced a practical guide to Christian fellowship entitled *Eshcol, a cluster of the fruit of Canaan . . . or rules of direction for the walking of the saints in fellowship according to the order of the gospel*.[24] This is an excellent piece of writing and was used by many Congregational churches in the seventeenth and eighteenth centuries as a practical guide to church membership and duties. It was prepared after he became a Congregationalist but it is of such an eirenical nature as to be useful to any Reformed church. It contains seven rules with explanations on the duties of church members to their pastor and fifteen rules on their duties one to another. Obviously he placed great importance on Christian fellowship and this book may be regarded as the statement of the aim of his pastoral and preaching ministry in Coggeshall. It described the type of church he longed to see.

Shortly afterwards a much more technical book came from his pen and was entitled *Salus Electorum, Sanguis Jesus; or the Death of Death in the Death of Christ* (1647).[25] It contains a dedicatory epistle to the Earl of Warwick in which Owen stated his desire to 'testify to all the world the answering of his heart unto that obligation which his lordship' placed upon him by giving him 'an entrance to that place for the preaching of the gospel, whither he was directed by the providence of the Most High, and where he was sought by his people'. The book also contains separate commendations by Stanley Gower and Richard Byfield, both members of the Westminster Assembly. The purpose of its publication was to prove that Christ died effectually only for the elect, those whom God chose in eternity to be His children. It sought to show the error of the Arminian and Remonstrant view that Christ died for each and every human being; but whilst containing a mass of learning, it is hardly readable since Owen's style is exceedingly heavy and his sentences long and cumbersome.

The whole of Owen's pastoral ministry had been conducted whilst the nation was torn by civil war. On several occasions he refers, with feeling, to his labours 'in the midst of a poor, numerous, provoking people'.[26] For about four months from June 1648 the people of

---

[24] In *Works*, Vol. XIII, pp. 52 ff.
[25] In *Works*, Vol. X. In 1650 John Horne of Norfolk published a reply to Owen's book under the title *The Open Door for Man's Approach to God*.
[26] 'Letter to the Commons of England' in *The Shaking and Translating of Heaven and Earth* (1649), in *Works*, Vol. VIII.

Coggeshall saw at first hand a meeting of the opposing forces. A royalist army was at Braintree, Essex, on 11 June intending to go direct to Norfolk and Suffolk where its leaders expected help from the gentry, but, at the suggestion of Sir Charles Lucas, they decided to turn aside to Colchester to try to attract recruits from the town. In Coggeshall Sir Thomas Honeywood waited on the night of the 11th with a trained band of soldiers but the enemy made a detour and reached Colchester the next day. After some hesitation by the townspeople the gates were opened to them. General Fairfax crossed the River Thames from Gravesend to Tilbury on the 11th and arrived at Coggeshall the next day where he met Honeywood and Colonel Edward Whalley. On the 13th he attacked the town hoping to repeat his recent achievement at Maidstone in Kent. But he failed and a long siege became inevitable. By the end of August many of the poor people within the town were beginning to eat dogs and horses since there was little food. Various attempts were made by the mayor and other leading citizens to relieve the situation through negotiations but Fairfax wanted a complete victory and news of Oliver Cromwell's victory at Preston served only to strengthen this resolve. Finally the royalist leaders gave way. On 27 August articles of capitulation were signed and on the next day Fairfax's army entered the town. The County Committee which had been captured at Chelmsford and held captive was released and three royalist knights, Sir Charles Lucas, Sir George Lisle and Sir Bernard Gascoigne, were executed. During the siege John Owen acted as chaplain to General Fairfax and ministered to the troops as well as to his own congregation. In an epistle to the General written a few weeks later he wrote, 'I had the happiness for a short season to attend your Excellency in the service of my Master, Jesus Christ'.[27] And referring to the siege he described himself as 'an endangered spectator'. Owen was the preacher at the day of thanksgiving held immediately after the end of the siege. Also he preached at another day of thanksgiving arranged by the County Committee at Romford a few weeks later. Both sermons were from Habakkuk 3:1-9.

The two sermons were printed as one discourse under the title *Ebenezer: a Memorial of the Deliverance of Essex County and Committee*.[28] The passage from the prophet Habakkuk contains a prayer which begins with a request for God to return to the nation in mercy, but it soon develops into a description of a theophany in which God displays His strength by visiting the earth in judgement. From these verses Owen drew out twenty-one observations or principles which the supporters of the cause of Parliament could take to heart. The

---

[27] This is prefixed to *Ebenezer: a Memorial of the Deliverance*, in *Works*, Vol. VIII.
[28] In *Works*, Vol. VIII, pp. 71 ff.

seventh is, 'Former mercies, with their times and places, are to be hed in thankful remembrance unto them who wait for future blessings'. It is followed by a prophetic application:

> Let former mercies be an anchor of hope in time of present distresses. Where is the God of Marston Moor, and the God of Naseby? is an acceptable expostulation in a gloomy day. O what a catalogue of mercies hath this nation to plead by in a time of trouble! God came from Naseby and the Holy One from the West. 'His glory covered the heavens, and the earth was full of his praise.' He went forth in the North and in the East he did not withold his hand. I hope the poor town wherein I live is more enriched with the store-mercy of a few months, than with the full trade of many years.[29]

The twelfth is a rather courageous proposition to affirm: 'The works and labours of God's people are transacted for them in heaven'. And it is followed by equally audacious language:

> Up and be doing, you that are about the work of the Lord. Your enemies are bread ready to be eaten, and yield refreshment. Do you think if our armies had not walked in a trodden path, they could have made such journeys as they have done of late? Had not God marched before them, and traced out their way from Kent to Essex, from Wales to the North, their carcases had long ere this been cast into the field. Their work was done in heaven before they began it. God was gone over the mulberry trees, 2 Samuel 5:24. The work might have been done by children, though he was pleased to employ such worthy instruments. They see, I doubt not, their own nothingness in his all-sufficiency. Go on, then: but with this caution, search by all ways and means to find the footsteps of the mighty God going before you.[30]

There is no doubt that John Owen saw the success of the parliamentary armies as the success of God's saints planned by Him before the foundation of the world, just as He had planned the salvation of the elect. Thus it was to God alone that all the praise, for the success of Generals Fairfax and Cromwell in their campaigns and battles, was due. Yet it would be a mistake to view John Owen as merely a political preacher. He was also an evangelist who was very conscious that God's greatest gift to mankind is salvation from sin, and eternal life.

[29] ibid., p. 88. Marston Moor and Naseby were, of course, scenes of great parliamentary victories.
[30] *Works*, Vol. VIII, p. 97.

Consider, if there be so much sweetness in a temporal deliverance, Oh! what excellency is there in that eternal redemption which we have in the blood of Jesus. If we rejoice from being delivered from them, who would have killed the body, what unspeakable rejoicing is there in that mercy whereby we are freed from the wrath to come. Let this possess your thoughts, let this fill your souls,—let this be your haven from all former storms.[31]

To look at the pastor from Coggeshall as a political Independent using religion to support his political views is to gain a totally misleading picture of him.[32]

Except perhaps in the summer of 1648 when army officers would have been guests, life in the parsonage must have been similar to that of many Puritan homes. The day began with family prayers conducted by the head of the house, in this case John Owen. Whilst he spent five or more hours in his study his wife contented herself with looking after the children and doing the housework. In the afternoon and early evening, parish homes were visited and families catechised. Perhaps one hour in the late afternoon or early evening would be given to playing with the children and talking with his wife. Once more in the evenings he would probably return to his books and his thoughts. From the parish registers of Great Coggeshall we know that at least three children were born to Mary Owen between 1646 and 1651. Mary was baptised on 4 July 1647 but died three weeks later and was buried on the 25th. Another Mary was baptised on 23 February 1650 and Elizabeth on 10 February 1651. There may have been other births or deaths; but, as the registers are very much faded in parts, it is now impossible to find out.[33]

(c) *Two famous sermons*

After the siege of Colchester, events moved quickly. The king was seized by the Army on 1 December. Five days late Colonel Pride, whose regiment was responsible for guarding the Houses of Parliament, 'purged' the House of Commons of about one hundred members, who were considered, by some army officers and Independent M.P.s, as likely to be unfaithful to the future cause of God and His saints in the nation. The king was brought to Windsor on 23 December in readiness for an early trial. On 1 January 1649 the Commons

---

[31] ibid., p. 126.

[32] For the problem of the identity of the Independents see J. H. Hexter, 'The Problem of the Presbyterian Independents' in *Reappraisals in History*, 1961, and G. Yule, *The Independents in the English Civil War*, Cambridge, 1958, and other studies mentioned in these books.

[33] I am grateful to the County Archivist of Essex, Mr F. G. Emmison, for sending me photocopies of pages from the registers.

declared it treason in the king to levy war on the Parliament and the kingdom and that he must therefore face trial. A special high court of justice was appointed and one hundred and thirty-five commissioners were nominated. Though General Fairfax and others amongst the commissioners stayed away from the trial it still proceeded and found the king guilty. On 30 January, outside Inigo Jones's handsome banqueting hall at Whitehall, Charles I was executed as a traitor to the Commonwealth of England.

The monthly fast for December 1648 came in the very week that the preparations were being made for the trial, and at least half of this day of fasting and prayer proved embarrassing to the Commons. Thomas Brooks, the morning preacher, sincerely believed that the cause of God could be, indeed should be, equated with the policy of the purged Parliament and he demanded that justice be done by punishing the king. Naturally he received the thanks of the House afterwards! The preacher in the afternoon was the Presbyterian, Thomas Watson, pastor of St Stephen's, Walbrook, London, and he had a rather different message. He preached a daring sermon about hypocrisy, suggesting that not a few in the Commons were hypocrites. They were making 'religion a cloak for their ambition'. Predictably he was neither thanked for 'his pains in preaching' nor was he asked to print his sermon. Yet it was published under the title, *Gods Anatomy upon Mans Heart;* Brooks published his sermon as *Gods Delight in the Progress of the Upright.*

With Watson's sermon still ringing in their ears the House of Commons had to decide on 30 December whom they would invite to preach at the monthly fast scheduled for 30 January. Clearly two ministers who were sympathetic to the aims of the purged Parliament must be invited. With the trial of the king and his possible execution looming ahead, no mistakes could be made. So two sound preachers were proposed by two safely radical members, Gilbert Millington and Francis Allen, both of whom were soon to sign the king's death warrant.[34] The ministers were John Cardell who preached at All Hallows, Lombard Street, London, and John Owen of Coggeshall. Sir Henry Mildmay, who had invited Owen to preach at Romford after the siege of Colchester, was asked to pass on the invitation of the House to him whilst Gilbert Millington was asked to contact John Cardell.

Since the execution of the king was fixed for 30 January, the monthly fast was delayed for one day. John Owen was probably in London to witness the spectacular yet dreadful ceremony on the 30th. Perhaps it is to the nights of the 28, 29 and 30th, which he spent in London, that he refers when he says his sermon was 'a hasty

[34] Millington was the member for Nottingham and Allen for Cockermouth.

conception, and like Jonah's gourd, the child of a night or two'. But even if the sermon was prepared in a hurry, the sentiments it contains were the result of several years of thought, observation and voluntary support of Parliament against the king.

The sermon when printed was entitled *Righteous Zeal encouraged by Divine Protection*[35]; it is from Jeremiah 15:19-20. The first part of the fifteenth chapter is taken up with a denunciation of the sins of Jerusalem and Judah, and the inevitability of forthcoming judgement from God. The second part contains the complaint of the prophet about his bitter circumstances but the passage ends with a promise from God to Jeremiah. 'I will make thee unto this people a fenced brazen wall; and they shall fight against thee, but they shall not prevail . . . for I am with thee to save and deliver thee' (v. 20). After an examination of the context, Owen's first theme is an explanation of the fact that God has many ways of punishing an evil nation and that there is no escape from His wrath, once He has decided to judge His people. In Jeremiah's own day, Jerusalem was destroyed and leaders of Judah taken into exile. But what caused the wrath of God to fall on the people? It was the sins of king Manasseh and the people of Judah. His subjects had made him king and could have removed him when they saw his wicked practices, but they did not. Thus they shared his guilt and the judgement of God upon the whole people became necessary. Not even the prayer of a Moses or a Samuel could have averted it.[36]

Owen's second theme is that in many ways England presented a similar picture to Judah. God's judgement upon her, though not yet as complete as Judah's, is already revealed (in the civil war and the execution of the king). There is, thanks be to God, still hope for England to avert a total ruin if Parliament quickly puts away the false worship, superstition, tyranny and cruelty that has hung over the nation for too long. Parliament should make no compromise with those who would divert it from its task of reforming the nation for the glory of God. Any such compromise would be to prefer the praise of man to that of God Himself. It should take a firm stand for righteousness in all departments of national life. It should not oppress the people in any way. Indeed Owen felt so strongly about this that he made a special appeal: 'I heartily desire a committee of your honourable House might sit once a week to relieve poor men that have been oppressed by men sometimes enjoying parliamentary authority'.[37]

---

[35] In *Works*, Vol. VIII, pp. 127 ff.
[36] Owen's views on the relation of king to people in Judah seem to have been affected by the contract theory of government which was then enjoying some popularity in Europe.
[37] *Works*, Vol. VIII, p. 148.

Members of Parliament, he went on, should beware of self-seeking and do their duty, desiring only the witness of their consciences that they had done their best. Finally, the Parliament must not persecute people either out of revenge for deeds of earlier years or because of religious principles.

Owen's third theme is that God will certainly give prevailing strength and unconquerable defence to persons who constantly discharge the duties of righteousness especially when these are undertaken in times of difficulty and opposition. This, of course, is what God promised to do for Jeremiah and, said the young preacher, God makes the same promise to the Parliament of England. 'An unbiased magistracy shall never want God's presence.'[38] The sermon closes with a word of exhortation. The position of Parliament in relation to England is identified with and compared with that of the prophet Jeremiah to Judah:

> All you, then, that are the Lord's workmen, be always prepared for a storm. Wonder not that men see not the ways of the Lord nor the judgements of our God:—many are blinded. Admire not that they will so endlessly engage themselves into fruitless opposition; they are hardened. Be not amazed that evidence of truth and righteousness will not affect them; they are corrupted. But this do; Come and enter into the chambers of God, and you shall be safe until this whole indignation be overpast. I speak of all them, and only them, who follow the Lord in all his ways with upright hearts and single minds: if the Lord will have you to be a rock and a brazen wall for men to dash themelves against, and to break in pieces, though the service be grievous to flesh and blood, yet it is his, whose you are. Be prepared, the wind blows—a storm may come.[39]

What has happened and is happening in England is of the Lord. 'It is the Lord's doing and it is marvellous in our eyes' (Psalm 118:23).

John Owen definitely saw the defeat of the royalist armies and the execution of the king as part of God's judgement upon a nation for its false and erroneous religion, cruelty, persecution, and shocking treatment of the poor. The purpose of the sermon was to make Parliament aware of the terrible position in which it stood in relation to God and His purposes. It could stand firm as a brazen wall and be the cause of bringing righteousness into the national life; or, if it compromised with evil and error, it could usher in further judgement from heaven. At a crisis in national history the young divine looked to the future

[38] ibid., p. 150.
[39] *Works*, Vol. VIII, p. 162.

and bade the leaders of the people go forward to do God's will in humility and with courage. It was an appropriate message in a difficult hour.

To the printed sermon he attached a dedicatory letter to 'the right honourable the Commons of England' and a tract 'Of Toleration and the Duty of the Magistrate about Religion'. The letter bears a somewhat apocalyptic character. 'God Almighty having called you forth, right honourable, at his entrance to the rolling up of the nation's heavens like a scroll (Isaiah 34:4-5), to serve him in your generation in the high places of Armageddon (Revelation 16:16), you shall be sure not to want experience of that opposition which is raised against the great work of the Lord, which generally swells most against the visible instruments thereof.' But, unlike some of his contemporaries, John Owen never allowed his vision of the end of the world to get out of control.

The tract on the magistrate's duty in religious matters is particularly important for it deals with a subject which the Westminster Assembly of divines had discussed and which had recently been fervently debated by members of the New Model Army.[40] Owen's own beliefs were similar to those expressed in the *Agreement of the People*, itself a production of army officers. He argued that it was the duty of individuals, magistrates, and churches to maintain truth and oppose error by the sword of church discipline and the hammer of the Word of God, that is by spiritual weapons. With many references to past history he showed that persecution of people who hold erroneous opinions has never achieved any lasting good. Further, he proved that the punishment of heretics is not required by God's Word unless they cause civil disorder. He outlined the duty of magistrates in six propositions.[41]

1. It belongs to the duty of the supreme magistrate, the governor or shepherd of the people, in any nation, being acquainted with the mind of God, to take care that the truth of the gospel be preached to all the people of that nation, according to the way appointed, either ordinary or extraordinary.
2. The gospel being preached and declared, as of right it ought to be, it is the duty of the magistrate, by the power wherewith he is intrusted, to protect and defend it against all or any persons that, by force or violence, shall seek to hinder the progress or stop the passage of it, under what pretence soever.

---

[40] Cf. W. Haller, *Liberty and Reformation in the Puritan Revolution*, New York, 1955, pp. 100 ff., 288 ff.
[41] In *Works*, Vol. VIII, pp. 189, 192, 194.

3. The providing or granting of places requisite for the performance of that worship which in the gospel is instituted, is the duty of the Christian magistrate.
4. Protection, as to peace and quietness in the use of the ordinances of the Lord Jesus Christ, from violent disturbers, either from without or within, is also incumbent on him.
5. Supportment and provision, as to earthly things, where regularly failing, is also incumbent on him.
6. It is the duty of the magistrate not to allow any public places for (in his judgement) false and abominable worship; as also, to demolish all outward appearances and demonstrations of such superstitious, idolatrous, and unacceptable service.

He concluded by suggesting that Parliament should organise and then listen to a debate about toleration in order that, having heard the arguments of learned men of different opinions, they might make up their own minds on the best evidence. Whilst not approaching the refined view of toleration expounded by John Locke, Owen's view was, in his day, a liberal and moderate attitude to a very difficult problem.

Whatever the M.P.s thought about this tract, the monthly fast for February was held as normal, though Parliament had some difficulty in finding willing preachers. The preachers chosen for the fast in March were John Warren of Hatfield, Joseph Caryl and John Owen, but it was postponed to 5 April and then once more to 19 April. It proved to be the last of its type, for on 23 April an Act was brought into the House to repeal the Act for the observation of a monthly fast. The reason given for the repeal was that the nation had seriously neglected the keeping of the fast. Henceforth, days of fasting were to be held as occasion demanded.

Omitting to mention that Caryl preached on the 19th, Professor Trevor-Roper states that Owen and Warren 'glorified in the prospect of further convulsions and looked forward to the triumph of radical heresy and the cause of the poor'.[42] This is not a fair description of the sermons. Owen took as his text Hebrews 12:27, 'Now God hath promised saying, Yet once more, I shake not the earth only, but also heaven. And this word, Yet once more, signifieth the removing of those things that are shaken, as of things that are made, that those things which cannot be shaken may remain'. The sermon was published as *Ouranōn Ourania: the Shaking and Translating of Heaven and Earth*.[43] He understood 'heaven' as referring not to celestial regions but 'to political heights and glory' which men have

---
[42] Trevor-Roper, op. cit., p. 341.
[43] In *Works*, Vol. VIII, pp. 242 ff.

framed for themselves. It meant the 'grandeur and lustre of their dominions'. 'The earth' referred to the people of the earth, the multitudes of men and women. So he explained the meaning of his text as follows:

> The Lord Jesus Christ, by his mighty power, in these latter days, as antichristian tyranny draws to its period, will so far shake and translate the political heights, governments, and strength of the nations, as shall serve for the full bringing in of his own peaceable kingdom;—the nations so shaken become thereby a quiet habitation for the people of the Most High.[44]

Later in the sermon he stopped to ask and then answer the question: What particular revelation is the Lord giving to His people in 1649? His answer was clear:

> Plainly, the peculiar light of this generation is that discovery which the Lord hath made to his people of the mystery of civil and ecclesiastical tyranny. The opening, unravelling, and revealing the Antichristian interest, interwoven and coupled together, in civil and spiritual things, into a state opposite to the kingdom of the Lord Jesus, is the great discovery of these days. Who almost is there amongst us now who doth not evidently see, that for many generations the western nations have been juggled into spiritual and civil slavery by the legerdemain of the whore, and the potentates of the earth made drunk with the cup of her abominations?—how the whole earth hath been rolled in confusion and the saints hurried out of the world, to give way to their combined interest? Hath not God unveiled that harlot, made her naked, and discovered her abominable filthiness? Is it not evident to him that hath but half an eye, that the whole present constitution of the government of the nations is so cemented with antichristian mortar, from the very top to the bottom, that without a thorough shaking they cannot be cleansed.[45]

Near the end of the sermon he exclaimed, 'Oh, that it might be the glory of this assembly, above all the assemblies of the world, that every ruler in it might be a sincere subject in the kingdom of the Lord Jesus'. His last warning to Parliament was that unless its members are sincere subjects of Christ the Lord, then the glorious but

---

[44] *Works*, Vol. VIII, p. 260.
[45] ibid., p. 274. It is interesting to note that this sermon was reprinted in 1793, 1794, and 1861 in the belief that its message could well apply to the political situation of those days.

unknown day of Christ's return to earth in glory will be for them a day of darkness not light.

The equation of the Papal system with that of the antichristian power described in the Book of Revelation was exceedingly common in Puritan theology of the seventeenth century. Therefore Owen was saying nothing new in equating the two. What he did fervently believe and feel was that in the events of the last twenty or so years, God had enabled the Christians of his day to see that not only had the Papal power infiltrated churches and their theology but it had also become part of the fabric of European civil affairs and politics. Thus the battle with Roman Catholicism was both a religious and political battle, and Parliament must root out of national life and religion all traces of Popery since no one knew the exact day when Christ would return to earth in glory to judge the living and the dead. For the next eleven or more years it was a belief to which he clung and which greatly influenced his view of politics and government.

CHAPTER III

Chaplain to Oliver Cromwell

IT was probably on 20 April 1649 that Oliver Cromwell and John Owen first met, and it was at the London home of General Fairfax. Before returning to Essex the young divine, whose sermon before the House had deeply impressed many M.P.s, called to pay his respects to the Lord General but was kept waiting. While Owen was waiting Cromwell arrived with some other army officers. When Cromwell saw him he immediately walked over to him, and laying his hand upon his shoulder in the familiar manner which he used to his personal friends, said, 'Sir, you are the person I must be acquainted with'. No doubt the sentiments expressed by Owen in St Margaret's Church were ones he heartily endorsed. To this unexpected compliment Owen modestly replied, 'That will be much more to my advantage than yours'. 'We shall see' came the reply as the general led him out into the garden where he told him of his intended expedition to Ireland and asked him to accompany it as a chaplain. When Owen did not express an immediately favourable response he was told that his brother was going as standard-bearer. The fact was that the pastor did not want to leave his flock even though he believed that the Irish expedition was necessary as part of the uprooting of the power of anti-christ from the nation. In the end he agreed but this was only after Cromwell had sent his brother to Coggeshall to persuade him and several brother ministers had advised him to go.[1]

(a) *A Day of Thanksgiving*

He was back in London again on 7 June 1649 to preach in Christ Church in the City of London at a special Day of Thanksgiving held to commemmorate the suppression of the Levellers at Burford by the army on 14 and 15 May. The Levellers were men with frustrations but they had a programme of political and social reform which included a widening of the franchise. They felt that with the Rump (the 'purged' Parliament) and its Council of State there was as much danger of despotism as under the king and his Privy Council. Their leaders made sure that their views were disseminated throughout the the army.[2] At Banbury in May 1649 a group of disaffected soldiers, led by William Thompson, drew up a manifesto entitled *England's*

[1] Asty, pp. 9–10.
[2] Cf. D. B. Robertson, *The Religious Foundations of Leveller Democracy*, New York, 1951.

Standard Advanced which contained the usual Leveller demands one of which was a call for the restoration of representation of soldiers by the 'agitators'. Cromwell and Fairfax feared anarchy and appealed for discipline and loyalty in the regiments. They hastily marched to suppress the mutineers. As they desired to maintain their own authority and that of the Rump this was the only course of action open to them.

The congregation which Thomas Goodwin and John Owen addressed was made up of the City authorities, the Council of State, the House of Commons, and all officers in London who were above the rank of lieutenant. For his text Owen chose Psalm 76:5, 'The stout-hearted are spoiled, they have slept their sleep; and none of the men of might have found their hands'.[3] He began by affirming that the care of the churches and the ordinances of the Gospel 'lies at the bottom of all God's powerful actings and workings among the sons of men'. He went on to remind his hearers that they were witnessing in their generation the glorious work of God in overthrowing ungodly tyranny, promised for the last days. Even so, the defeat of the Levellers, when compared with the victory over Charles Stuart and his armies, was 'as an appendix of good-will, for the confirming the former work which God Had Wrought'.[4] Thus the rise of the Leveller mutiny was to be regarded as a trial of the faith of God's saints. Owen evidently believed that the Levellers were enemies of the Gospel who had acted against the spiritual good of the Commonwealth, and who would have destroyed both the Parliament and their army commanders if left alone. The sermon ends with words of advice to the noble congregation: 'Be in the ways of God and do the things of God, and no weapon that is formed against you shall ever prosper'.[5] Thomas Goodwin preached on a similar theme.

The sermons were followed by a great feast provided by the City of London in Grocers' Hall. This sumptuous banquet was meant to serve as a farewell dinner to the army which was soon to leave for Ireland. Next day in the House of Commons Owen and Goodwin were thanked for their sermons and invited to print them.[6] Also an Act was read for the settling of £100 per annum on John Owen, Peter du Moulin and others. This money, in Owen's case, was for his services at the siege of Colchester in 1648. In 1657 Parliament also settled Irish lands upon him, perhaps in lieu of the money.[7]

According to the *Journal* of the Commons, the matter of placing

[3] The sermon was not printed until 1721 when it appeared in the volume of sermons.
[4] *Works*, Vol. IX, p. 207.
[5] ibid., p. 206.
[6] *C.J.*, Vol. VI, p. 226.
[7] ibid., Vol. VII, p. 535.

Thomas Goodwin in the headship of an Oxford or Cambridge College was referred to the Committee for regulating the Universities on 8 June.[8] Bulstrode Whitelocke[9] states that it was not only Goodwin's but also Owen's name that was put forward and the verity of this statement is strengthened by a report mentioned by Clement Walker that a committee had been appointed to consider how to prefer the two men to be heads of Oxford Colleges as a reward for their support of the parliamentary cause. Characteristically, Walker ended his reference to Owen and Goodwin by saying that 'it is not fit such men should serve God for nothing; in the times of St Peter and St Paul godliness was great gain, but in the days of the modern saints, gain is great godliness'.[10] Goodwin became President of Magdalen College, Oxford, on 8 January 1650, but Owen's preferment was delayed because he was already chosen chaplain for the Irish expedition with the special responsibility of looking into the affairs of Trinity College, Dublin.

(b) *In Ireland*

On 2 July, Parliament gave its approval for 'Mr Owen, Minister, to go into Ireland with the Lord Lieutenant of Ireland'.[11] At the same time it ordered that £100 per annum, payable in quarterly instalments, be allowed to his wife in his absence. It is very probable that private arrangements were made for Constantine Jessop[12] to look after the church at Coggeshall and to receive whole or part of the income during Owen's absence. By this time Mary Owen had several children as well as many local friends and relatives to prevent her from feeling too lonely in the absence of her husband. So with his affairs in order, John Owen was able to join Cromwell's army.

The departure from London was made the occasion of a solemn ceremony. At Whitehall three ministers, one of whom was probably John Owen, prayed for God's blessing on the expedition and Colonels Goffe and Harrison with General Cromwell expounded relevant

---

[8] ibid., Vol. VI, p. 226.

[9] Whitelocke, *Memorials of the English Affairs*, 1682, p. 391.

[10] Cited by B. Hanbury, *Historical Memorials relating to the Independents*, 1844, Vol. III, p. 394, from Walker's *History of Independency*. In 1653 Owen himself stated that he was 'first called from rural retirement' to the University but before he was able to take up his appointment he had to make journeys 'to coasts beyond the seas' and to 'the extremities of this island'. Preface to Reader, *De Divina Justitia*, (1653), in *Works*, Vol. X.

[11] *C.J.*, Vol. VI, p. 247.

[12] Jessop was born in 1602 and educated at Jesus College, Oxford, and Trinity College, Dublin. He was minister at Fyfield, Essex, until late 1647, after which he may have assisted Owen at Coggeshall.

passages of Scripture. Then the great procession began its journey to Bristol, with Cromwell riding in a carriage drawn by six whitish-grey mares. This was 11 July, and three days later the army arrived in Bristol, where it was delayed for a month before it set sail from Milford Haven on 13 August for Dublin, arriving there on the 15th.

How Cromwell and his army spent the next six months is well known, especially to the Irish. John Owen does not appear to have seen what happened at Drogheda and Wexford for he spent most of his time in Dublin living in the castle. No evidence now exists to prove that he actually investigated the affairs of Trinity College, but as he was appointed a commissioner in March 1650 for the University of Dublin it is possible that he fulfilled his commission from Cromwell. He certainly did much preaching and, according to two testimonies which have been preserved, proved of great spiritual help to certain people.[13] Also he found time to write a short book, *Of the Death of Christ, the Price He paid and the Purchase He made*, published after his return to London. It was a reply to criticism made by Richard Baxter against his earlier work, *The Death of Death* (1648).[14] The book was finished on 20 December 1649 in Dublin castle and its last paragraph contains a brief description of his life in the city:

> For the present, being by God's providence removed for a season from my native soil, attended with more than ordinary weaknesse and infirmities, separated from my library, burdened with manifold employments, with constant preaching to a numerous multitude of as thirsting a people after the gospel as ever yet I conversed withal, it sufficeth me that I have obtained this mercy, briefly and plainly to vindicate the truth from mistakes.[15]

It is regrettable that letters which he sent home to his wife and to people in London have not been preserved, since they would have helped us to gain a better picture of his life and work in that famous city.

The exact date of Owen's return to London is not known but it was certainly before the last day of February 1650 when he preached before Parliament. His dedicatory letter to the 'Commons of England' written on 8 March states that the burden of this sermon, entitled

---

[13] Dorothy Emett and Major Manwaring claimed that they owed their spiritual awakening to his preaching. Cf. J. Rogers, *Ohel or Bethshemesh* (1653), bk. II, ch. vi.
[14] Baxter made his criticism in an appendix to *Aphorisms of Justification*. For his theology see J. I. Packer, 'The Redemption and Restoration of Man in the thought of Richard Baxter', D. Phil. thesis, Oxford, 1955.
[15] *Works*, Vol. X, p. 479.

The Steadfastness of the Promises and the Sinfulness of Staggering,[16] was 'a serious proposal for the advancement and propagation of the Gospel in another nation'. The text was Romans 4:20, 'Abraham staggered not at the promise of God through unbelief'. The theme of the sermon is well expressed in its title. The following quotation comes from near the end. Not only does it show the preacher's desire to see the preaching of the Gospel in Ireland but it also reveals how he viewed the military success of Cromwell there.

> Be faithful in doing all the work of God whereunto you are engaged, as he is faithful in working all your works whereunto he is engaged . . . God's work whereunto you are engaged is the propagating of the kingdom of Christ and the setting up of the standard of the gospel. So far as you find God going on with your work, go you on with his. How is it that Jesus Christ is in Ireland only as a *lion staining all his garments with the blood of his enemies;* and none to hold him out as a *lamb sprinkled with this own blood to his friends?* Is it the sovereignty and interest of England that is alone to be there transacted? For my part, I see no farther into the MYSTERY of these things but that I could heartily rejoice, that, innocent blood being expiated, the Irish might enjoy Ireland so long as the moon endureth, so that Jesus Christ might possess the Irish. But God having suffered those sworn vassals of the man of sin to break out into such ways of villainy as render them obnoxious unto vengeance, upon such rules of government amongst men as he hath appointed; is there, therefore, nothing to be done but to give a *cup of blood* into their hands? Doubtless the way whereby God will bring the followers after the beast to condign destruction for all their enmity to the Lord Jesus will be by suffering them to run into such practices against men as shall righteously expose them to vengeance, according to acknowledged principles among the sons of men. But is this all? Hath he no further aim? Is not all this to make way for the Lord Jesus to take possession of his long since promised inheritance? And shall we stop at the first part? Is this to deal fairly with the Lord Jesus?—call him out to *battle* and then keep away his *crown?* God hath been faithful in doing great things for you; be faithful in this one—do your utmost for the preaching of the gospel in Ireland.[17]

And again:

> I would there were for the present one gospel preacher for every walled town in the English possession in Ireland. . . . The tears and

---

[16] In *Works*, Vol. VIII, pp. 211 ff.
[17] *Works*, Vol. VIII, p. 235.

cryes of the inhabitants of Dublin after the manifestations of Christ are ever in my view. . . . If their being gospelless move not our hearts, it is hoped their importunate cryes will disquiet our rest, and wrest help as a beggar doth an alms.[18]

Perhaps some of those present remembered how three years earlier he had made a similar impassioned plea for the preaching of the Gospel throughout England and Wales.

On 8 March an 'Act for the better advancement of the Gospel and Learning in Ireland' was passed in the Commons. It vested the property of the late Archbishop of Dublin and the Dean and Chapter of St Patrick's Cathedral in fifteen commissioners. John Owen was one of these along with Henry Ireton, Henry Cromwell, Jonathan Goddard, Hierome Sankey, Jenkin Lloyd and others.[19] The Act provided for the maintenance of Trinity College and also for the erecting and planning of another College and a Free School. On the same day Parliament resolved to send over six able ministers to Ireland and the Council of State appointed John Owen to be one of its official preachers at a salary of £200 per annum. He was required to preach every Lord's Day in the afternoon and was provided with lodgings in Whitehall. We do not know whether he brought his family to live with him. Probably they remained in Coggeshall and he visited them periodically.

(c) *In Scotland*

Oliver Cromwell left Dublin for England on 26 May. A month later the Council of State's Declaration of the justice and necessity of an invasion of Scotland was adopted by the Commons without a dissentient vote. Fairfax surrendering his commission, Cromwell was appointed Captain-General and Commander-in-Chief of the armies of the Commonwealth. Two days later he set out for the North, having with him Charles Fleetwood as Lieutenant-General and John Lambert as Major-General. On 19 July the army halted near Berwick and on the 22nd it entered Scotland. From two sentences in a dedicatory letter to Cromwell[20] it would appear that John Owen accompanied the army and preached to the troops at Berwick from Isaiah 56:7. 'For mine house shall be called an house of prayer for all people.' The

---

[18] ibid., p. 236.

[19] Ireton was son-in-law to Oliver Cromwell and Henry was Oliver's son, whilst Goddard was the general's physician. Ireton and Cromwell were army officers. Goddard became Warden of Merton College, Oxford, in 1651. Sankey was sub-warden of All Souls College, and Lloyd, bursar of Jesus College, Oxford. For the provisions of the Act see *Acts and Ordinances of the Interregnum*, 1642–1660 (eds. C. H. Firth and R. S. Rait), 1911, Vol. II, p. 355.

[20] The letter is prefixed to *The Branch of the Lord, the Beauty of Zion*, which is a discourse containing the sermon preached at Berwick and another preached later at Edinburgh. In *Works*, Vol. VIII.

theme was the relationship of the Church to Christ and the profusion of references to Biblical material shows that Owen believed that his hearers were men who had a very good knowledge of the contents of the Scriptures. God's spiritual house, he maintained, is Christ's Church of saints which is gathered out of all nations. This house is a living house, composed of spiritually-alive people, a strong house against which the gates of hell cannot prevail and also a glorious house.

> It is glorious in respect of the exaltation it hath above and the triumph over all its opposers. To see a house, a palace, hung round about with ensigns, spoils, and banners taken from the enemies that have come against it, is a glorious thing:—thus is the house of God decked: 'Kings of armies did flee apace, and she that tarried at home divided the spoil', Psalm 58:12. 'She that tarries at home', the mother of the family, the church of God, she hath 'all the spoils'. The Lord hath affirmed, that not only every one that opposeth, but all that do not serve this house, shall be utterly destroyed, Isaiah 60:12. There you have the spoil of Pharaoh, and all his host, gathered on the shore of the Red Sea, and dedicated to this house, Exodus 15. There you have the robes of Nebuchadnezzar, reserved when himself was turned into a beast, Daniel 4. There you have the imperial ornaments of Diocletian and his companions, casting aside their dominion for very madness that they could not prevail against this house. There is the blood of Julian, kept for a monument of vengeance against apostates. There you have the rochets of the prelates of this land, hung up of late, with other garments of their adherents, rolled in blood. There is a place reserved for the remaining spoils of the great whore, when she shall be burned, and made naked, and desolate, Revelation 11. Never any rose, or shall rise, against this house, and go forth unto final prosperity.[21]

He went on to explain that Jesus Christ Himself is the foundation and builder of this spiritual house. Also He dwells in it by His Spirit. To belong to the spiritual Body of Christ was infinitely more important than mere attendance at services of Worship. His sermon certainly encouraged the army to see its task as providing the peace and liberty in which the true saints of God could worship God aright and fulfil their Christian duties.

As John Owen travelled with the army towards the Firth of Forth he found the villages stripped of their male population whom the

---

[21] *Works*, Vol. VIII, p. 290. On the way to Berwick Owen visited the Congregational Church in Newcastle-on-Tyne. Cf. *Memoirs of Ambrose Barnes* (ed. W. H. D. Longstaffe), 1867, pp. 138 ff.

Scottish Commissioners of Estates had ordered to leave. On Friday 26 July he was probably with Cromwell at Dunbar where the fleet was waiting with provisions. By Monday he was in Musselburgh. The Scottish army under David Leslie was about four miles away entrenched between Edinburgh and Leith. On the night of the 29th the Scots made a surprise attack. Major-General Montgomery, with three colonels, Strachan, Lockhart, and Kerr, and a large body of their best cavalry, including many Cavaliers, set out for the English camp. They took Lilburne's regiment by surprise, defeated a detachment of Fleetwood's men, and rushed towards Musselburgh. By this time the English army was aroused and a counter-attack by their horse scattered the Scots, who fled towards Edinburgh. They were intercepted by a party of English dragoons who killed some of them and took a number of prisoners. John Owen witnessed these events and in a letter to John Lisle[22] at Westminster made reference to them. The letter was read in the House of Commons but only part of it has survived.[23]

> I dare not write the particulars of the fight, being assured that you have it from better hands: the issue, that they were repulsed by an handful, and a hundred and eighty taken prisoners; amongst them, Straughan's major, himself reported to be slain: the whole party pursued to their works: four ministers came out with them, but being not known, received the lot of war, three of them killed, and one taken.
>
> This was the party they most relyed upon, as being especially consecrated by the kirk to this service.
>
> Their ministers told the people before our army came, that they should not need to strike one stroke, but stand still, and they should see the sectaries destroyed.

Amongst those who sent a report of the fight was Cromwell.[24] Like Owen he referred to Major-General Montgomery and Colonel Strachan as 'two champions of the Church', on whom the Presbyterian Covenanters of the Scottish Church placed high hopes.

Before Cromwell's great victory over the Scottish army at Dunbar, Owen left the scene of war to return to London to his duties as preacher to the Council of State. But he was not allowed to stay there

[22] For Lisle see *D.N.B.*
[23] (Sir W. Scott), *Original Memoirs written during the Civil War*, Edinburgh, 1806, pp. 244–5. Cf. *A True Relation of the Proceedings of the English Army ... July 20–Aug. 5 ... Letters read in Parliament the sixth of August* (1650), and Abbott, Vol. II, p. 301.
[24] Abbott, Vol. II, pp. 299 ff.

for very long. At the request of Cromwell, who wished to combat the propaganda put out by the Scottish clergy, he was asked to return to Scotland with Joseph Caryl. On 13 September the Commons 'ordered that Mr Carill and Mr Owen be required forthwith to go into Scotland according to the desire of the Lord General'.[25]

The London ministers probably arrived in Edinburgh, which Cromwell had recently taken, just before 20 October on which day Caryl preached before the General and officers.[26] John Owen also preached before Cromwell between 20 October and 26 November. This may have been on 11 November when the Council of Officers kept a fast.[27] During this period, as before, Owen was on intimate terms with Cromwell, for when dedicating the printed version of the sermons he preached at Berwick and Edinburgh to the General he wrote:

> I do present them to your excellency, not only because the rise of my call to this service, under God, was from you; but also, because in the carrying of it on I have received from you, in the weakness and temptations wherewith I am encompassed, that daily spiritual refreshment and support—by inquiry into, and discovery of, the deep and hidden dispensations of God towards his secret ones—which my spirit is taught to value.

Being a chaplain who fervently believed in the justice of the cause of the Parliament and army he served, he entered into discussions with Scottish prisoners in order to show them how the providence of God was revealing itself in the movement of events. One of these prisoners, Alexander Jaffray, who was taken at Dunbar, has left an account in his diary of his talks with Cromwell, Fleetwood and Owen:

> During the time of my being a prisoner, I had good opportunity of frequent conference with the Lord General (Cromwell), Lieutenant General (Fleetwood) and Doctor Owen; by occasion of whose company, I had first made out unto me, not only some more clear evidences of the Lord's controversy with the family and person of our king, but more particularly, the sinful mistake of the good men of this nation (Scotland), about the knowledge and mind of God as to the exercise of the magistrate's power in the matters of religion—what the due bounds and limits of it are. The mistake and ignorance of the mind of God in this matter,—what evils

[25] *C.J.*, Vol. VI, p. 468.
[26] *Perfect Diurnall*, October 31.
[27] *Perfect Diurnall*, November 22.

hath it occasioned! fearful scandals and blasphemies on the one hand, and cruel persecution and bitterness among brethren on the other!²⁸

And Owen's growing influence as a theological spokesman for the army is seen in the contents of a letter dated 8 January 1651 from Robert Lilburne, the army commander in Hamilton, who wrote: 'I wish . . . I had some of Mr Owen's sermons and other books to disperse among them [the Scottish ministers and laymen] . . . many tell me they would gladly see and reade them'.²⁹ As we have seen, his sermons not only expounded various texts of Scripture they also argued the just cause of the Parliament and army.

Soon after the surrender of Edinburgh Castle to Cromwell, John Owen left Scotland for London to preach before the Council of State. On 8 March he was given permission 'to repair into the country for six weeks'.³⁰ Before he left Whitehall he heard that Oliver Cromwell had been appointed Chancellor of the University of Oxford. Whilst he was at Coggeshall with his wife and family the Commons voted by twenty-six votes to nineteen to appoint him the new Dean of Christ Church, Oxford.³¹ The small majority reveals how much uncertainty there was surrounding the appointment. In fact the House had debated the possibility of allowing the Presbyterian, Edward Reynolds, to continue as Dean even though he had not taken the Engagement, that is a promise to be faithful to the Commonwealth of England established without king or House of Lords. Also it had heard the report by James Challoner from the Committee for the Reformation of the Universities that Joseph Caryl had refused the position of Dean as he wished to remain in London. The confusion and negotiations which took place at Oxford before Owen's appointment are seen in a series of letters which Dr Robert Payne, an ejected Canon of Christ Church, wrote from Abingdon and Oxford to Gilbert Sheldon, the ejected Warden of All Souls. On 11 November 1650 he heard that Philip Nye and Stephen Marshall were being mentioned as possible successors to Reynolds. By 24 February the news was that Caryl was to be appointed although Reynolds still lived in the Dean's lodgings. Not until 24 March was he able to inform Sheldon that 'Owen, sometime scholar to Thomas Barlow of Queen's College is voted by the House (to which the business was devolved

²⁸ *The Diary of Alexander Jaffray* (ed. J. Barclay), 1833, pp. 58–9.
²⁹ J. Nickolls, *Original Letters and Papers of State* (1743), pp. 48–9.
³⁰ *C.S.P.D.* (1651), p. 74.
³¹ *C.J.* Vol. VI, p. 549.

from the Committee) Dean of Christ Church and that Reynolds must certainly leave it, after all the means he hath used to hold it'.[32]

According to Asty it was through a report in a news journal that Owen first heard of his appointment.[33] On 23 March 1651 Ralph Josselin noted in his diary that 'Mr Owen hath a place of great proffit given unto him, viz. Dean of Christ Church'.[34] In fact the profit was £800 per year. Soon afterwards the principal students of Christ Church wrote to Owen to express their great satisfaction that he was to be the new head of the College. This letter may perhaps be seen as both an indication of a measure of relief that at last an appointment had been made and also as a statement of confidence in the abilities and integrity of John Owen.[35]

---

[32] *Theologian and Ecclesiastic*, London, 1847–50, Vol. VIII, pp. 218–222. On 18 February Oliver Cromwell ventured the opinion that 'Dr Reynolds, Dr Wilkinson, Mr Curnett (Conant?) outed for not taking the engagement yet are useful and godly and willing to give satisfaction if means could be used to keep them in, it would be well'. He also suggested that he speak to 'Mr Owen and Sir Henry Vane'. Abbott, Vol. IV, p. 947. In fact it was Vane who acted as teller for the ayes on the division in the Commons which voted Owen in.
[33] Asty, p. 10.
[34] *Theologian and Ecclesiastic*, VIII, p. 222.
[35] No copy of this letter now exists but Asty affirms it was sent, Asty, p. 10.

PART II
Atlas of Independency
1651–1660

CHAPTER IV
Introductory

IN early May 1651 John Owen arrived in St Aldate's, Oxford, and entered the stately buildings of Christ Church to begin his work as Dean. Happily much progress in the way of reform and stabilisation after the civil wars had been achieved by Dr Reynolds. Apart from the delivery of lectures and sermons the duties before him to be undertaken in collaboration with the Chapter of eight canons included the oversight of lands and property, the maintenance of the fabric of Christ Church, the nomination of men to livings of which the College owned the patronage, the administration of discipline amongst servants and students, the annual election of students from Westminster School and elsewhere, and the provision of tutorial instruction and spiritual guidance of both undergraduates and Bachelors. In his capacity of Dean he also became a member of the Board of Visitors which had certain powers delegated to it by Parliament to settle internal matters of discipline and reform within the Colleges and Halls. From September 1652 his work and influence was increased by his becoming Vice-Chancellor through the nomination of Oliver Cromwell. Yet Owen did not seek these high offices; despite his 'most earnest requests to the contrary' they were entrusted to him. In addition to his work at Oxford he was often obliged to travel to London to settle University business or advise the government on religious matters.

(a) *Dean of Christ Church*

A good proportion of his time in Christ Church must have been taken up with administrative and financial matters. At least this is the impression one gets from reading the manuscript Chapter Book which is preserved in Christ Church Library.[1] Several pages, for example, are taken up with details of the problems connected with the tithes of Great Torrington in Devon. On 23 June 1651 the travelling expenses to Oxford of Mrs Smith, wife of the sequestered tenant of the rectory, were paid. Eventually in 1654 the Dean and Chapter successfully petitioned the Lord Protector for payment of tithes rightfully belonging to them. Then a few years later they discussed a petition from the people of Daresbury, near Runcorn, who wanted to secure a godly minister for their parish. Even so, they

---

[1] Canon Greenslade kindly allowed to me to read the Chapter Book and Dr Mason, Librarian of Christ Church, gave me the facilities needed to do so.

did not neglect the spiritual and intellectual life of the students, many of whom were only sixteen or seventeen years of age. On 5 May 1651 an order was made to the effect that senior members of College should preach in neighbouring village churches each Sunday. A month later the Dean and Chapter decided that pictures and windows representing God or the angels should be taken down. All undergraduates were expected to listen carefully to sermons and give an account of them to their tutors afterwards, and the conversation in Hall was to be conducted in Latin. Certain times for prayer were compulsory and tutors were expected to pray with their students regularly. Strict control was kept of the amount of money which was spent on food. On 29 September 1653 the following order was made:

> For the repressing the immoderate expences of youth in the College, that no gentleman commoner shall battel in the buttery above 5 shillings weekly; no under commoner above 4 shillings weekly; no scholar in the house above 3 shillings weekly; and the butler is hereby required to give notice to the Dean or Sub-dean at the end of the week of such as shall exceed this allowance.

Whilst Owen certainly made a lasting impression on such students as Philip Henry, John Locke, and William Penn, and passed on his Congregationalist principles to several others, he did not sufficiently impress and influence the majority of his students to cause them to share his dislike of Anglican rites and prelacy. Of the fifty or more Westminster students elected between 1651 and 1660 only one, Samuel Angier, became a Nonconformist from 1662. Perhaps this seeming failure may be attributed to his frequent absence from Christ Church when he travelled to London.

(b) *Vice-Chancellor*

As Vice-Chancellor Owen was the chairman of Convocation, the senate of the University. Although his behaviour at the meetings was in keeping with the high office he held, his dress was not conventional and this proved to be a source of annoyance to some of his colleagues. According to Anthony Wood he 'scorned all formality and undervalued his office by going in quirpo like a young scholar, with powdered hair, snakebone bandstrings (or bandstrings with very large tassels) lawn band, a large set of ribbands pointed, at his knees, and Spanish leather boots, with large lawn tops, and his hat mostly cock'd'.[2] In another important respect he differed from his predecessors in the office; he placed a much greater emphasis on preaching to students. With his friend, Thomas Goodwin, he preached regularly in St Mary's,

---

[2] Wood, *Athenae Oxonienses*, Vol. IV, col. 98.

which was the University church, and whenever else a suitable opportunity offered itself. Several books (e.g., *Of Temptation* (1658) and *Of the Mortification of Sin* (1656)) which were published by the University Press were in origin sermons preached to students. On several occasions he tried to set in motion reforms of the membership of the House of Convocation in which he believed there were too many flippant young men. Also he attempted to have abolished or simplified the annual University Act, held each July, since he felt, it encouraged sensuality and frivolity. On both these matters he was opposed and his resolutions defeated by a majority in Convocation. He used the powers invested in him as Vice-Chancellor both charitably and on one or two occasions harshly. For several years a large group of people met on Sundays in Oxford and held divine service according to the Book of Common Prayer. Although this was illegal he did not interfere with them. But when two Quaker girls tried to preach to the students he insisted that they be put in prison and whipped! Despite this apparently cruel treatment of the two girls, both his friends and foes admitted that he ruled the University from 1652 to 1657 both justly and efficiently.

Although the curriculum of the University during the Commonwealth was virtually the same as that used in the days of Charles I, a greater emphasis was placed on Reformed, Calvinistic doctrine in the 1650s. Owen himself lectured on the Sovereignty of God and published in 1653 a Latin treatise on the Justice of God. Perhaps Owen's aims for the University are usefully summarised in an order made by the Board of Visitors on 14 November 1653.

> Upon consideration that one maine end of the University is to traine up men as well in Divine as Humane learning that they may be able (when the providence of God shall call them) to publish the Gospell of Christ to the conversion and building up of soules to eternal life, and that exercise in the things of God doth much increase knowledge and savor therin: the Visitors thinke it meete that there should be frequent preaching in every College in this University, as far as the number of persons qualified for that service will beare.[3]

Thus to promote human and divine learning in the framework of the cultivation of godly living was the basic purpose of the University.

(c) *In London*

A deep concern for the progress of the Gospel and the extension of the kingdom of God lay at the heart of most of John Owen's

[3] *Register*, p. 372.

activities in London between 1651 and 1660. In his sermons before the House of Commons in 1651, 1656 and 1658 he called upon the leaders of the nation to promote the interest of the kingdom of Christ in the land. The pamphlet, *Humble Proposals for the furtherance and propagation of the Gospel*, which he produced in 1652, with the help of other ministers, sought to supply plans for a reformed national network of churches which would include Presbyterians, Congregationalists and Baptists. Its basic ideas were used by the Lord Protector two years later when he made his own Settlement of Religion. Owen dutifully served as a prominent member of Cromwell's Board of Triers which judged the fitness of men who sought to become parish ministers. Also he was an assistant to the commissioners for Oxfordshire whose task was to eject immoral, heretical and ungodly ministers in the county. He was a member of the committee appointed by the Protector to study the petition of Menasseh ben Israel for the readmission of the Jews into England. As many Puritans expected the imminent conversion of the Jews to take place at or before the overthrow of Roman Catholicism in Europe, the work of this committee was important from both a theological and economic standpoint. Another committee of which he was a member licensed translations of the Bible and yet another provided help for the suffering Protestants of Piedmont. A great part of his time was further spent as a referee in the conferences which sought to heal the divisions in the Scottish churches and reconcile the Resolutioners with the Protestors.

Unfortunately John Owen's Republican political views brought him into open conflict with Cromwell. Probably he did not approve of Cromwell being created 'His Highness the Lord Protector' in December 1653. Certainly he strongly opposed the move in May 1657 to make Cromwell into a king and he even wrote the petition against monarchy which senior army officers presented to Cromwell in that month. From this time until Cromwell's death in the following year the two men, who from 1649 to 1656 were such close friends, had little or no personal contact. After the important Savoy Assembly of Congregational elders in September 1658 and during the period when Richard Cromwell was Protector, Owen became deeply involved in political matters. He spent most of his time in London advising the senior army officers on the religious needs of the nation and of the churches as well as gathering a church in the home of General Fleetwood at Wallingford House. Thus he was connected with the moves and plots which led to the dissolution of Parliament in April 1659, the recall of the Rump of the Long Parliament, and the eventual resignation of Richard. Yet he was not connected with the closure of the Rump's sitting by General Lambert on 13 October. When the nation, on the verge of anarchy, began to look to General George

Monck, the army commander in Scotland, as the person who alone could restore order and civil government, Owen and his fellow London Congregationalists made several attempts to persuade the General to preserve the interests of their churches, but although Monck made vague promises, he was not able or willing to keep them after he had marched to London, and recalled the members of the Long Parliament. In March 1660, just before the return of King Charles and the restoration of the Anglican hierarchy, Owen was removed from the Deanery of Christ Church. He moved with his family to the house in Stadhampton which he had previously bought when he ceased to be Vice-Chancellor and where he had earlier held services of worship. For ten years he had exerted a powerful influence on the counsels of the nation and now, swiftly and tragically, he was silenced.

CHAPTER V

Correspondence 1651-1660

THE following letters, which comprise the extant correspondence of John Owen for the years 1651 to 1660 reflect a wide sphere of work and influence. Although they are only a small proportion of the very large correspondence with which he must have dealt in this extremely busy period of his life, they do mirror the variety of tasks and concerns which were ever before him in a complicated yet fascinating period of English history. It was in the expedition to Ireland in 1649 that Owen came to be well acquainted with Oliver Cromwell and from this association rise to high office in the Commonwealth; significantly the first letter is from Ireland. It was in 1660 that Owen fell into disgrace amongst Royalists and again, significantly, the last letter seeks to ridicule him. The rest of the letters show us the University teacher and administrator, the theologian, the preacher, the adviser of rulers and the evangelist with a deep concern for the growth of the Protestant Faith and the expansion of churches of the Congregational way. The correspondence is printed in chronological order, and the dates are according to modern style. The old spelling is in general preserved.

1. FROM THE COMMISSIONERS IN IRELAND[1]

Sir,

The Parliament, being desirous to advance religion and learning in Ireland, have commanded our endeavours to improve their interest for the promoting of that work according to the trust by them reposed in us. In pursuance of which trust we have inquired into the present state and condition of the College of Dublin and do find the said College furnished with very few officers or other members fit to be continued there. The consideration whereof (and the house being at

[1] A transcript of the copy of this letter is in R. Dunlop, *Ireland under the Commonwealth*, Manchester, 1913, Vol. I, pp. 10–11. All the Commonwealth records described in the 'Appendix' to *The Fourteenth Report of the Deputy Keeper of the Public Records in Ireland*, 1882, were destroyed by fire in 1922. Cf. also W. Urwick, *The Early History of Trinity College, Dublin*, 1892, pp 56–7, J. P. Mahaffy, *An Epoch in Irish History*: *Trinity College, Dublin*, 1903, pp. 295 ff., and St. J. D. Seymour, *The Puritans in Ireland*, Oxford, 1921, pp. 20 ff.

present visited with the pestilence[2]) moved us to dissolve that society until it shall please God to remove the sickness and some means found out to establish a course which may probably conduce to those good ends. In order thereunto we desire that you (whom we find to be one of the Trustees[3] of that College) upon advice with Mr Thomas Goodwin (or such other persons as you shall conceive fit) will seriously consider what laws, rules, orders and constitutions are fit to be established in the said College. Wherein we desire that the educating of youth in the knowledge of God and principles of piety may be in the first place promoted, experience having taught that where learning is attained before the work of grace upon the heart, it serves only to make a sharper opposition against the power of godliness. What God shall direct you in this matter we desire you to communicate to us with all convenient expedition, and likewise what qualifications are requisite in the admission of persons according to the course now used in the university. 2 July 1651

[2] According to Edmund Ludlow (*Memoirs*, ed. C. H. Firth, 1894, Vol. I, p. 261) the plague was believed to have been introduced into Ireland by a ship from Spain which docked at Galway.

[3] In March 1650 Owen was appointed a trustee for the University of Dublin. Cf. *Acts and Ordinances of the Interregnum, 1642–1660* (eds. C. H. Firth and R. S. Rait), 1911, Vol. II, p. 355.

2. FROM LEWIS DU MOULIN[1]

To the most Honourable and Distinguished Dr John Owen, Dean of Christ Church, Vice-Chancellor of the University of Oxford

Summary

He offers congratulations to Owen on his appointment as Vice-Chancellor, regarding it as a just and well-deserved reward for his merits and talents, and an office in which he will be of service to the University, rather than one who merely exercises authority only. He mentions Owen's works generally, his theological studies in particular, and sees him as a defender of scholarship and goes on to suggest that he has the support of the whole University who look to him for leadership and protection in their affairs.

Du Moulin refers to his own foreign origin and the affronts and difficulties he has had to endure on account of it. Referring to the overcrowding of students in the University he comments that the

[1] Dedicatory Epistle in Latin (comprising 12 pages) to Du Moulin's book, *Oratio Auspicalis* (1652). Lewis Du Moulin, for whom see *D.N.B.*, was appointed Camden Professor of Ancient History in September 1648. The book contains his inaugural lecture and seems to have been the only inaugural lecture of the period which was printed. Moulin used the name Ludovicus Molinaeus on the title-page.

lectures of foreign staff are not well attended. Though some people have blamed this on the difficulty of understanding a foreign accent, he feels it is rather the laziness of the students which is to blame. He points out that in the study of proper Classical Latin and Greek it makes no difference what is the nationality of the teacher as pronunciation of Classical languages is standardised in Europe. There follows a very detailed and rather technical analysis of the pronunciation of various Classical vowel sounds and the slight divergences among teachers.

The writer then answers another charge made against him that he is unsuitable for work in the University since he is French and people turn their dislike for France into dislike for him. This he rejects since his own father was exiled from France because of his work for the Church of England. Yet another charge which he finds made against him is that he, as a foreigner, should not be employed in an English University; but to this he answers that talent and ability should govern the requirements for appointments, not birth in a country. The introduction of a foreigner shakes native scholars out of their apathy since they are reluctant to admit the superiority of a foreign scholar, and conversely, the foreigner works harder to prove his worth.

The letter ends with further congratulations and a dedication.

September 1652

3. FROM OLIVER CROMWELL[1]

By his Exellency the Lord General Cromwell, Chancellor of the University of Oxon

Whereas diverse applications have been made unto mee from severall of the Members of the University of Oxford, concerning differences which have arisen betweene the Members of the sayd University about diverse matters which fall under my cognizance as Chancellor; and forasmuch as differences and complaints of the like nature may happen and arise between them. And considering that it would bee very troublesome and chargeable to the parties concerned to attend mee at this distance about the same, and the present burthen of publique affairs not permitting mee so fully to hear and understand the same as to bee able to give my judgement and determination

---

[1] Reg. Convoc., p. 173. For the University under the Commonwealth see Anthony Wood, *This History and Antiquities of the University of Oxford*, Oxford, 1796, Vol. II, pt. 2, and C. E. Mallet, *A History of the University of Oxford*, 1924, Vol. II. This and other letters from the University Archives are printed by kind permission of the Keeper of the Archives.

therein. I doe hereby desire and authorize Mr John Owen, now Vicechancellor of the University, and the Heads of severall Colledges and Halls there, or any five or more of them (whereof the sayd Vicechancellor to bee one), to heare and examine all such differences and complaints which have, or shall arise, betweene any of the sayd members, giving them as full power and authority as in mee lyes to order and determine therein as, in their judgements, they shall think meet and agreeable to justice and equity. And this power and commission to continue during the space of sixe months now next ensuing. Given under my hand and seale the 16th day of October 1652,

OLIVER CROMWELL

By his Excellency the Lord General Cromwell, Chancellor of the University of Oxon

Whereas within the University of Oxon there frequently happen severall things to bee dispensed, granted and confirmed wherewith the Vicechancellor, Doctors, Regent Masters and others of the sayd university in their Delegacy and Convocations cannot by their statutes dispense, grant or confirme without the assent of their Chancellor. And forasmuch as the present weighty affairs of the Common wealth doe call for and engage mee to reside and give my personall attendance in so neare London; soe that the Scholars of the sayd university and others are put to much charge and trouble by coming to London to obtaine my assent in the cases before mentioned. Therefore taking the premises into consideration for the more ease and benefitt of the sayd Scholars and university, and that I may with lesse avocation and diversion attend the councells and service of the common wealth; I doe by these presents ordaine, authorize, appoint and delegate Mr John Owen, Deane of Christchurch and vicechancellor of the sayd university, Dr Wilkins, Warden of Wadham Colledge, Dr Jonathan Goddard, Warden of Merton Colledge, Mr Thomas Goodwin, President of Magdalin Colledge, and Mr Peter French, Prebend of Christchurch,[2] or any three or more of them to take into consideration all and every matter of dispensation, grant or confirmation whatsoever which require my assent as Chancellor to the sayd university, and thereupon to dispense, grant, confirme or otherwise dispose thereof as to them shall seeme meet and to certifie the same to the convocation, and all and every such dispensation, grant, confirmation or disposition made by the aforesayd Mr John Owen, Dr Wilkins, Dr Jonathan

[2] John Wilkins, Jonathan Goddard and Thomas Goodwin are in the *D.N.B.*, but Peter French, the brother-in-law of Oliver Cromwell, who died in 1655, is not. See *Alumni Oxonienses*.

Goddard, Mr Tho. Goodwin and Mr Peter French or any three or more of them shall be to all intents and purposes firme and valid in as full, large and ample manner as if to every such particular act they had my assent in writing under my hand and seale, or I had been personally present and had given my voyce and suffrage thereunto. In writing whereof I have hereunto set my hand and seale the 16th day of October 1652.

OLIVER CROMWELL

4. FROM OLIVER CROMWELL[1]

For the Reverend the Vicechancellour and members of Convocation in the University of Oxford

Gentlemen,

I desire to bee tender in engaging you to conferre academicall Degrees upon persons who have not by converse amongst you, or performance of exercises according to the statutes of the university, approved themselves deserving the same: But there is a person Mr John Bunkley[2] by name whose eminent learning and worth is such that I account I may very freely commend him unto you and desire of you that hee may bee created Master of Arts; which degree in the judgment of learned men, to whom he is knowne, hee is like to adorne noe lesse, then that, to commend him, soe that it can bee noe act unworthy of your selves herein to answer the desire and expectation of

Your affectionate friend and Chancellour,
O. CROMWELL

Octob. 28th 1652

[1] Reg. Convoc., p. 176.
[2] For Bunkley (Boncle) see *C.R.* He received the M.A. degree on 22 December 1652.

5. FROM OLIVER CROMWELL[1]

To the Reverend the Vicechancellor and the Members of Convocation of the University of Oxford

Gentlemen,

I did not long since recommend unto you Mr Bunkley to bee created Master of Arts as a person who in respect of his singular worth was like to adorne that degree. I now understand that there is

[1] Reg. Convoc., p. 177.

a vacancy of one of the Esquire Bedles places;² and truly his eminent learning and piety being such as I am informed, I cannot but judge that, in that Station hee would be a very considerable ornament to your University; and that I may doe you a good office by recommending him to your Election into that place, and that by such an act as yours you would advantage your selves and doe that which would bee acceptable unto your best freinds as well as testifie your respects unto,

Your affectionate friend and Chancellour,

O. CROMWELL

² Boncle was elected as Superior Bedel in divinity for 1653. In 1654 he became Headmaster of Eton College.

6. TO THE MASTER OF BALLIOL COLLEGE[1]

At a meeting of the heads of Colledges and Halls in Christchurch the 22 of November 1652

Uppon the petition of Mistress Purefey desireing liberty to remoove her sonne James Purefey Batchelor of Arts from Brazenose Colledge,² to place him in some other Colledge or Hall in this University, by the authority of the Chancellor delegated unto us,³ it is ordered that the petitioner have liberty soe to doe.

Signed by apoynment

JOHAN OWEN: Vicecan: Oxon

I doe desire Doctor Savadge⁴ of Baylioll Colledge to admitt the person mentioned in the said petition into his Colledge.

JOHAN OWEN: Vicecan: Oxon

¹ Balliol College Register 1514–1682. The Librarian of Balliol, E. V. Quinn, kindly sent me a photocopy of this note which is in the handwriting of John Owen and was pasted into the Register, which is not paginated.

² For James Purefey see *Alumni Oxonienses*.

³ Cf. Letter No. 3.

⁴ For Henry Savage see *D.N.B.*

7. TO THE PARLIAMENT[1]

To the Supreame Authoritie of this Nation,
The Parliament of the Commonwealth of England

That the Fathers joy at the returning of a Spend-thrift Sonne, ought to have an influence upon the whole Family of Heaven and Earth, that is called after his name, to worke their suitable affections, and conformity to himselfe, cannot be questioned by any true childe thereof. Behold then, Right Honourable, a call thereunto, Poore Prodigalls, who have not only with our selves lost that rich Treasure of grace and holinesse, wherewith in our Common roote and Fountaine we were entrusted, but also in a course of Rebellion for many Generations wasted the remainder of Natures Riches to the utmost degeneracy that an Immortall rationall being is obnoxious unto, not returning a farre off, but rejoycing in the imbraces of their Father, and enterteined with his flesh and blood, who was slaine and sacrificed for them.

The ayme of our walking with God here is to come up to some conformitie to them, who behold his face and doe his Will in Heaven: amongst them there is joy at the Repentance of one Sinner, and shall not wee finde sweetnesse in the first fruits of a barren Wildernesse in the shining of a beame of light into the darknesse of another World, giving hope of a plentifull harvest, and a glorious day to ensue. Let men take heed, lest by despising the day, and opposing the Worke of the Lord towards those poore Sonnes of *Adam*, notwithstanding all their zealous profession, they proclaime themselves to pursue a Carnall Interest; by which they declare the enlargement of the Dominion of Jesus Christ is of no Concernment unto them.

Wee are by many Pledges assured better things of you Right Honourable, and such as accompany zeale for the House of our God, and therefore the ensuing Testimonialls of the progresse of the Worke of the Gospel being sent unto us, wee make bold humbly to present them to you; partly that we may invite you as the friends of Jesus Christ, to rejoyce with him that some sheepe of his, who were lost, are found; and partly to lay before you, some such fruits of the putting

---

[1] This letter first appeared in Henry Whitfield's *Strengthe out of Weaknesse* (1652) and it is also found in *Banners of Grace and Love* (1657) which seems to be a reprint of *Strengthe out of Weaknesse*. The purpose of both books was to stimulate interest in missionary work amongst the Indians of North America by allowing the reader to peruse various letters sent from New England to Henry Whitfield. These described the conversion of some Indians to Christianity. I am grateful to the Librarian of Harvard University for sending me a photocopy of this letter to Parliament.

forth of your Authoritie for the carrying on this most glorious undertaking, as may encourage you to goe on through him who doth enable you unto future reall expressions of your love and zeale thereunto. Wee shall not need to draw forth any particulars from the ensuing Narrative, to give you a taste of that Spirit whereinto these poore Creatures are sweetly baptized; Wee hope your delight in the Worke of God will inforce a leasure, to view the whole; this in Generall wee may say, that in the Wildernesse are waters broken out, and streames in the Desert, the parched ground is become a Poole, and the thirsty Land-springs of water in the Habitation of Dragons, where each lay, there is grasse with Reeds and Rushes, the Lord has powred water upon him that is thirstie, and flouds upon the dry ground; He hath powred his Spirit on the seeds of the Heathen, & his blesing on their Off-spring, they spring up as among the grasse, as willows by the water-courses: One sayes I am the Lords, and another calls himselfe by the name of *Jacob,* and another subscribes with his hand unto the Lord, and sirnames himselfe by the name of *Israel.* The Lord hath done a new thing, and wee know it, he hath made a way in the Wildernesse, and Rivers in the Desert, the beast of the field doth honour him, the Dragons, and the Owles because he gives waters in the Wildernes, and Rivers in the Desert, to give drinke to his People his chosen, so that upon the Report heere read unto us, wee cannot but glorifie God with those Primitive beleevers of old, and say, then hath God also to the poore naked *Indians* granted Repentance unto life. Their outward wants and streights have often been presented unto you; wee shall not need to repeat them, blessed be the Lord, and blessed be you of the Lord that your hearts have been stirred up to give encouragement unto this Worke, and to open a Doore for the reliefe of those Eminent Instruments in the hand of the Lord who carry it on, who though they communicate to them Spiritualls, yet are so farre from receiving of their Temporalls, that they impart unto them a Portion of their owne dayly bread, and provision necessary from their owne subsistence.

The good Lord lay the weight and concernment of this Worke upon your spirits, and wee no way doubt that you will in any way be wanting to the Publique improvement of this blessed opportunitie, for the enlargement of the Kingdome of him whom our Soules doe love: There is a vexation of spirit which through their formalitie and unbeliefe, hath encompassed many professors, that whereas they have with much seeming earnestness cryed out for mercies; when they have been bestowed, they have thought scorne of them: so did the *Jewes* in the busines of their Messias, and many at this day amongst our selves in the great workes of the Providence of God: It is so with some to this breaking forth of light amongst the *Indians,* desiring it before it began, despising it in its very beginnings, the Lord lay it not unto their charge, and keep all our spirits in an holy admiration and reverence of the powerfull efficacy of his eternall and unchangeable purposes, which through so many sinfull Generations (falling in their Rebellion) have preserved a seed to himselfe, whereof he will take care that one graine fall not to the Ground.

Your Honors humble Servants;[2]

JOHN OWEN	THO: GOODWIN
JOSEPH CARYL	SIDRACH SIMPSON
WILL: GREENHILL	PHILIP NYE
WILLIAM BRIDGE	WILLIAM STRONG
WILLIAM CARTER	HENRY WHITFIELD
GEORGE GRIFFITH	RALPH VENNING

[2] All the twelve ministers were Independents and are all in *C.R.* except Sidrach Simpson, who died in 1655, and for whom see *D.N.B.*

8. FROM THE COMMITTEE FOR PUBLIC REVENUE[1]

To the Deane and Prebends of Christ Church

Gentlemen,

Wee send you here inclosed the Petition of Henry Cornish,[2] the Certificate of Colonel Walton,[3] and the letter of Lord General Cromwell,[4] recommending Cornish unto us to have an Almsmans place in Christ Church Hospitall in Oxon.[5] Now understanding that there is noe Almsmans place voyd in the sayd Hospitall at present, wee desire you to conferre on him the first Almsmans place that shall next become voyd there, vouching the desert eroudition of the man, wee neede not say any thing, having soe ample testimony before you, soe leaving him to your especiall care,

We rest
Your very loving friends,[6]

Dated at the Committee
for the Publique Revenue
sitting at Westminster
the 14th day of Dec. 1652.

H. VANE
J. EDWARDS
H. MILDMAY
C. HOLLAND
J. TRENCHARD

[1] 'Christ Church Chapter Book, 1647-1658', p. 59. This and other material from Christ Church is printed by permission of the Dean and Chapter.
[2] This petition is no longer extant.
[3] Presumably Valentine Walton who married Margaret Cromwell.
[4] This letter is not in Abbott's collection of Cromwell's letters.
[5] Since its foundation Christ Church has been required to maintain 24 Almsmen (H. L. Thompson, *Christ Church*, p. 12.). The Almshouses on the west side of St Aldate's were sold to Pembroke College in the nineteenth century; the almsmen now receive small weekly pensions but no accommodation. I am grateful to Dr J. F. A. Mason for this information.
[6] For details of these men see M. F. Keeler, *The Long Parliament*.

9. FROM THE COMMISSIONERS IN IRELAND[1]

Sir,

We need not tell you of the great want of fit and able ministers for preaching the Gospel in this country. From our deep sense of it we formerly invited several to that work; but (to our saddening) find but a slow compliance. We do understand the inclination of some others for coming over; but most of them are strangers to us, so that we have enclosed these several letters directed to them, desiring that you would inform yourselves of them and their abilities, and as you shall find them qualified for the work to cause their letters to be sealed and set unto them, with such further inducements of your own as you shall conceive fit. We commit us all and our poor endeavours to the Lord, in whom we are your very loving friends.

For Messrs. OWEN, LOCKYER, AND JENKYN LLOYD[2]

31 August 1653.

[1] Cf. R. Dunlop, *Ireland under the Commonwealth*, Vol. II. p. 371, for a transcript of this letter, and see notes to Letter No. 1.

[2] For Nicholas Lockyer see *C.R.*, and for Jenkyn Lloyd, *Alumni Oxonienses*.

10. TO THE CITY OF LONDON[1]

To the Right honourable the Lord Mayor, Aldermen and Commons of the Citty of London

Right Honourable,

It hath been the usuall method of our infinitely Wise and Gracious God to open a doore of hope into his Church when it seemed to be shutt up, and He to have returned unto his place: Then will he arise and then will he be most exalted. We are called upon by an eminent providence to give testimony unto this goodnesse of the Lord in that he hath provoked that zeale for his glory and the wayes which he hath appointed and blessed for the advancement thereof, with tender affection to them whose hearts are upright with him in their Generation (which wee doubt not was longe before kindled in your breasts) to breake forth soe visibly in your late Addresse[2] to the great Councell of

[1] Reg. Convoc., pp. 221–2.

[2] The Address was entitled *To the Supreme Authority of the Nation, the Parliament of England* and was on sale by 2 September 1653. It was a protest against the sectarian party in the Barebones Parliament which was campaigning against tithes, universities, and any kind of public maintenance for the ministry. The petition pleaded that the precious truths of the Gospel should be preserved, that faithful ministers should be encouraged and their lawful maintenance and property preserved, and that the two universities should be zealously preserved and maintained. In 1653 the most debated religious issue was not between a Presbyterian or Independent Establishment but whether there should be any sort of State Church at all. The petition is printed in *The Parliamentary or Constitutional History of England*, 1757, Vol. XX, p. 219.

the Nation; wherein (all circumstances considered) you seeme to have out-done all those happy precedents of love to the Gospell which have made your otherwise renowned Citty soe justly deare to all the Churches of Christ. Those respects which are given to Religion when it thrives and prospers in the World are scarce thank-worthy, but to owne it in the midst of a crooked and perverse Generation, and to speake a word in its behalfe when all seem to have forsaken it, This is love unfeigned, and of a pure heart: And clearely such is yours. It was not because we are lesse concerned or more insensible then others that we did not prevent you in appearinge for a Cause so deare and precious: your wisdome and charity will readily suggest unto you the reasons of our silence to men, although to our God we are not, but in waitinge for him, whom it hath pleased to referre the greatest praise of soe blessed a work for you: which however it succeed (and why should there not be hope in Israel concerning this thing!) will certainly fill the hearts of all that wish well to Sion, with the sweet odour of your names and draw out their Spiritts in continual supplication at the Throne of Grace for a plentifull returne of blessings both upon your Persons and your honourable Citty. For our selves (however we may seeme more particularly concerned yet) our hearts assure us we drive noe interest but what is common to all men of sobriety and soundnesse in the faith of the Gospell in this our thankfull resentment of that your soe seasonable intercession for the Generall good: The Lord returne that exemplary labour which you have shewed to his Church and Gospell in this contending for the faith once delivered to the saints with the meanes of its orderly propagation according to the will of Christ with a bountifull encrease unto your bosoms fasteninge you as a nayle in a sure place and inspiringe you with yet more zeale for the honour of our God and the well fare of our Nation; that though the prince of darknesse (being full of wrath) bestirr himselfe never so much to extinguish the light and to throw downe the tabernacle of our Zion (the uncleane Spirit being not as yet caused to passe out of the Land) yet the glorious Lord may continually shine upon it, and through his mighty power in and by sure instruments not one of the stakes thereof may ever be remooved, nor one of its cords broken. For what relates to our endeavours that way, we humbly hope in the goodnesse of our God (without whom we are nothinge) that as he hath all ready breathed into our hearts some unfeigned though weak desires to lay out our selves for his glory soe he will further enable us to walke before him as such who should be lights unto others and to imploy all that wee are and have for the winninge of soules unto him whoe hath bought them with a price: and by this meanes as to justify the hopes of all the rationall and godly soe to silence the malice, envy and ignorance of unreasonable and self-seeking men. And as in generall we shall labour in the station allotted to us (in a troublous time) by the good providence of our God, to approve our consciences to him enduring with patience the contradiction of men, considering the end of the Lord; soe we will assure you that the publique testimony which you have been pleased to give concerninge your apprehensions of us, and expectations from us, doth exceedingly provoke us to a more earnest endeavour after the accomplishment of all those good ends whereunto we are appoynted, that you may have cause to rejoice and never be ashamed of your good thoughts concerninge us. That the Lord would preserve your famous Citty in the enjoyment of Truth, Righteousness, and peace and continually guide you by his Counsell in the government thereof, is the hearty prayer of,

Yours in all Christian observance,
The University of Oxford[3]

Oxford, from our
Convocation House,
September 13th, 1653.

[3] As Vice-Chancellor, John Owen was the person chiefly responsible for the writing of this letter. The ideas in it are in accord with the sentiments found in his sermons and books of this period; cf. especially *The Humble Proposals of Mr Owen, Mr Tho. Goodwin . . . for the furtherance and propagation of the Gospel* (1652), and his Latin Oration for 1654.

11. FROM BARON HERBERT OF CHERBURY[1]

For my Reverend Friend Doctor Owen; Dean of Christchurch, these

Mr Deane,

I am not a little troubled (that) your letter of the 29th August should surprise mee this day unprovided to give you any other satisfactory answer then that Mr. Palmer's[2] bill of Arrears due upon my son shall God willinge bee returned unto his tutor by All Hallows day; Bee pleased (in the last place) to take notice I labour at this time under great engagements for the late king as of other for myselfe and yet there are lands in Trust to lett for the payment of them which were unexpectedly obstructed in the sale very lately but these things

[1] Bodleian MS. Tanner 52, f. 48. Richard Herbert, second Baron Herbert of Cherbury (1600–1655) was the elder son of Lord Herbert: see *D.N.B.* s.v. Edward Herbert (1583–1648). Much of the property belonging to the Herberts around Montgomery was confiscated after the civil wars. Baron Richard Herbert had two sons, Edward, third Baron Herbert (d. 1678), and Henry (d. 1691), fourth Baron Herbert. This letter probably concerns the latter.

[2] Mr Francis Palmer was a Student of Christ Church and a tutor.

now removed, I expect by Gods assistance a speedy issue to all troubles of this nature which are otherwise insufferable in conscience and honnor.[3]

Your affectionate friend and humble servant,

Montgomery
23 Sept 1653
R. HERBERT

[3] Not only is this letter now badly faded but it is also written in poor English.

12. FROM OLIVER CROMWELL[1]

For my Reverend and worthie friend the Vice Chancellor and Convocation of the University of Oxford, these

Gentlemen,

Hearinge that a Bedles place in the University is Vacant by the resignation of Mr Boncle whome I formerly recommended unto you, and having Information of the fitnesse of Leonard Lichfield, Printer to the University,[2] for the discharge of that place, that it may be an encouragement to him to be further serviceable unto you in his faculty soe neerly related to your Studies. I doe recommend him unto you for that imployment not doubting but that if you shall judge him meet for the place, he will faithfully discharge it, and by his diligent service in the performance of his duty answere the recommendation from

Cockpitt,
Octob: 14: 1653.

Gentlemen,
Your lovinge friend,
O. CROMWELL

[1] Reg. Convoc., p. 224.
[2] For Leonard Lichfield see *D.N.B.*

13. FROM OLIVER CROMWELL[1]

To my Reverend and worthie friend the Vice Chancellor & Convocation of the University of Oxford, these

Gentlemen,

I understand that the time for the nominatinge a Vice Chancellor for the next year is now approachinge, and consideringe how great need there is of continuinge the governement of the University in an able and faithfull hand I doe hereby nominate and appoint the present

[1] Reg. Convoc., p. 223.

Vice Chancellor Mr John Owen to the place of Vice Chancellor to your University for the yeare following: not doubtinge but he will answer that Care and Vigilancy which the service and occasion of the Place doth call for wherein allsoe you shall not want the ready assistance of

Gentlemen

Your lovinge friend & Chancellor

Cockpitt
October 24th 1653

O. CROMWELL

14. FROM THE VISITORS OF THE UNIVERSITY OF OXFORD[1]

Upon consideration of a speech lately made by Mr Busby,[2] Student of Christ Church, at the funerall of Mr. Hoult[3] of Balioll Colledge, at Magdalen Parish in Oxon: contayning matter of profanation and abuse of Scripture, tending much to the palliation and extennuation of grosse miscarriages, to the strengthening of the hands of the wicked and sadning of the hearts of the godly, whereby God hath beene much dishonored, and the University scandalized and prejudiced. And all this after his restauration to his Student's place, out of which hee had formerly beene ejected: wee the Visitors of the University of Oxon doe hereby order: That the said Mr Busby be deprived of all the profitts and priviledges of his Student's place in Christ Church for a full halfe yeare after the date hereof, and that hee be not then restord but wholly ejected, except he shall so approve himselfe to the Deane and Prebendaries of Christ Church, as they may judg him likely to be serviceable to God in his place and generation. And it is further ordered: That a coppie of this Order and his speech[4] be herewith sent unto the said Deane and Prebendaries of Christ Church aforesaid.

The Visitors

November 8th 1653

[1]There are two copies of this letter. One is in the 'Chapter Book of Christ Church', p. 63, and the other is in Burrows, *Register*, p. 370.

[2]John Busby was a Westminster student in 1647. He proceeded B.A. in 1650 and was soon after expelled and then restored.

[3]John Hoult became a member of Balliol College in 1651 and was made a Fellow in 1653. He died on 23 Oct. in a fall from a horse. Cf. *Wood*, p. 184.

[4]This speech does not seem to be extant.

15. FROM OLIVER CROMWELL[1]

To my worthy friends the Vice Chancellor and Venerable house of Convocation in Oxon

Gentlemen,

Having received a good Character of Mr. John Windebanke,[2] Master of Arts, and beinge desired by a worthy friend to recommend him unto you, I shall make it my request that he may receive the favour of a Degree of Dr in Physick from your University. I am certainly informed that he hath been a Student in your University this Twenty yeares and hath since his leavinge it spent some time in forraigne parts, and that he hath been a Practitioner for some yeares in that science with much credit and reputation; soe that he hath all ready gained the repute of one worthy for his Knowledge and abilitys upon whom you may conferr this Title. And in regard his Place of Practice & residence is soe far distant from the University, I shall desire he may have his Grace granted Simpliciter without any further Occasion of Trouble, or Attendance to him. I can assure you I doe very much avoyd Occasions of Trouble in Requests of this extraordinary nature, be pleased therefore to excuse this given to you at present by

Gentlemen,
Your assured friend & Chancellor to serve you
O. CROMWELL

[1] Reg. Convoc., p. 241. No date is given but it was probably written just before Cromwell became Lord Protector; it was read in Convocation on 5 April 1654.
[2] John Windebank was the son of the old Secretary of State, Sir Francis Windebank, for whom see *D.N.B.*

16. TO THE LORD PROTECTOR[1]

To His Highness Oliver Lord Protector of the Common-Wealth of England Scotland and Ireland and Chancellor of the University of Oxford, these present

Most Serene Lord,

Amongst the signs of peace and tranquillity about to be sealed, we see that you are placed at the head of affairs so that in your wisdom you may calm and compose everything which is troubled by rebellion.

[1] Reg. Convoc., pp. 226–7. Original in Latin. This letter was written after Cromwell became Lord Protector in December 1653.

And so let it be fitting that in the Public Rejoicing, the University, your foster-child, (to whom your good fortune extends first and foremost) should respectfully approach you and join with the rest in congratulation. And indeed, as your more loyal supporters we cast ourselves before you, offering our respects to your greatness. For being now accustomed to your patronage, we pay honour to a name well known and loved in the world of letters, a man heavy with praise for his civil and military deeds, bred for learning and for weapons, under whose protection may the weakness and anxiety in our affairs die away. We owe it to your favour that the University survives today: that ignorance and unruliness do not dishonour our company; that these insolent men of Rhetoric (with their awkward eloquence which the wretched men drew from public springs) should not overshadow the noble arts. And we thank you in the name of this learned and indeed universal body that you should have taken into your care the floundering world of letters; because of your care we have not seen the Prefects and Public Procurators of our piety go hungry and be exiled; because in your lifetime, the military glory of Britain's name has risen again; and so if anyone criticises the achievements of the State which you have made great, let him consider the world beyond, for we see our naval triumph, which was snatched away and shattered by a rival nation, brought back under your auspices, bearing a crown of laurel; and our waters not lying freely open to pirates and enemies hemming in our shores.

But it is not right to touch further on these things at random, nor by our own trifling affairs to disract you as you watch over the public good. . . . It is our greatest wish that with you as Guardian and Guide of affairs, Religion, Learning and the Public Peace may continue harmoniously for as long as possible, and that, in the dignity of your office, you may consider us worthy of your protection.

December 1653.
Your most devoted servant,
The University of Oxford

17. FROM THE LORD PROTECTOR[1]

For Mr John Owen Vice Chancellor and the rest of the Convocation of the University of Oxford, these

Gentlemen,

Understandinge that there hath been an Augmentation of Allowance granted unto five of the Bedles of the University of Oxon by the Convocation of the same, and likewise by the Committy of Parliament

---
[1] Reg. Convoc.. p. 231.

for the Universitys after a serious and strict Examination of their severall Fees and Allowances which said Augmentation continued according to the said Committees Order till the 13th day of November last; And finding that the same grounds do remaine as formerly for the Continuance thereof; And that their Care ought to be taken into Consideration and owned, I therefore desire you on their behalfe to Continue the said Augmentation unto them, and that till a larger and more Competent Subsistance be found out for them. Not doubting but it will bee a great encouragement to them faithfully to serve the University in their severall places and you will hereby oblige me to remaine

Your very lovinge friend and Chancellor

Cockpitt
December the 28th 1653

O. CROMWELL

18. TO THE CONGREGATIONAL CHURCHES[1]

Beloved and deare Brethren,

We have had it long in our thoughts and mutually in our discourses to make known our judgments concerning those high and open attempts of some of our Brethren in London: who in pursuit of an opinion concerning the Kingdom of the saints, or fifth monarchy, to be administred by the Saints, by immediate Commission from Jesus Christ, having decryed all other Government that is the ordinance of men, as peices of the fourth monarchy, to which Christ in this juncture of time they must suppose hath put a period.[2] If to no other end but only to clere our selves before the Churches & the world, from any participation with them in that judgment & endeavour; And being also

[1] Bodleian MS. Carte, 81. ff. 16r–17r.

[2] The opinions of the Fifth Monarchy men were taken from a particular interpretation of the Books of Revelation and Daniel. In chapter two of the latter, four kingdoms (the Babylonian, Medo-Persian, Greek and Roman) are described. The Fifth Monarchy men held that the Roman Empire had continued through the rule of the Papacy and the Roman Catholic Church and that after the overthrow of this system 'the God of heaven will set up a kingdom which shall never be destroyed, nor shall the sovereignty thereof be left to another people; but it shall break in pieces and consume all these kingdoms, and it shall stand for ever' (Daniel 2:44). Since Papal (and Laudian) influence had seemingly been eradicated from English religious and political life, they expected that the rule of Christ and His saints would soon begin. They referred to this rule of Christ as the Fifth Monarchy. A recent book which describes the rise of this movement and its views is P. G. Rogers, *The Fifth Monarchy Men*, 1966, but L. F. Brown, *The Political Activities of the Baptists and Fifth Monarchy Men*, 1912 (reprinted New York, 1965), is still useful. Cf. B. S. Capp 'Extreme Millenarianism' in *Puritans, the Millenium and the Future of Israel* (ed. P. Toon), 1970.

some of us acquainted with the endeavor of some, upon generall pretence to draw sundry Churches into a conjunction with them in their disorderly and unwarrantable practices; we thought it incumbent on us, in discharge of that duty we owe to our Lord Jesus Christ, the King of Peace, to bear our testimony against the irregularity of the proceeding before mentioned, and being occasionally met here at London (the place of the residency of some of us) to take the advantage of humblie presenting our thoughts unto the Churches of Christ with whom we desire to have communion throughout the nation. For the opinion it selfe the Iniquitie of it falls thus heavy upon our spiritts that as thus stated, (and as thus stated is that thing by us generally contended against) it doth not only cut the sinews of all Magistracy whatsoever, in these our present times, and sett them as Magistrates in opposition to Jesus Christ, as enimyes to him and his immediate government (according to their opinion by the Saints onely and that as Saints) but further it doth without evasion bring this horrid scandall upon all those that profess holynes, that after all occasions that have been layd unjustly upon them as the sole cause of all the alterations of Government that have been made, and exasperation of all sorts of men and partys of men that have followed there upon, that in the closure of all they should lay an immediate claim to the Government of the whole world, and a soveraigne right and power in the name of Christ to dispose of all mens estates and lives in order to the affairs of Christ, as they shall stand in opposition to or as they may be subservient thereto. What hath been the frame of spirit wherewith this busines in publiq assemblies in this City hath been carryed on, what the deportment therein of the chiefe leaders towards their brethren and with what daingerous commotions of mind and spirit it hath been attended, we presume you are in some measure acquainted. That the Gospell hath been dishonored, the way of Christ evil spoken of, the power of Magistracy weakened, and the Civil peace of the Nation endangered (the gilt of all which and sundry evills of the like nature the men of the world would gladly find occasion to discharge upon the Churches of Christ) is much more evident and naked to the view of all, than that we are able to cover it with that garment of love and forbearance which our soules desire to extend unto all that with us call upon the name of the Lord. It is now above a yeare since sundry persons engaging in publick meetings and otherwise in an entrance in to this busines which is now grown up into so much offence and scandall, some of us in sundry conferences dealt with them upon the account of the whole matter, labouring to diswade them from that their undertaking, as a thing in it selfe unwarrantable and whereunto it did not appeare to us that they had received any call. This not succeeding we have thus far waited in patience, expecting the further dealings of the Lord with them and the Nation. What in this issue it is grown up into we have in part intimated unto you, and we are not able to judge but that the further procedure of it, if not through the good hand of God prevented, would prove pernicious to the Churches of Christ, and well faire of this Nation. That the Lord Jesus Christ, who walketh in the midst of the golden candlesticks, would through the effectuall presence of his spirit with you, keep you from every evill way enabling you to keep the word of his testimony, and preserve you blamelesse to his comeinge, is the prayer of

                                        Your loveing Brethren
                                        JOHN OWEN
                                        THO. GOODWIN
London   PHILIP NYE
Jan. 9 1654   SID. SIMPSON

19. TO THE EVANGELICAL CHURCHES OF EUROPE[1]

At a time of so many great changes among all peoples and of cunning and violent conspiracies against the Evangelical Cause by the enemies of the Gospel, the Church of God is visible everywhere and not as a fugitive in the desert. This we recognise is to be attributed to the outstanding providence of God towards us. And although in many places pastors have worn away their strength with their own disputes and thereby exposed their flanks, not so much with subversive action as with open disturbances, still through all this, by God mercifully blessing us, the fundamental teachings of faith and morals and the reformation of divine worship already achieved have remained sound and unblemished. Thus even in these fiery trials of the people of God and pure religion, His great name has not been extinguished; moreover, in these trials the Church has become purer, and has not been destroyed—just as the burning bush which appeared to Moses in Egypt was not consumed.

With reference to the European Churches all is well but with our English Church all is very well since it should be confessed that our God and Saviour, giving us power through His outstretched arm,

---

[1] The original is no longer extant. This translation is made from the Latin copy in the Staatsarchiv, Zurich (E. II. 457 b, f. 1. Duraeana), and is printed by kind permission of the Keeper of the Archives. John Durie left England on 5 April 1654 on his mission to seek to arrange an Evangelical Protestant Alliance. For details of his life and of this mission see J. Minton Batten, *John Dury, Advocate of Christian Reunion*, Chicago, 1944, and for the political background see Abbott, Vol. III, pp. 232ff.

has saved us from the fateful fire more miraculously than He has saved others, like as a brand snatched from the burning. Therefore it is our necessary duty not only to bear witness to the praise we owe to God with a joyful heart and confess the same in the whole congregation of His people (that is in the Evangelical Churches of Europe), but to shew our true thanks by undertaking labours which glorify His name and which bring about meetings of our brethren, and which lead to very important matters in the present situation.

We think these efforts will be a means of bringing an agreement between all Evangelicals for the propagation of the truth and for brotherhood of Christians, promoting a strong coalition against the pernicious, superstitious traditions of Antichrist, as well as the errors which undermine faith and the fraudulent wiles of Satan. In these endeavours we have devoted and consecrated ourselves to calm all internal disagreement, and to remove all cause of offence and disturbance. We are keen that our aspirations will wholly succeed, and especially for this reason, that we find true Christian unity of mind and judgment in the midst of our differences; for this we earnestly ask all the faithful to rejoice and give thanks to God.

Our beloved brother in Christ, John Durie, minister of the Word of God, well-known for faithfully proposing this pursuit of unity for many years, has now offered himself to take up, once more, his earlier attempts. He is a man who has, by the grace of God, toiled not without fruit both in this land and on the Continent of Europe, and his mission has provided us with the desired opportunity of promoting the search for Evangelical Unity. We cannot refrain from praising him both to our own countrymen and to the Evangelical Churches, and we must bear witness to all people that our work is joined with his.

And so we ask all to whom these words commend themselves that they shew faith in the things which he (John Durie) puts before any religious conference in our name. On those matters about which they wish us to be informed and concerning which they desire us to be associated with him, we ask likewise that they acknowledge his counsels, namely, that praying to God, the author of our salvation, we may serve Him with a pure heart in our ministry and in our concern on behalf of men; and with one accord, acknowledging our own weakness, perform these things which (with the help of God) can be made to flourish in the pursuance of the goals set before us. To shew our faith in this mission we have put our signatures to this letter."[2]

---

[2] All the names in the three sections are in *C.R.* or *D.N.B.* except four. These are Peter French, Canon of Christ Church; William Carter, preacher at Westminster; Samuel Fisher, preacher at St Bride's, London; and Richard Minshall, Master of Sidney Sussex College.

1. Professors and Heads of Colleges at Oxford.
    JOHN OWEN, EDMUND STAUNTON, ROBERT HARRIS, HENRY WILKINSON (Canon of Ch.Ch.), GERARD LANGBAINE, DANIEL GREENWOOD, JOHN WILKINS, HENRY LANGLEY, PETER FRENCH, THOMAS GOODWIN, THANKFUL OWEN, HENRY WILKINSON (Magdalen Hall).
2. Pastors and Preachers.
    EDMUND CALAMY, RICHARD VINES, PHILIP NYE, THOMAS MANTON, STEPHEN MARSHALL, WILLIAM CARTER, SAMUEL BALMFORD, PETER WITHAM, ROGER DRAKE, JAMES NALTON, SAMUEL FISHER, GABRIEL SANGAR, JOHN MERITON, SAMUEL AUSTIN, SIMEON ASHE, THOMAS GATAKER, JOHN FULLER, SAMUEL CLARKE, JOSEPH CARYL, WILLIAM COOPER.
3. Professors and Heads of Colleges at Cambridge.
    LAZARUS SEAMAN, RICHARD MINSHALL, JOHN ARROWSMITH, ANTHONY TUCKNEY, THOMAS HORTON, SAMUEL BOLTON, JOHN WORTHINGTON, WILLIAM DILLINGHAM, SIDRACH SIMPSON, RALPH CUDWORTH.

(Dated March 1654?)

20. FROM CHARNELL PETTY[1]

To the Vicechancellor of the University of Oxford, greeting

Sir,

Whereas I have received a writt from Oliver Lord Protector of the Common wealth of England Scotland and Ireland and the Dominions thereto belonging to mee directed for the election of one Burgesse in your university of Oxon to come to the Parliament to bee held at the Citty of Westminster upon the third day of September next coming and there to advise with the Knights Citizens and other Burgesses of this Common wealth.[2] These are therefore by vertue of the sayd writt to command you firmly enjoyninge that upon the receipt hereof you make Proclamation of the same, and of the certain day for the sayd election to bee made in your said university, and that you cause to bee freely and indifferently chosen by those of your sayd university who shall bee present at such election one fitt and discreet person

[1] Reg. Convoc., p. 249. Petty was the sheriff of Oxfordshire. Cf. *Wood*, p. 184.

[2] On 27 June 1654 the Convocation unanimously elected John Owen to be the burgess. When he went to Westminster in September the question of his eligibility to be an M.P. was raised on the grounds of the Clerical Disabilities Act of 1642, and he was not allowed to take his seat. On 21 November Convocation sent a petition concerning this matter to Parliament. Cf. M. B. Rex, *University Representation in England, 1604–1690*, 1954, pp. 188ff, and p. 119 below.

to serve as Burgesse for your sayd university, and the name of such Burgesse soe to be chosen, whether hee bee present or absent, you cause to bee inserted into certaine Indentures thereuppon to bee made between you and them who shall be present at such choyce and that you cause him to come at the day and place aforesayd, soe that hee, the sayd Burgesse, may have full and sufficient power for himselfe and the people of the University aforesayd to doe and consent unto those things which then and there by the common councell of the sayd Common wealth in Parliament (by gods blessing) shall bee ordained upon the weighty affairs aforesayd, soe that for defect of such like power by reason of impoudent choyce of the Burgesse aforesayd, the sayd affairs may not remayn undone. And you are not to chuse any Sheriffe of the sayd Common wealth. And the sayd Choyce distinctly and openly soe to be made, you certifie to me under the hands and seals of them who shall be present at such Choyce within twenty days after the sayd Election; that I may returne the same to the sayd Lord Protector into his Chancery and hereof fayle not. Given under the seale of my office the tenth day of June in the yeare of our Lord, 1654.

CHARNELL PETTY

21. FROM HENRY LAWRENCE[1]

Sir,

The bearer hereof Richard Griffith[2] being lately a member of Eaton Colledge hath been represented to his Highness the Lord Protector as a person of merit and by his piety, proficiency in his studyes and other qualifications very capable of preferment in the University which (as is informd) he had ere this obtayned had not his Highness respect to Mr Moshe (grounded upon the merit of his fathers memory who for adhering to the truths of the Gospell lost his life in the Romish Inquisition) interposed for the said Mr Moshes admittance into Kings Colledge. His Highness hath therefore been pleased to referr it to the Counsell to recommend him (in his Highness name) to your favour. That he may be admitted to some preferment of the Colledge upon the first occasion or opportunity. And the Counsell doe accordingly hereby recommend it to you that he may be effectually provided for not doubting but being thus tendered you will be very mindfull of him and the rather as it will be an occasion of giving

---

[1] *C.S.P.D.* (1654), p. 294. S.P. 25/75, f. 479. For Henry Lawrence, President of the Council of State, see *D.N.B.*

[2] The Board of Visitors for the University of Oxford placed Richard Griffith in a Fellowship at University College from 1 September 1654, *Register*, p. 399.

encouragement to learning and to future diligence both in him and in others,

    Signed in the name and by the order of the Counsell,
            H. LAWRENCE, President

For Dr Owen, Deane
 of Christ Church in Oxford.
For Dr Arrowsmith, Master
 of Trynity Colledge in Cambridge.

22. TO THE LORD PROTECTOR[1]

To his highness Oliver Lord Protector of the Comon wealth of England Scotland and Ireland and the Dominions thereunto belonging

The humble petition of the Collegiate Deane and Chapter of Christ Church in Oxon

Sheweth

That your Petitioners Rectory of Great Torrington in the County of Devon was sequestered in the yeare 1646 from Richard Smith gent. (tenant to your petitioners) for his deliquency.

That out of the said Rectory (during the time of the sequestration) three hundred and two pounds nineteen shillings and two pence of rent is in arrears to this foundation: which (as we have been informed) hath been received by the commissioners for sequestrations in the said county and accounted for to the Commissioners of Haberdashers Hall and never paid to your Petitioners. By reason whereof (and other like arrears) the Colledge remaynes much dampnified and indebted unto this day.

Whereof the patrons humbly pray your Highnes to give order to the Commissioners of Haberdashers Hall to examine the grounds of the petition and according to the truth and justice thereof to make payment of the money due to the patron,

            And they shall ever pray[2]

JOHN OWEN	HENRY CORNISH
PETER FRENCH	HENRY WILKINSON
JOHN WALL	AMBROSE UPTON
CHRISTOPHER ROGERS	

August 9, Christchurch

[1] *C.S.P.D.* (1654), p. 345. S.P. 18/75, f. 110. A note attached to the petition in the Public Record Office, London, reads, 'His Highnes pleasure is to referr this petition to the Councill for them to direct the Treasurers at Goldsmiths Hall to repay to the use of the Colledge the Arrears of the Rent mentioned in the petition'. John Howe went to Great Torrington in May 1654; see *C.R.*

[2] For John Wall see *D.N.B.*, for Christopher Rogers, Henry Cornish and Henry Wilkinson see *C.R.*, and for Peter French and Ambrose Upton see *Alumni Oxonienses.*

23. FROM EDWARD LOWE

Sirs,

The Deane and prebends of Christchurch in Oxford thirty yeares since (at least) gave an organ to the University which was planted in the University Church: the Universitye in requitall settled tenn pounds per annum upon the organist of Christchurch for the time being; to have the tune of a psalme (sung before and after sermon) playd by the said organist. This stypend was paid quarterlie by the Vice Chancellor to the said organist and acquittance given for the receipt though the organist had for his owne share but eight pounds thirteen shillings fower pence by the yeare for the sayd service, the remainder of the tenn pounds was paid by him to a Clarke for nameing the said psalme. This my predecessor received in his time and my selfe in my time received it fifteen yeares without interruption which was till the year forty eight; then for two yeares by reason of the troubles I received nothing. But in the yeare 1650 I received my two yeares arrears (by order of the delegates) from Dr Reynolds then Vice Chancellor. From that time by reason of fresh troubles I received nothing till the yeare 1652 and then my arrears were granted me by the Delegates and payed me by Doctor Greenwood, Vice Chancellor. The next yeare 1653 the Delegates agreed the Vice Chancellor Doctor Owen should pay mee tenn pounds and made a private order I should have no more without giving anie reason or laying aniething to my chardge since which time I have not had a penny.

My humble petition to the Honourable Chancellor is, that he would be pleased to recommend a review of this busines to the Delegates of the University. And desire if he soe pleases that either cause be showne how the said Organist did forfeit his title to the said stypend being a part of his lively hood and subsistence; or else, that the arrears be paid and his stypend continue during his naturall life; he behaving himselfe in all things as he ought to doe in relation to the present Government,

EDWARD LOWE,

Organist of Christchurch in Oxford

To the Vice Chancellor & Delegates.

Sept? 1654.

[1] *C.S.P.D.* (1654), p. 425. S.P. 18/77, f. 216. For Edward Lowe see *D.N.B.* He succeeded Dr William Stonard as organist of Christ Church in 1630. He resigned in 1656 and was appointed professor of music in 1661. Cf. *Wood*, p. 205.

24. FROM THE LORD PROTECTOR[1]

For our worthy friends the Vicechancellor and Convocation of the University of Oxford

Gentlemen.

Considering how necessary it is that the government of the University bee continued in an able and faithfull hand wee doe hereby nominate and appoint Doctor John Owen Deane of Christchurch to the place of Vicechancellor to your University for the yeare following not doubting but hee will answer that care and vigilance which the service and occasions of that place doth call for, wherein also you shall not want the ready assistance of

                                Gents

Whitehall,   Your loving freind and Chancellor

October 31st 1654   OLIVER P.

[1] Reg. Convoc., p. 255.

25. TO HENRY WILKINSON[1]

For my worthy and reverend friend Dr Henry Wilkinson at Christ Church in Oxford, these

Sir,

Some friends of the bearer (Mr Ireland[2]) have procured a mandamus from his Highnesse for his restoration to his place in Christ Church; as things now stand I am unwilling either to admit of, or to dispute the mandamus: and therefore when it was brought unto me by Colonel Cook[3] I refused to receive it, but withall told him that he need not make any such returne until I had advised with you what were meet to be done. That which is purposed by him at present is a resignation of Mr Godolphin[4] who will not otherwise leave his place. If you and the rest of the company think fit to leave out Mr Godolphins

---

[1] Bodleian MS. Tanner 69, f. 182. Henry Wilkinson was a Canon of Christ Church and Lady Margaret Professor of Divinity from 1652 to 1660.

[2] Thomas Ireland went to Christ Church in 1649 as a Westminster Student and was expelled in 1652. In 1654 or 1655 he was restored to his place.

[3] For Colonel Thomas Cooke see C. Firth and G. Davies, *Regimental History of Cromwell's Army*, Oxford, 1940, Vol. II, pp. 578ff.

[4] William Godolphin kept his place as a Westminster Student and remained at Christ Church until the Restoration. In later life, whilst an ambassador to Spain, he became a Roman Catholic and chose to live in Spain. See *D.N.B.*

name, and to put his in, you have hereby my consent; if you think not good soe to doe, pray impart your thoughts unto me and what you would advise upon the whole matter: they profess they got the mandamus, rather to countenance us in our desires of doinge him good, than to contend with us, wherein indeed I do believe him. Excuse me I pray that I write you no news at present; I judge it not meet by this opportunity. I wonder I have nothing from your selfe and your cousan about the students petition.

Your very affectionate and humble friend,

JOHN OWEN

Pall Mall
Mr Cookes House
Monday Morning

26. TO THE PARLIAMENT[1]

To the Parliament of the Commonwealth of England.
The humble petition of the University of Oxford

Sheweth,

That your Petitioners understanding that out of your pious inclinations towards the advancement of the publicke Good, You have beene pleased to take into consideration a petition presented by the Doctors of the Civill Law residing in London, wee are imboldened to adde our humble requests for some encouragement to that Profession, beinge one of the principall parts of Learning for which this University hath been anciently famous and where there still is a Publicke Professor, Doctor of that Faculty, who is obliged to read and hold publicke disputations in the same, and where severall Colledges by the statutes of their respective Founders are bound to have some of their Societies to bee students and Graduats in that Law. Which as it is a distinct body from the Cannon Law wee humbly conceive to bee very suitable to the present government, and a profession of much use and publike concernment as well for forraigne Commerce and negotiations abroad (being generally received and practised in other Nations) as alsoe for many questions, debates and decisions fitt to bee knowne and made use of in this Nation, not only in causes maritime, but alsoe in causes Matrimoniall and testamentary and others, the cognizance whereof hath formerly beene held proper for, and allowed to, Persons of that Profession, which if in your wisdome you shall think

[1] Reg. Convoc., p. 251. For the political background to this letter see S. R. Gardiner, *History of the Commonwealth and Protectorate*, Vol. III, 1653–1655, pp. 167–225. A similar petition was sent by Cambridge University. Cf. C.J. VII, pp. 382, 407, 457, 462, and B. Whitelock, *Memorials of English Affairs*, p. 592. Also *Wood*, p. 187.

fitt to restore, it would bee a great encouragement to all students of that Faculty in this place to endeavour to enable themselves by their studyes here to become hereafter serviceable to the Commonwealth in those affayrs. Which your Petitioners shall acknowledge as a reall Testimony of your care and respect to Learning and shall bee obliged to pray for a happy successe upon all your undertakings.

THE UNIVERSITY OF OXFORD
18 November 1654.

27. TO BULSTRODE WHITELOCK[1]

To the Right Honourable the Lord Commissioner Whitlock

Most Honourable Sir,

For your generosity, by which we have been quite overwhelmed, we respectfully hasten at last to offer you our thanks (which is all we can do) though we have been slow and over-reticent, just as when we are making a request of you. However, lest you should bestow your favours on bankrupts who pay out under compulsion what they prefer to hold back, let us say this: we have not taken great pains to pay our debt not because we underrated your generosity or wished to take advantage of your kindness, but so that we remain bound to you for ever by right of being your clients (if such we are) when you distribute your property. They are uneasy in their debts who pay back at once. A man is ashamed of his patron and seems to resent the favour when he draws up his accounts and pays out immediately. We have restored your name to the list of patrons and have put aside the gold you sent in its own package with the remaining money—it is good even though it bears the king's effigy on it—nevertheless all the more precious for being a token of your favour and a reflection of your goodwill towards the world of letters.

Those who pile up their money, watching over it with great care and unable to keep away from it, are condemned to misery and torment. We, on the other hand, make careful but full use of our resources. Our money and gold (which, though anxious to possess, we seek honestly) yields us out of almost every generation Great Men, Leaders who once held the world's affairs in their charge, now finding peaceful recreation in this shrine of scholarship amid letters and books; and when they themselves are the equal of Annals and History, it is

[1] Reg. Convoc., p. 252. Original in Latin. For Bulstrode Whitelock see *D.N.B.* He was made a commissioner for custody of the Great Seal in April 1654 and was deprived of the office in June 1655 upon his refusal to execute the ordinance for reforming the court of Chancery. In 1654 he gave some gold and silver coins to the University, cf. *Wood*, **p. 188.**

the rightful inheritance of the Human race to gather from them the chain of events and records of the world: that which is in our keeping here should be a public heritage, something which belongs to everyone. Although you have not poured out your gifts to us merely to win popularity, yet this is what will happen. You yourself benefit when you endow the Muses. For such things are appreciated among generations to come and they think highly of people on that account and extol their names so that they endure for posterity.

This and future ages will tell of the impartiality with which you presided in court, with what integrity you conducted state affairs, how well you exercise your power and with what ease and success you bring together the boldest people into peace. You have set up for yourself the greatest monuments of your boundless wisdom.

'Nothing is more welcome on a tossing sea than to know that a firm hand is at the helm.' So we humbly pay you in thanks (in which alone we have plenty) and still we are in your debt. We place before you this pledge of our respect but the chief thing remains and our obligation to you grows day by day.

Your most devoted servant,
THE UNIVERSITY OF OXFORD

26 November 1654

28. TO SIR THOMAS WIDDRINGTON[1]

To the Right Honourable the Lord Commissioner Widdrington

Most honourable Sir,

You have won the affection of the university by a debt of obedience and continual gratitude (you yourself stand out as a leading example of justice to be counted among the acknowledged prides of our public figures), because you have undertaken the care of learning in the Council of State and by further proof of your goodwill have given us cause to approach you as our patron with still greater confidence. To you and other men who have shown us generosity we owe a debt indeed. As you very well understand in your wisdom, some encouragement by way of honour is due to talent; and the noble arts, placed dishonourably on the lowest step, and hard-pressed by lack of money, rise with difficulty. And so we publicly declare our thanks to you as a man of learning because you have seen to it that we may maintain

---

[1] Reg. Convoc., p. 253. Original in Latin. For Thomas Widdrington see *D.N.B.* Like Whitelock, he was a commissioner for custody of the Great Seal and was dismissed in June 1655 for refusal to execute the ordinance for the reform of the court of Chancery. Cf. *Wood*, p. 188.

our high standards and because you think it fit that Learning should have a place in the Assembly of the People.

Whilst Mars rules the sky it would be wrong for us to pick out one virtue when we see so many before us, but from a distance we have every respect for your justice and the integrity with which you conduct civil affairs in that most distinguished court, and your eloquence rising from the innermost heart of jurisprudence, the means by which you hold and regulate the reigns of government. For you are indeed a distinguished man to whom the people look for wise counsel and guidance and, as we know what is good for us, we recognise, in you the judge and protector of our affairs. With your encouragement we hope that each university will look ahead independently with its own eyes and enjoy as their two Chancellors men who will take charge of and protect the public business of learning in the councils of the nation.

You invest yourself with honour and glory while you endow learning. May you enjoy the expectation of a name that will long endure, certain of posterity which will grant you acclaim and renown as you race on in your present course of honour.

26 November 1654.

Your most devoted servant,
THE UNIVERSITY OF OXFORD

29. TO THE LORD PROTECTOR[1]

To the most gracious Oliver, Lord Protector of the Republic of England, Scotland and Ireland, Chancellor of Oxford University

That your University of Oxford should seem late to come to you with its customary praise is on account of our wonder at the great benevolence with which you conduct affairs, from which we could not be roused save by constant rejoicing. At last we have been stirred by the applause of men congratulating each other, and by voices re-echoing the peace on land and sea; and rushing forward in perhaps a somewhat impetuous fashion, we cast ourselves before your Excellency and pour out the prayers we conceived on waking from our sweet sleep.

Brought ashore, the Salii[2] feel for some time a lingering giddiness from the tossing and not until they have recovered do they walk

---

[1] The original in Latin forms the dedicatory epistle in *Musarum Oxoniensium*, Oxford, 1654, which contained verses by members of the University to celebrate peace with the Dutch. Owen also has a poem in it.

[2] The Salii were a College of priests, whose religious ceremonies involved leaping and jumping.

straight. So it was with us not very long ago, for we live among men ignorant of our ways, making our position slippery and uncertain. Then it came about that by listening carefully we heard a calumny. Once the pride and delight of the nation we were soon almost a laughing stock. To be sure, not for nothing do those who fear to be known to Posterity hate Learning. The University has survived only by the grace of everlasting God, by its own standing and through You. Let them say what they will in praise of the times, by no other means did the well-being of the University stand firm in this tempest. At last, snatched away from the cruel dangers in a sudden impulse and urgency, we break out with these prayers. We hope for no-one to suffer save he who wishes the war to linger on and on until wild beasts, driven from their caves occupy the deserted cities and men, expelled from the cities, take over the caves. For Learning has no place among that sort of men who, though unfit for the control of affairs, yet aspire to it all the more boldly.

Truly we seem to be placed beyond the reach of weapons because you do not disdain to grant the closest protection for our safety—nor do we need any other with you as our Guardian. Generally, there is but forlorn hope for mediation unless they catch a man by surprise, especially in the halls of the Leaders where there is little thought for the absent. And so we humbly beg that you will graciously accept praises for the peace, which are offered to you, a greater man in war than all our praise could describe, for a peace sought by so many victories and which will be celebrated for ever as far as the Christian world extends, praises for peace which your University echoes in harmony.

Your most devoted servant,
In your most renowned university,
JOHN OWEN

December 1654.

30. FROM PHILIP HENRY[1]

Most honoured Sir,

Being importuned to improve my interest for the supply of a vacant curacy in these parts, I make bold to acquaint you with the state of it, that, if you know of any, either in your own college or

---

[1] A transcript of this letter is in J. B. Williams (ed.), *The Life of the Rev. Philip Henry by the Rev. Matthew Henry*, 1825, pp. 27–29. For Philip Henry, curate of Worthenbury in Flintshire, see *C.R.* He was a student of Christ Church, Oxford, and whilst keeping this position went in 1653 to be a tutor to the sons of Judge Puleston of Emeral, who owned the tithes of Worthenbury parish.

elsewhere, that is willing to accept of it, you would please to be instrumental in sending him hither.[2]

The place is called Holt, it is in Denbighshire; but I think a man may throw a stone out of it into Cheshire; it is distant from Wrexham about three miles, and from Cheshire five; the situation of it for convenience is beyond exception; there are but few such hereabouts, only the salary, I fear, somewhat too small to come so far for. It is as yet, upon certainty, but £45 per annum, but it is probable may be made, ere long, £65, paid in money, and no deductions out of it for taxes; for the place of his abode, if he be a single man, the Major of the town, a very godly person, hath promised it in his own house, till such time care be taken to provide for him otherwise. For his qualifications, Sir, he must, in a judgement of charity, be one that fears God, in regard he comes, not to a place that never heard of Christ (as many such there be in Wales) but to a knot of eminent, discerning Christians, scarce the like anywhere hereabouts, among whom there are divers able, indeed, to be themselves teachers of others, so that if he himself be one that hath no savour of the things of God, he will be no way acceptable or useful there. He must, moreover, be either fitted already for the administration of the ordinances or in a capacity of being suddenly fitted; if he make haste hither, he may have an opportunity shortly of being ordained here in Shropshire.

Sir, if God, the Lord of the harvest, shall make use of you in his providence, as an instrument of thrusting forth a faithful labourer into this corner of his vineyard, I no way doubt but you will be often mentioned by some of them with rejoicing at the throne of grace, and that you, yourself, when you shall have reaped the fruit of their prayers, will bless God for putting such a prize into your hands.

Sir, craving your pardon for my boldness in troubling you, I leave the matter with your care, and yourself, and all your relations and concernments, with our ever good God.

Your Servant very much obliged,
PHILIP HENRY[3]

Sir, since my purpose of writing to you about the business above mentioned, I have received information from Christ-Church of a summons to appear personally there, before Michaelmas Term: whereupon my request to you is, that by a line or two you would please to acquaint me, whether I may not obtain to be dispensed with.

---

[2] From September 1654 to January 1655 Hugh Bethel seems to have acted as the Curate of Hale before moving to Burton in Cheshire. Therefore it would seem that this letter was written early in 1655 before, or just after, the departure of Hugh Bethel, for whom see *C.R.*

[3] Philip Henry is mentioned also in Letter No. 56.

1. In regard I was so lately there. 2. In regard of the great distance I am now at from thence; above four score miles. 3. Of the unusual unseasonableness of the ways and weather: and 4. Which is most of all, my very great indisposedness in point of health. If I may be excused, I would intreat you, Sir, to endeavour it for me; if not, that you would please to send me word,—1. Whether it will not serve if I came sooner: and 2. How long it will be required that I make my stay there. Sir, I have more reason to beg your pardon for this latter trouble than the former.

31. FROM GEORGE GALE AND EDWARD FARRAR[1]

In the name of God. Amen. Before you a Publike Notary, a publike and authentick person and the witnesses here present: Wee, George Gale, B. of Phisick and Edward Farrar, Mr of Arts, both Fellowes of University Colledge in Oxon, and under that title joyntly and severally, principally and equally, complaining of the nullity and nullities, injuries and greivancess hereafter set forth by all ways and meanes which wee or either of us better may or can and to all effects of Law and justice that may ensue doe joyntly and severally say and alleadge and in due form of law propose: That the right worthy Dr John Owen, the ViceChancellor, the Doctors of Divinity and Proctors of this University and Visitors of University Colledge in the sayd University (or at least pretending themselves soe to be) in a certaine cause concerning a pretended, illegall and unstatutable election of one, Thomas Thornton, Mr of Arts and Fellow of our sayd Colledge into the place and office of Master or Governour of our Colledge aforesaid, made and voted by an incompetent and unconsiderable number of the Fellows of our sayd Colledge, without any notice or intimation given to any of the absent Fellows, being the major part, contrary to the statutes, customes and usage of our sayd Colledge, which cause hath beene agitated before them and doth as yet depend before them undecided, have illegally and unjustly (all due reverence to their respective persons now and at all times reserved) by a certaine pretended vote or decree but in itselfe altogether null and invalid, as much as in them lieth allowed, approved, and ratified the aforesaid illegall and unstatutable election of the sayd Thomas Thornton into the sayd place of Master or Governour of the sayd Colledge, whereupon wee the sayd George Gale and Edward Farrar finding ourselves

---

[1]Reg. Convoc., pp. 259–60. The Public Notary was G. Ballard and this statement was made on 22 February 1655 and read in Convocation on 2 March 1655. There is no reference to this episode in the Register of the Visitors but it seems that Thornton was removed.

G

joyntly and severally by the declaring and pronouncing of the aforesaid vote and pretended decree, and by severall other nullityes and greivances of this processe as out of the acts thereof may be deduced and collected, to be much injured and oppressed, doe by this present writing joyntly and severally appeale to the Venerable House of Convocation of Doctors, Masters, Regents and non Regents of this University, their delegates or any other Judge competent in Law. And wee doe joyntly and severally protest that three days are not fully expired from such time as the aforesaid nullityes and greivances were made knowne and did appear unto us or either of us, and lastly wee doe protest that wee will correct and reforme this our instrument of appeale by adding unto and subtracting from the same and reducing the same into a better and more competent forme of Law, and that wee will intimate the same to all persons herein concerned as wee shall bee thereunto advised by our Councell, learned in Law, according to the course and stile of this University.

32. TO JOHN THURLOE[1]

For the Honourable John Thurloe Esquire Secretary of State to his Highnesse, these

Sir,

I heartly thanke you for the account you were pleased to give me of the Lords gratious dealinge in his beginning to manifeste himselfe once more in our behalfe. He is the same, and he changeth not. We are here in a quiet condition. I have raised and nowe well settled a troope of sixty horse, besides their officers.[2] The towne also hath raised some foote for their defence. We have some persons in custody on verry good grounds of suspition, and shall yet secure them. There is much riding to and fro in the night in the villages near us; but as yet I cannot learne any certaine place of their meetinge, soe keep a continual guard, and hope that some good service towards the publique peace hath been effected by our arming ourselves: the justis of the county have mett: are backward and cold; but something we have gotten them to engage for towards the raysing of some troopes. Had I a blank commission or two for horse, I could (as I suppose on good grounds) raise a troope in Barkshire, sundry good ministers and others

[1] Bodleian MS., Rawlinson A.24, f. 336, and *Thurloe State Papers*, Vol. III, p. 281. For John Thurloe see *D.N.B.*

[2] In March 1655 there was a minor Royalist uprising in Wiltshire led by John Penruddock. Cf. A. H. Woolrych, *Penruddock's Rising* (Historical Association), 1955. Owen saw it as his duty to make preparations to put down any rising that might occur near Oxford.

having been with me to assist you to that purpose, if you think it necessary to have the worke goe on, (as surely it is, at least to engage men in such a citie as this, wherein self-preservation helps on the publicke interest) pray send me downe one or two commissions to the purpose. One thing I must needs trouble you with: there are in Barkshire some few men of mean quality and condition, rash, heady, enemys of tiths, who are the commissioners for the ejecting of ministers. They alone sitt and act, and are at this time casting out on slight and trivial pretences very worthy men; one in especial they intend the next weeke to eject, whose name is Pococke;[3] a man of as unblamable a conversation, as any I know livinge, of repute for learning throughout the world, being the professor of Hebrew and Arabicke in our university; so that they do exceedingly exasperate all men, and provoke them to the height: if any thing might be done to cause them to suspend actinge untille this storme be over, I cannot but thinke it would be good servis to his highness and the commonwealth to doe it. Pray, Sir, excuse this scrible from,

Your most humble and faithfull servant,

Oxford.   JOHN OWEN
March 20. 1655.

[3] Edward Pococke was Rector of Childrey. See *D.N.B.*

33. FROM THOMAS DOWN[1]

To the right Reverend and Honourable the [Vice-Chancellor] and Schollars of the University of Oxford for the time being

I Thomas Downe Clerke Rector and Incumbent of the Rectory and Parish church of Goodlye alias Goodleigh in the County of Devon for diverse causes mee hereunto moving doe freelye and absolutely by these presents graunt yeild up and resign all my righte title and interest of, in, and unto the church and Rectory of Goodlye alias Goodleigh aforesayd withall the profitts, benefitts and appurtenances thereunto belonginge. And doe hereby humbly desire that this my resignation may bee admitted and accepted of and the sayd church may thereupon been pronounced voyd according to due forme of lawe. And I doe by these presents constitute and appoint Edward Eabery and John Saunders-gent. my true and lawfull Attorneys joyntly and severally for mee and in my name to appeare before the Chancellor and Schollars of the University of Oxford aforesayd to desire that this

[1] Reg. Convoc., p. 261. For Thomas Down see *C.R.* In August 1657 he became Rector of St Edmund's with St Mary Steps, Exeter. Down was succeeded at Goodleigh by Lewis Bradford.

my present Resignation may bee admitted and accepted of, And the sayd church to bee thereupon pronounced void and farther to doe and performe all things necessary in and about the premises and whatsoever my sayd Attornyes or either of them shall doe in and about the premises, I hereby ratifye, allowe and confirme, witnes my hand and seal the thirtieth day of March in the yeare of our Lord one thousand, sixe hundred, fifty-five, 1655.

THOMAS DOWNE

Witnes hereunto,
  Thos. Westlake
  Wm. Michell
  Arth. P. Litton

34. TO JOHN THURLOE[1]

Sir,

You were pleased at my comeinge out of towne, to speake with me about my worthy neighbour Mr Unton Crooke[2]; and to consider the character, which upon knowledge and consideration with respect to what was in your thoughts about him, I then gave. I have not since seene, or spoken with that gentleman but my knowledge of his worth, and integrity, and repute in his countey is such that I cannot but assume the boldnesse to renew my testimony concerninge him, knowinge that it is a businesse wherein I would not, for respect to any person in England, be the least occasion of a mistake unto his Highnesse. Pray excuse this boldness in

Sir, your most humble and most affectionate servant,

JOHN OWEN

Ch. Ch. College
May 29 1655

[1] Bodleian MS. Rawlinson, A26, f. 413, and *Thurloe State Papers*, Vol. III. p. 488.

[2] Unton Croke, fourth son of Sir John Croke, was a sergeant-at-law and the father of Unton Croke who played a leading part in putting down the rising led by Colonel Penruddock. See *D.N.B.* s.v. John Croke.

35. FROM THE LORD PROTECTOR[1]

To the Reverend the Vice Chancellor and the Convocation of the University of Oxon, these

Gentlemen,

We understand that the time for the Nominatinge a Vice Chancellor for the next yeare is now approachinge, and consideringe how necessary

[1] Reg. Convoc., p. 269.

it is that the Government of the University be continued in an able and faithfull hand; We doe hereby nominate and appoint Doctor John Owen Deane of Christ Church to the Place of Vice Chancellor to your University for the yeare followinge, not doubtinge but he will answer that Care and Vigilancy, which the service and occasions of that Place doth call for, wherein allsoe you shall not want the ready assistance of

Gentlemen,

Your loveinge friend and Chancellor,

OLIVER P.

White-Hall,
August the 22 1655

36. TO THE LORD PROTECTOR[1]

May it please your Highnesse,

Your Highnesse was pleased to favour me not long since in my request on the behalf of Mr Serjeant Crooke,[2] and to mention your good intendments towards him. Least in the multitude of your weighty affaires, he might be forgotten, duringe the present opportunity of making him one of your judges, I am bold to remind your Highnesse of your thoughts towards him, being fully assured, he will never really forefeit them. I dare not with any confidence assume unto myself a judgement of the fittnesse of any person for such an employment; yet I have most good grounds to continue in my former perswasion of his ability and integrity; so that I am most confident, your Highnesse will never have cause to repent of your doinge him this favour, and that he will in his place performe that which is the true service unto you in an upright administration of justice. That you may have the presence of our good God in a living sense of his unchangeable love in Jesus Christ to your person, and a gracious assistance in all your affairs, is the daily prayer of him, who is to your Highnesse,

most humbly and faithfully devoted,

JOHN OWEN

Oxford

Octob.2.1655

[1] *Thurloe State Papers*, Vol. IV, pp. 65–6.

[2] Although he was not made a judge, he was appointed in 1656 a commissioner for trials of persons charged with treason.

37. FROM JOHN WALLIS[1]

To the most worthy gentleman John Owen, Doctor of Sacred Theology Dean of Christ Church, Oxford, Vice Chancellor of the University

In letters of this sort (dedicatory letters) it is usual (most worthy Sir) to fill each page with a eulogy and request for patronage. It seems to me that both these should rather be omitted. For although there is much that may be said, you are so much better known on other accounts than you could ever become through my dedication so that by speaking of who and what you are, I should be holding a candle to the sun. But, however, as far as this matter is concerned, much as a person wants the services of a patron this is what happens; either the patron does not need them or he seeks them in vain. In Geometry, indeed, if there are no strong proofs, in vain may anyone think the deficiency may be made up on his own authority or that of his patrons. Therefore, leaving out these things, I have decided in preference that I should give a brief account of the work I have undertaken; for as it is a requirement of my office that I should do this, so it is that I should deliver it to you.

No-one can doubt how puffed up with pride and arrogance is the man who gives but slight consideration to what has been written. For it is rather to be grieved over than doubted that quite on his own authority he should despise equally all things human and divine, aweful and dreadful about God, Sin, the Holy Scripture, all things material and immaterial generally, about the immortal soul of man and other weighty topics of Religion. (I myself touch on a few of these several times in sections 18 & 20 and finally in passing at the end of the work.)

When I looked at him, the equal of 'Leviathan' (which made his name for him) or rather 'Goliath', parading with such arrogance, I decided that he should be thoroughly attacked so that he may see he cannot do anything he likes without being called to task, not proudly give himself airs above other men. But why should I undertake to refute his Geometry, leaving out Theology and other Philosophies, when there are other things in which he has made far more dangerous errors? There is more than one solitary reason but the most important is this: there are plenty of men all around us who also wish, if it seems necessary, to reprove that man for his impudence

---

[1] The original in Latin forms the dedicatory epistle to Owen in *Johanni Wallisii . . . Elenchus Geometriae Hobbianae* (1655). John Wallis (for whom see *D.N.B.*) was the Savilian Professor of Geometry at Oxford. He had a long controversy with Thomas Hobbes (for whom see *D.N.B.*), the author of *Leviathan* (1651).

on this matter; but since there are fewer men who engage in this study, I felt a strong sense of obligation to undertake the burden myself. I would not wish it to be thought that I alone in the University am fit to undertake this for there are many others (whatever that man may imply to the contrary). For it is sheer calumny which he is doing his best to persuade people, that there are no distinguished mathematicians, or at least not in this University; for although we have few men like him, we have many who are better. Indeed this man here, having re-established Philosophy, has formed an extremely high opinion of his own expertise in Mathematics and, (as if he alone understood these things) looks down from afar on everyone else, whether Philosophers or Mathematicians, to such an extent that if he sees anyone disagreeing with him in Theology or Philosophy he thinks they should be sent away with this supercilious reply, that since they are unlearned in Geometry they do not understand these things. And all the time he himself is so completely ignorant about these things that whatever he publishes on this question is clearly nonsense and pure rubbish which calls for ridicule rather than refutation. For my part I have judged that these things should be speedily opposed, not, to be sure, because I think that Geometry should be protected lest it take harm (indeed this of all disciplines has least to fear from logical fallacies), but so that when this balloon has been burst, that man, so full of airy talk, might be quite deflated and that others, less skilled in Geometry, may know that there is no more to be feared from this Leviathan on this account since its armour (in which he had the greatest confidence) is easily pierced: and also so that outsiders (if they saw him maintain such things unchecked) might not think all men who practise Geometry here are like him. So I completed in the July and August following a refutation of the book published in the June, that is when other business permitted. As far as the style is concerned, it is considerably more bitter than is my usual practice but necessity forced me against my will. For I had learnt from Proverbs 26 v.5 that one should sometimes reply, not according to our own manner, but in the style of those we are able to contradict. And to reply more mildly to this man would be like treating a stinging nettle with gentleness. Indeed, nothing could be more bitter than a reply to this man in his own words, and if he thinks there are cutting remarks to what I say, he should realise that they are only the same as those he used to wound other people, but with less justification: he is being stabbed with his own weapons and should not take it amiss. We have not covered everything which could be said in refuting him, but as much as is necessary. And if anyone else has the time to expose this nest of his errors in Theology and Philosophy by the same evidence with which we have refuted his

Geometry, I reckon that there will be little left for him to pride himself on in the future.

JOHN WALLIS
Savilian Professor of Geometry

October 10, 1655
Oxford

38. FROM HENRY LAWRENCE[1]

Sir,

His Highness the Lord Protector and the Council having determined of a certain number of persons (whereof yourself is one) to meet with a Committee of the Council on Tuesday the fourth of December next in the afternoone neare the Council Chambers in Whitehall to the intent some proposalls made to his Highness in reference to the nation of the Jews may be considered of, you are therefore desired by his Highness and Council to take notice thereof and so meet at the said time and place for the purpose aforesaid.[2]

Signed in the name and by order of the Council

Whitehall　　　　　　　　　　HENRY LAWRENCE, President
16 November 1655

[1] *C.S.P.D.* (1655–6), p. 23. S.P. 25/76, f. 366. For Henry Lawrence see *D.N.B.* From 16 January 1654 he was permanent chairman of the Council of State.

[2] For the mission of Menasseh ben Israel to London in 1655 and details of the conference on the readmission of the Jews see *Menasseh Ben Israel's Mission to Oliver Cromwell* (ed. Lucien Wolf), 1901.

39. FROM HENRY LAWRENCE[1]

Gentlemen,

A Petition hath been presented unto his Highness the Lord Protector in the name of the Fellows of Jesus Colledge in Oxford containing some complaints against Doctor Roberts[2] the principall of the said Colledge, which being referred by his Highness to the Counsell and they upon consideration of the matter finding it proper for your cognizance and determination, the Counsell have therefore thought fitt to transmitt the same to you to the end you may consider thereof and upon due examination of the Fact proceed to a determination therein according to justice and the powers intrusted to you which

[1] *C.S.P.D.* (1655–6), p. 29. S.P. 25/76, f. 387.

[2] Dr Michael Roberts became Principal in 1648. For details of this dispute in Jesus College see *Register*, pp. 401–8.

you are desired to doe accordingly with your most speedy opportunity that so the Colledge may not receive prejudice by the long dependance thereof.

    Signed in the name and by the order of the Counsell,
              H. LAWRENCE, President

Whithall 20 November 1655.

To Doctor John Owen Vice Chancellor of the University of Oxon, Dr Thomas Goodwin President of Magdalen Colledge in Oxford and the rest of the Visitors of the said University appointed by ordinnance of his Highness the Lord Protector and Counsell unto any one to be communicated to the rest.[3]

[3] For details of the new Board of Visitors see *Register*, p. 400.

40. FROM ROBERT WICKENS[1]

To the Reverend & Learned John Owen D.D. Deane of Ch.Ch. and Vice-chancellour of the University of Oxford

Most Honoured Sir,

When the child *Obed* was new borne, he was presented unto *Naomi*, to be nursed on her knee, & to sleep in her bosome: yet had he no great relation to her, save only that he was borne of a woman that had lived in her house, and had been sheltred under her Roofe. This booke, that here desires to come under your wings, and lodge there, hath the same interest, and many more, to draw it to your hands, and to cause it to sanctuary under your Patronage. For it hath been Press-borne in that University, which in sacrificing her *Optima*, lookes upon you as one of her chiefe *Stators*, And may blesse God, that you, and some other worthyes have sate Governours there: else she her selfe might long ere this have *sate in the Dust, and the delicate woman, that was brought up in scarlet, embraced the Dung*. Besides, the Authour must Acknowledge all the comforts of his Nursing dayes to that house, where you now by the good hand of God peculiarly preside.

Now for the worke and Subject in hand I need not preface much, It being in it selfe but a Preface; yet a preface to that $\pi\alpha\mu\mu\epsilon\gamma\epsilon\theta\epsilon\varsigma$, that song of Songs, the great and sacred booke the word of God,

[1] This letter is found in Wickens' book, *A Compleat & Perfect Concordance*, 1655. He matriculated in 1632 and received his B.A. and M.A. degrees from Christ Church. Then he was a schoolmaster before becoming Rector of Todenham.

which as farre excells all the Daughters that have done worthily, as *Saul* overtopt the multitude in Mizpeh, when he stood among the people, head and shoulders above them all. Now if the Kings daughter be so glorious within, her clothing of Broidered gold, and her raiment of needle worke, needs must the virgins also, her Companions, have their Beauty, their Perfection. Among these Companions, these handmaids of the Word of God, I reckon Commentatours, Common-places, Scripture-Dictionaryes, and all Gospell Tracts, and all the Labours of those Holy Ones, that have knowne the way of the Vine-yards, at what houre soever they entered. In which number Concordances have their knowne and excellent uses, guiding to all the Depths and Treasures of the word; as those poore Lepers, that sate in the outgates of *Samaria*, were made Instruments to the whole Citty, to lead them to rich and well victuall'd Tents, where they might safely and fully satisfy their hunger. A little Cloud, that an hand might have covered, was enough to foretell those of more fruitfull wombes, that within an houre covered the face of the whole Heavens. And Concordances for their use may be compared to the Top of *Pisgah*, which, though it selfe was barren and Rocky, yet was it able to shew the Discoveryes of the whole Land of *Canaan*. But all this, and what ever else may be spoken, as to the usefullnesse of Concordances, I know will be easily granted: Only the quarrelsome age, and the spirit of gainesaying will be apt to reply, that there is no need of multiplying bookes: Seeing others have already done so excellently upon this Subject; Seeing *Cushi* is run before, and runs so well, what need *Ahimaaz* trouble himselfe to be a messenger? But Sir, to satisfy these, and all that may aske a reason, I shall desire leave to open the true Causes, and first Motives upon my heart, that I am persuaded were wrought there by the spirit of God, and by his providence have drawne me forth to this laborious, and tedious taske.

First, I was sorry to see such helpfull expedients wanting to so many men that might have made dayly use of them: for Concordances were growne so bulky, and so deare, that young men seldome had them, poore men could not have them: though the one had most need of them, being yet by reason of age but babes, and inexpert in the word of righteousness; and the other were like to make the most use of them, because their family-wants, and urging necessityes would not permit to furnish their studies with any great variety and choice of other Authours.

Secondly, I found that our Concordances, not being portable, nor fit Companions for a journey, and necessary absence from bookes, were often farthest off, when a man would most wish their helps. *The oile was to fetch when the poore Virgins should have made use of it.*

Thirdly, they were books (that whether for their price, or for their lumber I know not) yet commonly were shut out of private families: where what good they may do, will be easily found by every faithfull *Abraham, that desires to command his sons, and teach his household to know the Lord and to do righteousnesse.*

Fourthly, I had been puzzled my selfe, and had heard others complaine too; that upon heads, which were very large, and tooke up many leaves, and were cut out into many subdivisions, they were often compelled to give over a word in the search, or else to spend more time in the pursuit of it, then their streightnings would well admit. Now to help these inconveniences, I have by the assistance of God found a new method, never yet pitched upon by any; which by superscribing the head, to be repeated to every subsequent line, conteining some most significant word, and signall expression in the verse, doth very much contract the worke, and lessen the volume of it. The work I confesse hath been wearisome and long, & the bare correction, and proving of the coppy cost more houres then the makeing of some bookes hath done, though of a treble magnitude. But if God get any glory by it, and his servants any help, I shall remember the Toile but as waters past, and like a *woman after Travaile,* quickly forget the pain *for joy a Child is borne.*

Sir, I humbly aske pardon for the boldnesse of my addresse, and commit you into his hands, that hath engraved upon his Palmes the names of all his Saints. The Lord remember all your worke, and labour of love in the Gospell of Jesus Christ.

    So Prayes,
        The least and unworthiest of all your Fellow-labourers in the Ministry of the Word.
                ROBERT WICKENS

41. FROM THOMAS GILBERT

In his *Vindiciae Supremi Dei Dominii* (1655), which is written in opposition to Owen's own *De Divina Justitia,* there is a Latin letter from Gilbert to Owen. Their scholastic debate was concerned with the question as to whether Divine Justice has necessarily to be satisfied for human sin before the elect can be forgiven. Owen maintained that God cannot forgive sin without atonement being made on behalf of humanity whilst Gilbert, who remained a lasting friend of Owen, argued that God could, if He wished, forgive the elect without atonement being made, although He had chosen to let His Son die. Because of the technicalities of this subject the Latin letter is not translated here. For Gilbert see *C.R.*

42. FROM THE LORD PROTECTOR[1]

To our trustie and welbeloved John Owen Doctor in Divinitie Vice Chancellor of our University in Oxford.

Trustie and welbeloved,

We greet you well. Whereas we have been moved on the behalfe of Mr Oliver Pocklington[2] of Nottingham Physician (of whose worke and learninge We have received ample testimonie) that he may be admitted to the Degree of Doctor in Phyicke. We have thought fitt to recommend him unto you and our University of Oxford for that purpose, with our desire that he may be admitted to the Degree of Doctor in Physicke accordingly.

Given under our Signet at our Palace of Westminster: the fourth day of March 1656.

OLIVER P.

[1] Reg. Convoc., p. 283.
[2] Oliver Pocklington was the son of John Pocklington, D.D., for whom see *D.N.B.* He received the degree on 25 April, 1656.

43. FROM THE LORD PROTECTOR[1]

For Dr John Owen, Dr in Divinity, Vice-Chancellor of our University of Oxford

Sir,

We have received very good satisfaction from severall hands touchinge Mr Peter Vashon[2] Practitioner in Physicke as to his sufferings for his Religion in his owne Nation, his service in the late Warrs to this Common-Wealth, his skill in the Faculty he professeth, and success (through the blessinge of God) in the Practice of it, together with the unblameableness of his Conversation.

We are pleased out of our especiall favour and regard had to a Person under soe good a Character to vouchsafe him this our especiall Recommendation to you, and by you to the rest into whose hands our power to that purpose is delegated together with our house of Convocation in the University of Oxford, to be created Batchelour in Physicke for his more free and undisturbed Practice in that Faculty.

Your loveinge Friend

Whitehall
25 of March 1656

OLIVER PR.

[1] Reg. Convoc., p. 279.
[2] For Peter Vashon see *Alumni Oxonienses*. He received the degree on 10 April 1656 and then received the Doctor of Medicine degree on 4 July 1659.

44. FROM FRANCIS MARTYN[1]

To the vicechancellor of the University of Oxford, greeting

Sir,

Whereas I have received a writt from Oliver Lord Protector of the Common wealth of England Scotland and Ireland and the Dominions thereto belonging to mee directed for the election of one Burgesse in your university of Oxon to come to the Parliament to bee held at the Citty of Westminster upon the seventeenth day of September next coming and there to advise with the Knights Citizens and other Burgesses of this Common wealth[2]. These are therefore by vertue of the sayd writt to command you firmly enjoyninge that upon the receipt thereof you make Proclamation of the same, and of the certain day for the sayd election to bee made in your sayd university, and that you cause to bee freely and indifferently chosen by those of your sayd university who shall bee present at such election one fitt and discreet person to serve as Burgesse for your sayd university, and the name of such Burgesse to bee chosen, whether hee bee present or absent, you cause to bee inserted into certaine Indentures thereuppon to bee made between you and them who shall be present at such choyce and that you cause him to come at the day and place aforesayd, soe that hee, the sayd Burgesse, may have full and sufficient power for himselfe and the people of the University aforesayd to doe and consent unto those things which then and there by the common councell of the sayd Common wealth in Parliament (by gods blessing) shall bee ordained upon the weighty affairs aforesayd, soe that for defect of such like power by reason of improudent choyce of the Burgesse aforesayd, the sayd affairs may not remayn undone. And you are not to chuse any Sheriffe of the sayd Common wealth. And the sayd Choyce distinctly and openly soe to be made, you certifie to me under the hands and seals of them who shall be present at such Choyce within twenty days after the sayd Election; that I may returne the same to the sayd Lord Protector into his Chancery and hereof fayle not. Given under the seale of my office the seventeenth day of July in the yeare of our Lord, 1656

FRANCIS MARTYN

[1] Reg. Convoc., p. 289. Francis Martyn was the sheriff of Oxfordshire.

[2] Convocation elected Nathaniel Fiennes for whom see *D.N.B.*

45. FROM THE LORD PROTECTOR[1]

To the Reverend the Vicechancellor and the Convocation of the University of Oxon. These

Gentlemen.

Wee taking notice that the time for nominating a Vicechancellor for the next yeare is now approaching and considering how conducing and necessary it is for the good of the University, and for carrying on the worke of Reformation there, that the Government thereof bee continued in an able and faithfull hand; And wee having had abundant Testimony and experience of the abilities and faithfullnes of Dr John Owen Deane of Christchurch. Wee are very willing and desirous that Dr Owen (though hee hath susteyned the burden and duty of the sayd place for severall years last past) should for the Publiq good bee continued therein. And wee doe hereby nominate and appoint the sayd Dr Owen to the place of Vicechancellor to your University for the yeare following, not doubting but hee will continue his wonted care and diligence in the discharge of the sayd trust. And wee hope you will bee ready in your severall places and stations to contribute your endeavours for the carrying on of the worke of Reformation, and good Government of the University wherein you shall not want all due encouragement from,

Gentlemen.

Your loving Friend and Chancellor.

OLIVER P.

[1] Reg. Convoc., p. 290. The letter is not dated but it was read in Convocation on 7 October 1656.

46. TO NATHANIEL FIENNES[1]

Most honourable Sir,

We beg you to pardon us for troubling you and disturbing you as you watch over the public good; we applaud from afar as you race over that exalted course of virtue; for we truly cannot do other than honour and greet you repeatedly as our patron through whose auspices we may review and acknowledge the money for which we are indebted to you.

[1] Reg. Convoc., p. 300. Original in Latin. For Nathaniel Fiennes see Letter No. 44 above. He had defended the teaching of Civil Law in the University. Cf. *Wood*, p. 210.

Gladly we acknowledge that we have had fulfilled those wishes which we conceived long ago when, with the votes of everyone gathered together and with all voices in favour, you were chosen to protect the interests of learning in Parliament; being a man, long renowned, into whose care, moreover, the University might commend itself; one in whose wisdom and good faith it might confidently entrust whatever in any way appertains to learning. We all offer you our thanks that we have not found our hopes vain nor requests ignored: we thank you because you grant your protection in all things if ever an intruder breaks into the privileged domain of the people and because you apply yourself in person to our affairs if ever they are uncertain or go amiss, and, by your advice and authority, you give your support to Learning, as a patron and example among distinguished men.

However, you can do us no greater kindness than by taking care (as you are doing) lest any debauched young men, companions of Bacchus (scholars cast out from the garden of Learning and the Muses) returning here as by right should continue to be a bad influence on those who belong here: nor let it go unchecked that anyone for his own amusement force the officials of the University in charge of discipline and government to rush to and fro through the courts, a spectacle for others, a shameless source of amusement for a late hour. Without doubt a man keeps by him a copy of *Oeconomicus*[2] and just as this is indispensable to the head of a household, similarly a University of young men must have guidance when it stumbles, and the structure of discipline will fall apart if those in charge of studies are dragged through the courts with the grievances of all for the purpose of speaking out, and are forced to come out in public to join argument as of equal right with any nobody: than such inequality indeed nothing could be more unequal.

And so on this account we appeal to you as the upholder and vindicator of our liberty to do all you can to stop this contention and dissoluteness lest we have here one long Christmas revelry and the whole year becomes as December. Yet in spite of our concern about these things we will put an end to our requests or we may see your favour taken from us and your kindness all sold out by our constantly bidding for it. And so we place before you this most urgent of our requests for your help,

Your most devoted servant,

THE UNIVERSITY OF OXFORD

9 February 1657.

[2] Presumably a book by Xenophon on domestic and estate management.

47. FROM JOHN BEVERLEY[1]

Dearly Reverend in our Lord,

Suffer, I beseech you, an abrupt yet humble Word of Exhortation, from one tho' personally unacquainted, yet emboldened to this Undertaking by the common Law of a joint interest in, and special Affection to, the solemn Work of Christ's visible Kingdom. I most thankfully to Almighty God confess, he hath caused the Lustre of this Truth to break thro' a great Part of that slanderous Heterodoxy, Prejudice, and general Obloquy wherewith Satan subtly and maliciously over-clouded it in this first Dawning of our England's disciplinary Reformation, when it groaned under that Hell-hatch'd Nick-name, that *infamia nominis*, as *Blondel*[2] terms Independency. But yet, how too-considerable a Part of the same sad Cloud stands over the Head of this choice Cause of Christ, among the Reformed Churches, both Abroad and at Home, what need I tell you? Have you not read; or rather, how could, or can, your Bowels rest in reading so many dismal Abominations charged, even after all that precious *Hooker* or *Cotton*[3] have said, to the continued Disparagement of so innocent a Cause? Truth itself, so far as we understand in this Cause, not mainly calls and cries, by these importunate Lines, upon you, for a more full Vindication. And whom should such a Truth, in such a Extremity, betake herself for relief unto, among all her children, rather than to yourself; or such as you can prevail with, and judge, if you can justly, any more fit than yourself, even yourself, who have such a Name in the Learned and Christian World already, as that your very appearing might be sufficient Vindication? May I not charge you in Christ's Name, to rise up once more for Christ, and for this Part of his Truth also, even as in a former Church-Case? *Esther* iv.14. What Account can be given but that God, foreseeing how useful you might be in such a Juncture, for Relief of his Truth now abused,

---

[1] Matthias Maurice, *Monuments of Mercy*, 1729, pp. 10–14. At its formation in 1655, John Beverley became pastor of the Rothwell Congregational Church and one year later, on the presentation of the Protector, he became Vicar of Rothwell. Cf. G. F. Nuttall, *Visible Saints*, Oxford. 1957, p. 38. The purpose of this letter is to persuade Owen to defend the principles of the Congregational way against the attacks of Daniel Cawdry, Presbyterian minister at Great Billing, which was near Rothwell in Northamptonshire. Cawdry accused the Congregationalists of being schismatics and Owen engaged in controversy during 1657 and 1658 with him. The book which Owen wrote because of this letter was entitled *Review of the true Nature of Schisme*, which was a reply to Cawdry's *Independencie a Great Schisme*, 1657.

[2] i.e. David Blondel (1590–1655) a professor at Amsterdam.

[3] For Thomas Hooker see *D.N.B.* and for Cotton p. 20 above.

did chuse to set yourself in that signal Place at *Oxford,* even for so signal a Service, to such a signal Portion of Truth? And can you forbear to extend your Hand in such a Case? Who can dispatch so noble Work, even *verso pollice,* with such Ease and Facility? What Wonder if the Memory of such a Cause rot with Posterity, when such as have tasted the glorious God therein, do themselves so slightly regard it, not improving the least of their many Talents in Vindication of it. Oh what manner of Zeal have others had, and is promised to such as you the Chieftains of Israel. See *Isai.* lxii.1. with v 6,7. *Zeph.* iii.18. *Hagg.* i.4. Is this a time, when such Reproach and Gloominess covers the Face and Mountain of Truth? Is this a time for you, O ye Heads of Colleges, the Principal of the Flocks, to dwell in your own cieled Houses, and however pompous and stately Possessions! When we, poor Under-Shrubs, have our Heads bowed down with Grief, after continued Implorings of God for his stirring up some eminent Instruments; tho' we dare not be diffident, or desert the Truth, resolving rather to die, and be (if so it must be) buried with our Mother *Naomi;* yet how unsufferable is it that Truth should thus be torn in Pieces, while such Cedars are standing! If the Children alas of *New England* (as my Soul bled to read in *Cobbet* of late)[4] be under such Guilt, by Degeneracy after their Parents are dead; how much more monstrous for you Fathers in *Old England* to degenerate, even while you live, from others, or your own former Zeal in vindicating the Truth! And for you, who see more, and have more Advantages every way, than any before you, for whom even to appear in the Cause, is in effect to gain the Victory; for you to be now silent, under whatever Pretence, what is it but to render all former Attempts by ever-glorious *Hooker,* &c. for the Truth, as it were ineffectual; than which, what can be more lamentable? What, dear Sir, if we were all, as some such as yourself are, personally promoted? What Satisfaction is this, when the Cause of Truth lies bleeding, stinking, and rotting, without Care, Cure or Vindication? Or shall common Excuses and Put-offs shroud the declining so necessary a work? How many empty Compliments, it's like, you have time for; and not Vacancy enough for such Work as would live after, yea, procure Life to the Cause after Death? Or will you put it off to those of *New England*? Have they not already done their Part, (Glory to God) while the Prime of them lived! Is not this their triumphant Defence, that they have not in the least been wanting to answer every Book, as then put out against them? Ah! what have we in *Old England,* who are not in a Wilderness, we may blush! What have we come near them in, for Christ and his Truth's Vindication? I hope God the Father will at length hear the many Cries and Tears in secret

[4] For Thomas Cobbet see *Dict. Amer. Biog.*

poured forth, in Behalf of what I have thus writ. If I lose this my Labour, as to Man, I shall as he said, *Isai.* xxxviii.15. *go softly*, all my few remaining Days, *in the Bitterness of my Soul;* and at my last Gasp, or departing Sob, rejoice that I am going to the blessed Souls of *Shepherd*,[5] *Hooker, Cotton,* &c. Pardon, dear Sir, my *Errata* in all this, for either Matter or Form; but as you love Christ Jesus, and dread that *Anathema,* I. *Cor.* xvi.22. let it be duly improv'd. In hope whereof, thus rests, praying, a Lover of, and Servant to, all the Flocks of Christ's Companions,

JOHN BEVERLY

Rothwell,
Feb.24.1657

[5] For Thomas Shepard see *D.N.B.*

48. TO GEORGE KENDALL

In Kendall's book *Fur Pro Tribunali* (1657) there is a long Latin letter specially written by John Owen and addressed to Kendall congratulating him on his decision to oppose the Arminian sentiments of the book *Fur Praedestinatus* (1651), which contains a satirical dialogue between a Calvinist minister and a thief and is intended to bring disrepute on the orthodox Calvinist doctrine of predestination. *Fur Praedestinatus* was originally written in Dutch by Henricus Slatius as *Den Ghepredestineerden dief* (Antwerp, 1619) and it is possible that the Latin translation was made by William Sancroft—at least this is the view of Thomas Birch, *Life of Tillotson,* p.160 Cf. also J. B. Mullinger, *The University of Cambridge,* Vol. III., p. 438.

As Owen's letter is very long and full of technical theology it is not given here in translation.

49. FROM THE LORD PROTECTOR[1]

To our trustie and welbeloved the Vicechancellor and Convocation of our University of Oxford

Trustie and wellbeloved,

Wee greate you well. Amongst the many parts of that Government which is intrusted to us, wee doe looke upon the universities as meriting very much of our care and thoughts; and finding that the place of Chancellor of our Universitie of Oxford is at present in our selfe, and withall judging that the continuance thereof in our hands may not bee soe consistent with the present constitution of affairs; wee have therefore thought fitt to resigne the sayd office, as wee

[1] Reg. Convoc., p. 305.

hereby doe, and to leave you at freedome to elect some such other person thereunto as you shall conceive meet for the execution thereof. Our will and pleasure therefore is that you doe proceed to the election of a Chancellor with your first conveniency.[2] Not doubting but you will in your choyce have a just regard to the advancement and encouraging of Pietie and learning, and to the continuing and further setling of good Order and government amongst you, which you may easily find yourselves obliged to have principally in your consideration and designe whether your respect the University it selfe or the good of the Common-wealth upon which it hath soe great an influence. And although our relation to you may by this means in some sort bee changed yet you may bee confident wee shall still reteyne a reall affection to you, and bee ready upon all occasions to seeke and promote your good. Given at Whitehall, this third day of July, 1657.

OLIVER P.

[2] Convocation invited Richard Cromwell, son of the Lord Protector, to be Chancellor. See p. 121 below.

50. FROM HENRY LAWRENCE[1]

Sir,

His Highnesse the Lord Protector with the advise of his Privy Councill hath beene pleased to passe the inclosed order touching some matters in difference betwixt the Ministers of Scotland[2] for hearing whereof it is conceived fitt the Referees begin their meeting on Tuesday next at that Roome in Whitehall where the Commissioners for approbation[3] used to sitt, and it is desired that in order thereunto you will come up with your most speedy conveniency, and so I rest,

Your very loveinge friend,

H. LAWRENCE

Whitehall,
July 16th 1657

[1] C.S.P.D. (1657/8), p. 30. S.P. 25/77 f. 495.

[2] From 1650 Scottish ministers and laymen were divided into two parties, the Resolutioners, who were prepared to accept any help in their opposition to the English rulers, and the Remonstrants or Protestors, who signed a Remonstrance against all, including the young Charles, who were not wholeheartedly for the Covenant. On 14 July 1657 the Council of State appointed referees to hear proposals from each party in order to reach a settlement.

[3] These were the backbone of the Cromwellian Settlement of Religion who gave permission for a man to be allowed to take a living.

51. FROM RICHARD CROMWELL[1]

To the right worthy the Vicechancellor and the rest of the Convocation of the University of Oxford

Gentlemen,

Having from severall eminent persons in your university received an ample Testimony concerning Mr Robert Whitehall,[2] Fellow of Merton Colledge, that hee is one well deserving his degree of Bach. in Phisicke, it is therefore my desire that hee may have free creation thereunto. To that purpose I doe recommend him to the next Convocation for their concurrence herein and present admission to that degree. I rest

Your loving friend and Chancellor.

Whitehall
July 29th, 1657

R. CROMWELL

[1] Reg. Convoc., p. 309.
[2] For Robert Whitehall see *D.N.B.* In the British Museum Lansdowne MS. 822. f. 166 there is a letter from Richard Cromwell to Henry Cromwell commending Whitehall, and requesting that suitable work be found for him in Ireland.

52. TO HENRY CROMWELL[1]

For his Excellency, the Lord Henry Cromwell, these

My Lord,

I received your commands by Mr Wood,[2] in reference unto the Statutes of this university, to be sent unto you. I shall with the first convenient opportunity endeavour to send or bringe them unto your Lordship. I am glad to heare of your indeavour to dispose of that university to the interest of piety and learninge; and am bold to informe your Lordship, that out Statutes, as those also of the other university, beinge framed to the Spirit and road of studys in former days, will scarsly upon consideration, be found to be the best expediente for the promotion of the good ends of Godlinesse and solid literature which are in your ayme. I could much rather wish, that if the great employments of your Lordships servants in that place will not afford them leasure to attend such a worke, that you would be pleased to send your commands to some of your friends and servants in England, men of Ability, wisdome, and piety, to

[1] British Museum Lansdowne MS. 833. f. 179.
[2] This Mr Wood was probably Robert Wood, Fellow of Lincoln College, Oxford, for whom see *C.R.*

compose a body of orders and statutes suited to the present light, interest of state and advantagious discourse of literature in the ways and expedients of it which we do enjoy that may be submitted to your Lordships judgement. It is not impossible that somethinge not unworthy your owninge might be presented unto you; and that returninge with the advantage of your acceptance and approbation it might get esteeme here also where, inveterate prejudice, beaten good customes and in many an affection for an old interest will not safely permit them most evidently usefull tenders of alteration to take place;[3] I hope your Lordship will pardon this boldness in him who prays for your dayly,

    and is,
     My Lord,
      Your most humble and most faithfull servant,
              JOHN OWEN

Ox: Ch: Ch: Coll.
Septemb: 9th: 1657

[3] In 1657 John Owen was encountering opposition in Convocation for his plans to reform that body and the statutes of the University.

53. FROM RICHARD CROMWELL[1]

To the Reverend the Vicechancellor Doctors and other the Members of the Convocation of the University of Oxon

Gentlemen.

 Whereas by the statutes and Constitutions of your University, it doth appertaine to the Chancellor to nominate and appoint yearly the vicechancellor there, being sorry that the doeing thereof hath beene soe long deferred, which may have beene some prejudice to your affairs. I doe hereby nominate Dr Conant[2] Rector of Exeter Colledge to bee Vicechancellor of the sayd University for the yeare next ensuing: and desire that accordingly hee may bee admitted to the exercise and enjoyment of all the Powers, rights and Priviledges unto the sayd office any wayes belonging or appertaining, I am,

    Gentlemen,
     Your affectionate friend and Chancellor
             R. CROMWELL

Southampton,
Octob. 5th 1657

[1] Reg. Convoc., p. 309.
[2] For the career of John Conant see *C.R.* and *D.N.B.*

54. TO JOHN MAIDSTONE[1]

For the right worthy John Maydston Esquire and Cofferer to his Highness at Whitehall, these

Sir,

Upon the account of that acquaintance which some of us have with you and your known respect to things of honesty and good repute, we are emboldened to intreat your favour and assistance in a businesse wherewith you are not altogether unacquainted. The honourable persons unto whom his Highnesse hath referred this businesse concerning the election in All Souls have appoynted thursday the 11th of Febr. for the hearing of it and to that end have sent a letter unto us requiring the presence of us at that tyme; the matter is of great importance unto the whole good interest in this place; the season is such as makes travayling dangerous, some of us are actually indisposed as to health and scarce any of us able to take such a journey at present. There are important matters of fact that must be proved by the witnesses whom we have no power to cause to appeare without a summons from above; and being Fellows of that Colledge they will not appeare of their owne accord. The statutes of the Colledge which most evidently impoure us to the whole of what we have done in that businesse must be brought up upon which severall accounts being sundry of us very desyrous to wayte in person upon the honourable referees.[2] We hertily desire you to attend our Noble Chancellor and the Lord Fiennes and in our name to begge the favour of putting off the hearing to some further day by them to be appoynted. We hope they will not deny us this favour: but if for reasons which at this distance we cannot apprehend it may not be granted we humbly desyre that the Honorable referees would send a summons for Mr. Panton and Mr Bond Fellows of that Colledge and also an order for the bringing up of the Booke of Statutes. Sir if you shall please to put your selfe to this trouble and to give us an account of their Lordships determination by the next post you will exceedingly oblige.

Your very humble and affectionate friends
JOHN CONANT
JOHN OWEN, THANKFULL OWEN,
CHRISTOPHER ROGERS, HENRY WILKINSON,
JAMES BARRON, FRANCIS HOWELL[3]

January (?) 1658

[1] *C.S.P.D.* (1957/8), p. 277. S.P. S.P. 18/179, f. 102.

[2] For the discussions of the Visitors concerning All Souls see *Register*, pp. 434ff.

[3] For the members of the Third Board of Visitors, appointed 2 September 1654, see *Register*, p. 400.

55. TO LADY ELIZABETH PULESTON[1]

Madam,

Whilst I was in hopes to have waited upon you, and your worthy husband at your owne house, I reserved my begginge of your pardon that I had not made my acknowledgement of your favour in owning and minding a relation of kindred, and sundry other respects, unto that season. Beinge by the providence of God prevented as to those resolutions, I am bold to lay hold on this opportunity of returninge my hearty thanks for your kind remembrance of him, who is no way able to deserve your respects, though he will at all times owne as hearty and entire an honor and regard to your Ladyship and your noble husband as any person living; I hope you both, with my Cousins, your sons, are in health; and am resolved (if the Lord please) to see you in the beginninge of this Springe. My wife presents her faithfull service and respects to your Ladyship and is glad to hear of your name. For my part, it is some contentment to me, that whilest I am in this place, I have some little opportunity to express a regard to that relation you are pleased to allow me the honor of by taking the best care I can of him who bears the name of your family, my young cousin—Puleston[2]—I humbly begge your pardon of this trouble, and leave to subscribe myself,
    Madam,
       Your most humble servant and affectionate kinsman,
                                  JOHN OWEN

My most humble service of respects with many thanks
for his kind invitation to your worthy husband.
Ox: Ch: Ch: Coll:
Jan. 26th, 1658

[1] Bodleian MS. Eng. Lett. c. 29, f. 145. Cf. also *Diaries and Letters of Philip Henry* (ed. M. H. Lee), 1882, p. 31, and Letter No. 30 above.
[2] Roger Puleston entered Christ Church in February 1656.

56. FROM LADY ELIZABETH PULESTON[1]

My much honored Cosin,

I was in hopes that I should have seen you here, as you proposed, the last Spring, and am very sorry it fell out otherwise; it hath pleased the Lord to lay mee low under his hand by much payn and many months sickness from a cancer in my breast, and I am wayting every day till my change cometh; but if we meet no more on earth I hope wee shall in the arms of Jesus Christ.[2] There is a friend of mine,

[1] A transcript of this letter is in *Diaries and Letters of Philip Henry*, p. 32.
[2] Elizabeth Puleston died on 29 September 1658.

whose name is Edward Thomas of Wrexham,³ who brings his son to your Colledge, and I request you to countenance him with your favour. The youth is very hopeful both in learning and grace and his father an ancient professor of Godlinesse in these parts, and one of approved integrity; and I know, Sir, that such and what concerns them lyes near your heart upon far greater and other interests than mine; and I persuade my selfe what your opportunityes will permitt you to do on his behalfe, you will receive a full recompense of reward for, from him who hath promised to requite even a cup of cold water given in the name of a Disciple.

Mr. Henry⁴ is here with mee, much my comfort in my present affliction; what my husband intends concerning him is not yet settled, but I hope shortly it will bee. In the mean time I am lothe he should lose a certainty in the Colledge for an uncertainty here: and doe therefore desire you to continue his place to him for a while longer, that seeing the Lord hath made him willing to lay out himselfe in the work of the gospel so far remote from his friends, in this poor dark corner of the land, hee may not in any thing be prejudiced for our sakes (who do esteem him highly in love). My husband is at London or in his way home. We and ours are much engaged to you for your love and I should have beene very glad if it might have fallen within the compass of my abilityes to make known other than by words my sense of your many kindnesses: but 'tis the Lords will I should dye your debtor. With my unfayned respects and service to your Lady,

I rest,
Your affectionate Cosin and Friend,

August (?) 1658   ELIZABETH PULESTON

³ For Edward Thomas see A. N. Palmer, *A History of the Older Nonconformity of Wrexham*, Wrexham, 1888, p. 31.
⁴ It was not until 1659 that Philip Henry was legally installed into the living at Worthenbury. See *The Life of the Rev. Philip Henry* (ed. J. B. Williams), p. 29. Cf. p. 79, n. 1.

57. FROM RICHARD SALWEY¹

For Dr John Owen Deane of Christ Church and Mr Thankful Owen²
President of St Johns Colledge in Oxon.

Sent,

The Counsell being desirous that you would afford them your labours in preaching at Whitehall on the Lords dayes betweene this

¹ *C.S.P.D.* (1659/60), p. 221. S.P. 25/98, f. 240. For Richard Selwey, President of the Council during the rule of the restored Rump, see *D.N.B.*
² For Thankful Owen see *C.R.*

and the first of December next hence thought first hereby to signify their desire therein unto you not doubting of your readinesse to answer their call to such a Worke. And that they will expect you on too morrow sevennight and if your owne occasions shall at any time require your absence from that work they shall leave it unto your especial care that the same may be supplied by such person of eminent godliness & gifts as you judge meete for that work.

Signed &c
RICHARD SALWEY, President

Whitehall,
24 Septem. 1659

58. TO GENERAL MONCK[1]

To the Right Honorable General Monck and the officers of the army in Scotland

My Lord and Gentlemen,

Your Declaration to the Churches of Christ in the three Nations,[2] having been delivered to us and considered by us, wee hold it our duty in a businesse of soe great importance and consequence to communicate unto you our sense thereupon; which that it might more fully bee imparted wee have desired some of our Brethren in person to make theire repair unto you, to witt Lt. Genll. Whalley and Major Genll. Goffe,[3] together with Mr Joseph Carrill and Mr Matthew Barker,[4] pastours of neighbouring congregations, who as they are deare unto us and of esteeme in the Churches, soe are able to relate unto you our mindes and apprehensions in this busines; and therefore wee earnestly desire yow to receive them with good affection, and to give credit to what they shall represent unto yow in our names. The shortnes of the tyme would not permitt us to take with us the concurrence of more Churches in remote parts of the Nation, whose

---

[1] *The Clarke Papers* (ed. C. H. Firth), Vol. IV, 1901, pp. 81–2. For General George Monck see *D.N.B.* He was the commander of the army in Scotland. This and the following five letters can only be understood against the political background of the last four months of 1659. Cf. I. Roots, *The Great Rebellion*, 1642–1660, 1966, pp. 242ff.

[2] A copy is in the British Museum.

[3] For Edward Whalley and William Goffe, both regicides, see *D.N.B.*

[4] For Joseph Caryl and Matthew Barker see *C.R.*

sence wee doubt not but wilbee the same as ours, who subscribe ourselves,

My Lord and Gentlemen,

Yours to serve you in the Lord,

JOHN OWEN
PHILIP NYE
JOHN ROWE
SETH WOOD
THOMAS SMALLWOOD
JACOB WILLER
HENRY SCOBELL
WILLIAM HOOKE
THOMAS BROOKS
WILLIAM GREENHILL

MATTHEW MEADE
ROBERT GOUGE
HUMPHREY DAVYE
NICHOLAS ROBERTS
NICHOLAS JUXON
WILLIAM VINER
ROBERT NEWMAN
THOMAS CHANDLER
THOMAS ONGE[5]

From the Savoy,
31 October 1659.

[5] This list includes both ministers and lay elders. All are in C.R. except Willer, Scobell, Roberts, Juxon, Viner, Newman, Chandler and Onge.

59. TO GENERAL MONCK[1]

My Lord,

I had made bold to have written unto you att the beginning of the late differences that have falen out betweene you and your freinds heere in England, but that I feared least prejudices and mistaikes might have rendred my soe doing only troublesome unto your Lordshipp and uselesse in its selfe; for though I knew my selfe to bee an utter strainger to that which was the occasion of the breach betweene you,[2] yett the misrepresentations of things that I found prevaileing amongst ous would not suffer me to be confident that I should escaipe from a share in itt. But now, finding the infinitely wise and gratious providence of God working things towards a closure betweene yow, I could not withold from contributeing my mite also unto soe good a worke, haveinge already laboured unto my utmost in this place for the furtherance of a mutuall condescension, which must bee the meanes of a freindly composure and end of this bussinesse, their being then a resolucion on all hands of fixing on a free Commonwealth; and in such a way, as that whatever wee have yet attained hath bin but a shaddow of what is now aimed att, and care to bee taken therein for the true interest of Christ, and that of men sober and

[1] The Clarke Papers, Vol. IV, pp. 121-4.
[2] This was the employment of military rule instead of civil.

godly. I cannot apprehend that any just and warrantable cause of difference can remaine amongst yow. Their are, my Lord, two evills that wee have cause to feare: the one is the prevailing of the Comon Enemy over ous; the other the prevailencie of fanaticall selfe seeking persons amongst ous. By your union both of these through the mercy of God, wilbee prevented. By a continuance in your breaches, I cannott say both (because they are inconsistant), but one of them, that is one or the other, will certainly ensue: either the Comon Enemy will devoure ous all, which is the most likely, or another sort of men will have opportunity to lay hould on that power which will not easily be wrested from them. However, this is vissable to the whole world, freinds and enemies, nor can it be gainesayed by any with the least couler of reason; if the armies ingage in blood, their is a grave maid for our whole cause and interest, and a doore of ruine opened to all the sober godly in both Nations; which the old enemy is soe sencable and assured of, that his hopes and feares goe upp and downe, according as the differences of the army seemes to widen or close, noe otherwise then if that difference were an army for Charles Stuart, and these men are wise in their generation. It is certaine, my Lord, that God hath putt an opportunity into your hands to be eminently servicable to the interest of good men in these Nations, for your cordiall closing with your friends heere, carrying on things of common advice and consent, will exceedingly strengthen their hands in opposeing things distructive to the liberty of the Commonwealth and true interest of the saints, which are attempted to bee imposed on them by multitudes of men, and a continuance at this distance wilbee certainely ruinous, both to the armies and their freinds; nether are they able to prevent itt, who desire most to see yow both ingaged in blood, while they intend to warme themselves by the fires that [you] kindle. Finding then by the Declaration and letters, and some conference with the Commissioners sent by yow hither, that your principalls and those of your freinds here are universally the same, I cannott conjecture what cause of difference should remaine; but because the sitting againe of the last Parliament is by some spoken of as a sufficient cause of itt, I shall offer my thoughts to your Lordshipp on that particular. Most of the persons of that number are my old freinds and acquaintance. I may say freely that I ventered somewhat for their sitting. I know nothing at all of their dissolution, being for about five weekes before absent from this place; nor shall I take off from their esteeme by a review of their actings during their session. Yet this I shall say, that it were better that both they, and I, and hundreds of better men then my selfe were in the ends of the earth, then that this [cause] should be ruined by the armies contest about them. For my owne part I am satisfied with these two things: first, that without there restauration a free state or Commonwealth may be setled, the Common Enemy defeated, the ministry preserved, reformation carryed on, and all the ends of our ingagements satisfied, if your Lordshipp and those with you concurre in the worke; and, secondly, that their reinvestiture cannott be effected without the blood of them whose ruine I am perswaded you seeke not, as on other accounts soe because I find them cordially assert and honour yow, as also the enslaveing of these Nations forever to the will of the major part of that small number.[3] For that they should sitt downe againe, with thoughts of passing by what is past, looking onely forwards future settlement and issuing their power therein, cannott fall on the imagination of any wise man, but only those who are distant from this place, nor doe any amonge themselves pretend to such resolutions. I have spoaken my heart plainely and honestly unto your Lordshipp in these things, as in the presence of God, without respect to persons or parties. And much more I would willingly add, were it not for feare of being esteemed importunate to presse on you in your weighty affaires. Yea, out of that sincere honour I have long borne you, [I] would willingly waite on yow in person, should yow command it, for the assurance of the assured setlement of love betweene yow and your freinds in this Nation. My Lord, yow shall on all occasions find me a true lover of my countryes liberties, an enemy to all usurpations upon itt, and one resolved to live and dye with the sober godly interest; and, finding your Lordshipp on the same principles, I have bin free with yow beyond the rules of that cautiousnesse which the difficulties of the season seemes to call for; but I walke by now such rule. The manie things of all lawfull difference betweene yow and your freinds heere being secured by the agreement of your Commissioners, let me in the name of our Lord Jesus Christ, and on the account of his interest in the whole earth, in the name of all the trembling saints in these Nations, begg of you to bee instrumentall in putting a perfect issue and perpetuall oblivion to the late breach and division, as the only visable medicin, under the providence of God, to prevent the utter ruine of all that is deare unto you and ous. I have only to add my desire that yow would believe mee to be what in sincerity I am,

        My Lord,
               Your Lordshipps most humble, faithfull
                  and affectionate servant,
                          JOHN OWEN

Westminster,
November 19, 1659.

---

[3] The Rump was restored in December.

60. FROM GENERAL MONCK[1]

For my Reverend Friends, Dr Owen, Mr Hook, and Mr Greenhill; to be communicated to the Churches in and about London

Honoured and dear Friends,

I received yours, and am very sensible of your Kindness which you have expressed to the Army in Scotland, in sending down such Honourable and Reverend Persons so long and tedious a Journey, whom we have received with Thankfulness and great Joy, as your Messengers of the Churches, and Ministers of Christ; and have taken Notice of this Office of love, and of your Care of these three Nations. I do promise for my Trust and the rest of the Officers here, that your Interest, Liberty and Encouragement shall be very dear to us; and we shall take this as a renewed Obligation to assert to the uttermost what we have already declared for the Churches of Jesus Christ. I doubt not, but you have received satisfaction of our Inclination to a peaceable Accommodation, and do hope, that some difficulties being united, we shall obtain a fair Composure. I do assure you, that the great things which have been upon my Heart to secure and provide for, are our Liberties and Freedoms, as we are the Subjects and Servants of Jesus Christ, which are convey'd to us in the Covenant of Grace, assur'd in the Promises, purchased for us by the Blood of our Saviour, and given as his great Legacy of his Churches and People; in comparison of what, we esteem all other things as Dung and Dross, but as they have Relation to, and Dependence upon this most noble End. The other are our Laws and Rights as Men, which must have their esteem in the second Place, and for which many Members of the Churches have been eminent Instruments, to labour in Sweat and Blood for these eighteen years past, and our Ancestors many hundred Years before. The Substance of which may be reduced to Parliamentary Government, and the People consenting to the Laws by which they are to be Governed; that this Privilege of your Nations, may be so bounded, that the Churches may have both Security and Encouragement, is my great Desire and of those with me. So that I hope you will own these just things, and give us that Assistance which becometh the Churches of Christ, in pursuance of this Work. And we do assure you, that we shall comply as far as possible, with respect had to your Security, and Safety of these Nations, and the Preservation of our ancient Birth-rights and Liberties; and we shall pray that we may be kept from going out of God's Way, under Pretence of doing God's Work. I do, in the name of the whole Army, and for my self,

[1] J. Toland, *Letters of General Monck*, 1714, No. XII. A reply to No. 58.

give you all our affectionate Thanks, for this your Work of Love; and though we are not able to make such Returns as are in our Hearts and Desires to do, yet we shall endeavour by all Means and Ways, to express our Care and Love to the Churches, and shall leave the Reward to him, who is the God of Peace and Truth, in special assured a Blessing to the Peace-makers: And conclude with the Words of David, I.Sam.25.32. Blessed be the Lord God of Israel and blessed be your Advice, and blessed be you all. Now the Lord be a Wall of Fire round about you, and let his Presence be in his Churches, and they filled with his Glory. I have no more, but to entreat your Prayers for an happy Issue to these unhappy Differences which is the Prayer of him who is,

                        Reverend Sirs,
                              Your very Affectionate Servant,
                                        GEORGE MONK

Edinburgh, Nov.23.1659

61. FROM GENERAL MONCK[1]

For my Reverend freind Doctor John Owen, Deane of Christ Church at Westminster, these

Deare Freind,

You will receive by those honourable and reverend Gentlemen who were appointed by the Churches to speake with mee a letter directed to your selfe, Mr Greenhill, and Mr Hooke, which I intreate you to see communicated to the Churches in and about London. I have therein, and in other printed papers, faithfully stated the reall and sinceare intentions of the army heere with me; and if you have any credit for mee, I beseech yow to beleeve that wee have declared to the world the very resolutions and thoughts of our hearts. I thanke you for your very free and kind letter of the 19th of this instant. I doe confesse I have received therein very much satisfaction as to the greate cause of my owne feares—I meane the fanaticall and selfe seeking party, which doe threaten much danger to these three nations, for the prevention of whose dominion I dare assert it in the presence of God I have hazarded all that is deare to mee. And let me friendly tell yow that itts not imadginable the highth theire spiritts weere arrived, from what incurragements I know not; but I doe assure you that one of them, being accused before a Court Martiall for maintaininge that our blessed Lord and Saviour Jesus Christ (I tremble to

---

[1] *The Clarke Papers*, Vol. IV, pp. 151–4. A reply to No. 59.

write it) was a bastered, and this wicked and ath [eistical] expression proved by very sufficient witnes, yet was carried off by his owne party, with many other insolencyes not to bee remembered in this paper. Now, haveing such knowledge of your worth and piety, I earnestly begg of you to bee an instrument with my Lord Fleetwood[2] to bee carefull of the safety of sober and judicious Christians, which can noe otherwaise bee obtained then by bringing the army to obedience to the civill authority. I know the goodnes and credullousnesse of his spiritt is such, that he hath too greate latitude of charity for such as designe his ruine; and, I must speake it boldly, hee hath not a faithfuller friend in the three Nations then my selfe, nor one that shall more truly serve him; but in such darkewayes I cannot follow him. Hee knowes with what zeale and importunity I urged my dismission from the deceased Protector, and very lately from this Parliament; but now, being at the heade of a part of the army, I dare not sitt still and let our lawes and liberties goe to ruine. I take God to witnes I have noe pleasure in these differences, but I cannot yet say that wee have received any assurance of Parliamentary authority by the late pretended agreement, but shalbee willing to have further treaty for satisfaction. I am ingaged in conscience and honnour to see my Country freed (as much as in mee lies) from that intollerable slavery of sword Government, and I know England cannot, nay, will not endure it; and if this army here had concurred with them in England, wee had bin all exposed to the fury of the three Nations, which they would some time or other have executed. I see nothing will content some men but the inslaveing of all our consciences to theire pleasure. I had thought so many changes would have taught us to rest some wheare; but I shall leave it to yow, whome I know to bee of sober principles and of a publicque spiritt, to represent these things to our freinds in England. As to the Cavaliers interest, I think I may modestly averre it hath not a greater enimy in the three Nations then my selfe, soe that I shall not trouble my selfe to confute those slanders that fanaticall spiritts would asperse mee withall. I doe assure yow in the presence of God that I shall oppose it to the last dropp of my bloud; but I must plainely tell yow that theire hopes are nurished by our unsettlement. Nothing can gratifie them more then the interruption of this Parliament. Could wee once come to a fixt point in a Commonwealth way, wee shall soone engage the body and bulke of the Nation against them. I am sensible of the same feares with your selfe, that the engageing of the armies in bloud will make a grave to bury our whole cause and interest; but the Lord bee judge who hath necessitated us to this hazard. I should bee as willing to bee serviceable to the interest of good men in these nations as any

[2] For General Charles Fleetwood see *D.N.B.* and letters 85, 96, 97 below.

other, but I cannot act against my conscience and commission; neither can I see any legall foundation for a free state, unles this Parliament sitts downe againe, or some other legally called; neither is that necessity of runing into bloud for the attaineing it soe visible unto me, when most of our friends who were demitted their commands may bee restored by our interposalls. I should bee very willing to relinquish all publique imployment as soone as I shall see a good security to our lawes and libertyes, spirituall and civill; and none shalbee more ready to imbrace peace upon those termes; but otherwise I must sadly assure yow that I cannot but appeare for my poore country, and must referr my selfe to the righteous God, with this resolution, 'If I perish, I perish'. Now, haveinge dealt thus plainely with yow, I must reassume my former desire, knowing that interest yow have in the Lord Fleetwood, that yow would let him know what God, the saints, and the world expects at his hands: that hee should restore the Parliament to sitt with safety and freedome, and incurrage men of sober principles in the army; for I must bee free with you, that his enimies doe already publish that hee laid aside his Brother for other than publique ends. I have experienct abundance of love and respect for him and should bee very sorry that soe good a man should bee abused to serve the passion and lust of others. I have noe further but to begg your prayers, and remaine,

Your affectionate friend and servant,
G.M.

Edinburgh,
29 November, 1659.

62. TO GENERAL MONCK[1]

My Lord,

Wee have received your Lordship's letter of November the 23rd by the Honourable and Reverend Brethren sent by the Churches to waite uppon yow, directed to some of us to bee comunicated to the Churches from whome they were sent, the Elders and Bretheren whose names are subscribed being convened, and haveinge duly weighed your Lordshipp's letter with the report made unto us by the Bretheren, wee made bould to give the ensueing Result of our thoughts. Wee doe humbly acknowledge your Lordshipp's respects unto the Churches of Christ expressed both in your letters, declarations, and kinde acceptance with friendly respective entertainement of their messengers, whereof they have given a full accompt unto us, and wee are glad to heare of the clearenes of your lordship's intencions

[1] *The Clarke Papers*, IV, pp. 184–186.

both as to the peace of these nations and the preservation of the old interest of the good people of them and the Saints of God in them; and wee must alsoe assure yow that wee are abundantly satisfied with the intention of the army heere in England as to the same ends, which they have manifested in their late resolutions for the speedy calling of Parliament, wherein if any thing seeme to bee wanting on your parts it will bee your serious interposition that it may bee sure as may preserve the good people from being made a prey to the common enimy, neither doe wee see any thing like to be insisted on by them detrimentall to the godly ministry. In the meane time wee cannot but sadly informe your Lordship that by your divisions not onely incurragement hath bin given to the common enimy, but they have made such a progresse in pursuite of their designe, as that if there bee a continuance for a few days in these breaches it will bee out of your power and theires alsoe to shew the least part of your intended kindnes to the people of God, who are in danger now every moment to bee destroyed and slaine by their inraged enimies.

We are perswaded that if yow were in this place, and saw the tumults, rage, and combination of the old enimies, with the probability they have to accomplish their desires every day, you would not defer one moment to put your selfe into a posture of opposeing them, which in the condition in which yow are, yow are not onely uncapable to performe but alsoe occasionally give them incurragement unto. The state of the quarrell in these parts now is not a Parliament or none, the last Parliament or not, but [the preservation of] our lives from the common enimy or not; and wee would be sorry on your account that the bloud of the Saints of God and of all that hath bin ingaged in our common cause, should with soe much coller bee laid at your doore, as it wilbee if things continue in the present posture a few dayes longer. But yow there and the army heere fixing uppon the same things, all particular centring and a Parliament not to close imediatly soe as to unite in the defence of the common interest, and of the Saints of God, is soe strange a judgement as noe age can pairolele.

Wee cannot but acquaint your Lordshipp that all the feares of the people of God at this day, yea, and all their danger, arrise mearely from the differences yow abide in, which if not speedily remedied will prove the utter ruine of that magistracy and ministry which on both sides are pleaded for.

Wee have not more to add but onely to reminde your Lordshipp of that portion of Scripture wherewith yow close yours to us: I Samuel 25. And wee can with confidence assure yow that it will one day bee noe griefe at heart unto yow that yow have bin prevented from shedding bloud, and made instrumentall for the recovery of the portion of Christ in these nations from the mouth of that greate destruction whereinto it is now cast. With our prayers for your Lordship, that God will guide yow into strate paths, wee rest

Your Lordshipps most humble servants[2]

EDWARD WHALLEY	WILLIAM GOFF
JOHN ROWE	JOHN STONE
MATTHEW BARKER	THOMAS OWEN
JOHN OWEN	JOSEPH CARRILL
PHILIP NYE	WILLIAM BRIDGE
WILLIAM GREENHILL	ISAAC KNIGHT
WILLIAM HOOKE	SETH WOOD

Westminster,
December 13, 1659

[2] For Stone and Thomas Owen see *C.R.*

63. FROM GENERAL MONCK[1]

For my Honourable and Reverend friends, Lieut.Generall Whalley, M. G. Goffe, and Dr Jno. Owen, to be communicated to the congregated Churches in London

Honourable and Reverend friends,

I received yours of the 13th instant, and doe assure yow that my intention and indeavours for the good old cause and the good people of the Nation is still the same as it was when those honourable and reverent persons from yow were with mee, and I could have wished yow had thereby furnished mee with some likelier and readier expedient for accomplishing those desires of mine then that I am now useing; but I must frely confess to yow that I am not soe fully satisfied with the intentions of those whome you call the army in England as yow seeme to bee, nor can I thinke that I have the same apprehencions which you have of that new state of the quarrell in your parts, or of the danger the good people are now in from the Common Enimy. Would they, if they thought the people of God were in soe greate danger, and that a few dayes continuance in these breaches might make that danger past remedy—would they, I say, think now at last of calling a new Parliament, the verry calling and chuseing of whose Members would take up some weekes tyme, though there were noe limitations nor restrictions to bee agreed uppon, or though there were noe necessity for us to interpose as yow desire for the preservation of the good people? Or would they keepe this designe of theires soe secrett that wee should heare of it from you onely, and not from themselves, least, perhaps our consent might [not] bee soe soone gained? Or would they not rather support the present Parliament to sitt downe againe quietly, which might bee done in few dayes tyme, and would ymediately putt an end to all these unhappy controversies, and make that posture of ours, which yow now think gives advantage and incurragement to the Common Enimy, a posture formidable to them, and most convenient to oppose them? What coloures may bee made use of to lay the bloud that may bee spilt in the quarrell at my doore I know not, but this I know, that God who judgeth righteously, and whome noe colloures or pretences can deceive, will in tyme beare witnesse to the innocency and uprightnes of my heart; and I am confident it cannot bee unknowne to you, nor to the greatest part of the people of the Nations, that the late force uppon the Parliament was the begining and cause of these contentions, and that it was done to preserve in theire imployments a small number of officers, not more considerable or better deserveing of the common cause then the like number of those whom themselves have since laid aside, and that they have to this end espoused the interest of a party with whose designes Magistracy and Ministry can noe more stand then with those of the Common Enimy, and to gratifie them have declared publicquely that they would take away tythes, and have now proceeded soe farr as to open againe that issue of bloud which had for a good tyme (through mercy) bin stop't, and was in a hopefull way to have bin altogether healed. For my part, I can safely say that God and my owne actions will beare mee witnesse how carefull and solicitous I was to bring the last treaty to a perfect close, and all our quarrells to full and speedy composure. I think those honourable and reverend Brethren of yours can remember, uppon the first receipt of the late agreement, though it was such as I could not in honour or justice ratifie, yet being uppon my march, to shew my desire to peace, I ymediately returned to Edinburgh, and drew back my forces out of England, and made an offer to the Lord Lambert that the forces on both sides might bee drawne backe according to the tennour of the agreement; which offer of mine his Lordship did not onely consent too, but while wee thought ourselves heere secure and the treaty still continued, yea, even while Col. Sankey was heere from his Lordshipp with the highest expressions, protestations, and offers of peace, advanced upon us in such a manner as wee had just cause to think his intentions were otherwise; yet since that tyme I have not bin wanting in any thing that might on my part promote that good end; but understanding that a quorum of the Commissioners for the government of the army constituted by an Act of Parliament of the 11th of October last, were now sitting at Portsmouth, I imediatly dispatched a messenger to them to perswade them to an accomodation, and directed letters to the Lord Lambert and the officers at Newcastle to let them know as much, and to desire that they would permitt him to passe. If they would refuse it, I leave it to your selves at whose doore the bloud will lye. They have declared for the same things that I have, and now they act by their commission are my lawfull superiors, soe that I am not now in a capacytie to make any agreement without theire consent. Gentlemen, I have now farther to trouble yow, but to presse yow againe to bee perswaded that the cause wee are now contending for is your owne cause, and the cause of all the good people, and that as there was noe occasion given by us at first to the beginning of these unhappy contraversies, soe there shalbee nothing now omitted on our parts that wee think may bee a meanes to bring them to a speedy and a happy period, and to bee earnest with yow to possesse those that have bin the authors and are still the continuers of the force uppon the Parliament with a true and deepe sence of the dangers and inconviencyes that are like to follow, in case this debate bee by them continued any longer, and to assist us with your prayers to the throne of grace that all these controversyes may bee ended without the effusion of any more Christian bloud, and that they may produce to the Nations liberty and prosperity, to Parliaments theire just power and authority, and their duty, priviledges, and encurragements to the people of God, which is the utmost of the desires and wishes of

Coldstreame,
22 Dec. 1659

Your very humble servant,
GEORGE MONK

64. FROM THOMAS TRUTHSBYE[1]

A SERIOUS LETTER TO DR JOHN OWEN
Sent by a small Friend of his, relating to the intendments of Wallingford-house; Also a short friendly reply to a late Pamphlet of his concerning Tithes.

Sir:

Immediately upon my arrival at this floating and giddly Island, I thought it incumbent on me to inquire after the Men whose spirits began, and were lead forth to the late revolutions in *England*; After heard of those barbarous and Apocryphal names, of *Fleetwood*, that man of War; *Lambert*, that aspiring Commander; *Desborough* the Clown, and blinde *Hewson* the Cobler, that accurate and dexterous translator of Government; the two former were represented to me as *English* Gentlemen, and so our Friends in the *Netherlands* imputed their actions to noble and generous designs, hammered on the Anvil

---

[1] This letter was printed on a single sheet and may be read in the British Museum. Thomas Truthsbye is obviously a pseudonym used by a man who had Quaker sympathies—possibly Thomas Taylor, cf. *D.N.B.*

of their profound Intellects; where note, that I account *Fleetwood* a grand Politician, by a Figure the Learned call *Irania*, or if you will *Synedoch*, as Captain *Allen*, or Colonel *Parker*[2] lately had it in one of their University Sermons; but to proceed, what these Rustical Plebeians *Desborough* and *Hewson* proposed to themselves, we admired, never conjecturing that this Meal-man would either Sift out a Government, or this Lord bring his Ends so together as to stitch it up, though a man that ever managed his All very well. From these Peasants I further enquired, what Clergy-men were famous, and notorious in these Usurpers account, presently a Friend of mine nominated Thankful *Owen*, late Ambassadour to Gravesend, and your Worship was cried up as high as Tyburn, as well known, and as little trusted; in my Travels Westward they call'd you *Quaker*, Northward *Anabaptist*, in *Oxford* a State *Independent*, in *London* a *Jesuite*, beyond Seas a conscience-mender; I can scarce visit a Tavern, or Country Ale-house, but forth comes some of the Learned Works of *John Owen*, a Servant, &c. as if you were cut out to entertain all sorts of Guests; if I send for Tobacco, your Books are the inclosure of it, and there I finde your name stinking worse than that *Indian* Weed; the Cooks dare not venture it at the bottom of their Pyes, lest it should either spoil their sale, or stick as close to them as you doe to *Wallingford-house*. Sir, I am unwilling (being the first time I ever Epistoliz'd to you) to divert you from your more weighty concernments, *viz.* The upholding of your Deanary at *Christ-Church*, taking sanctuary at *Amsterdam*, should the Saints Kingdom be overthrown, or Dominion expire; If you ask, why I make so bold with you, as to inform you, how odious you are to all persons, who cannot so sordidly comply with every Government, pray and teach to every Faction, side with all Innovators; how you are by all serious men thought the scorn of Religion, a man either of a very wide or seared Conscience, this and much more I could tell you, but I presume you know them sufficiently: The slender acquaintance I have with you, and those small obligations, your deceitful promises, and contradictory practices to piety and honesty have imposed on me, may equally plead for my saying thus much, and no more

Yours.

Sir,

Since the writing of this, there is come to my hand a short reply to a Paper of yours, about Magistracy and Tithes,[3] the man claims

[2] Details of all these army officers may be found in C. Firth and G. Davies, *Regimental History of Cromwell's Army*, Oxford, 1940.

[3] Late in 1659 Owen produced a tract on tithes and the role of magistrates. It was entitled *Two Questions concerning the Power of the Supreme Magistrate about Religion*.

acquaintance and familiarity with you, being a Gifted Brother, and *Quaker*, as I guess by his style.

Brother *John Owen*, I have a Message to thee, let not thy carnal mind cheat thee; Is Magistracy an Ordinance of God? then either in *Capite*, or *Corpore*, in a single Person, or Parliament, but in neither of these, *ergo*. 1. Does not the light within thee witness to thy wrinckled face, that thou *John Owen* wast instrumental, and by thy close jugling with a gathered Brood in *Wallingford-house*, didst countenance, promote, vigorously act to the downfall of timerous *Richard*, and dissolution of that famous Parliament? 2. As for Parliaments, didst thou not preach up and down the Rump? After its resurrection thou calledst them dry Bones breathed into, and in a short time with *Lambert, Desborough*, &c. help rebury them, and preach their second Funeral Sermons.

1. Are Tithes due to those the world calls Ministers, and Parsons? then why did Christ rebuke those that Tithed Mint, Annis, and Cummin? and if these are forbidden, then sure greater matters.

2. Tithes is an Old Testament word, and (as a Sadler in *Oxford* said of Christmas) then it was abolisht at Christs coming.

3. The Tithes in *Malachies* Prophecy were commanded to be carried into God's Store-house, *ergo* not the Parsons Barn.

4. Suppose I have nine Hens, and they drop from their rumps but nine Eggs a year, ile not give a turd for the Parsons tenth.

When you have answered these Arguments, ile peruse your Book, and if there be anything worthy a farther reply, you shall have it, with that sweetness and gravity as becomes your Person and cause,

Vale,

THO. TRUTHSBYE
a Gifted Brother

FURTHER MS MATERIAL FROM OXFORD ARCHIVES

65. From 'Christ Church Chapter Book' when Owen was Dean.

1. The following authorisation is found eight times betwen 1651 and 1658. The first was made on 7 December 1651.

To all to whom these presents shall come: know ye that I, John Owen, Deane of Christ Church in Oxon of the foundation of King Henry the Eight, have nominated made and constituted and doe by these presents nominate, make and constitute my welbeloved in Christ, (Ralph Button), one of the Prebendaries of the said Church, my true and lawfull proxie giving him full power and authoritie for mee and in my name and stead (being absent) to manage and transact any businesse or affaires of the said Colledge: to go after with the rest of the Prebendaries as fully and absolutely as I myself could doe with them if present. To have and to hold this power in the premises untill . . . day of . . .[1] next ensuing the date hereof and noe further. In witnesse whereof I have put my hand and seale the seventh day of December in the yeare of our Lord, 1651.

2. The introductory words 'To all to whom these presents shall come; Wee the Deane and Prebendaries of Christ Church Colledge in Oxon send greeting' appear at the beginning of the following documents.

   a. 18 July 1651. Permission for Tenants of the Manor at South Stoke in Oxfordshire to plough certain areas of land. p.44.

   b. 9 December 1651. Christopher Rogers, Treasurer of Christ Church, cleared of charges of debt. pp.49–50.

   c. 8 May 1653, An attorney is appointed to look after College lands and property in Yorkshire. p.58.

   d. 8 August 1657. A lease of land in Middlesex is granted to Sir Gilbert Gerrard of Harrow-on-the-Hill. p.80.

3. The following indentures were also contracted.

   a. 21 September, 1655. With John and Arthur Clarke, Thomas Bromfield and Lawrence Marsh for tithes at Kirkham in Yorkshire. p.69

   b. 22 October 1656. With Isabella Chamberlaine for lease of lands at Stratton Audley in Buckinghamshire. p.73.

66. From 'The Register of Convocation' whilst Owen was Vice-Chancellor.

1. The petition of Convocation to Parliament when Owen was not allowed to take up his seat as the elected representative of the University.

---

[1] The date is not filled in here but in later authorisations it is filled in. Each lasted from six to eight weeks during which time Owen was presumably in London. On February 26 1652 he nominated Peter French; on 27 July 1652, 16 December 1652 and 25 July 1653, Henry Cornish; on 3 October 1653, 10 May 1655, 10 April 1658 and 26 February 1659, Henry Wilkinson; and on 28 July 1654, Ambrose Upton.

To the Right Honorable the Committee for Priviledges.
The Humble Petition of the University of Oxford.

Sheweth,

That whereas your Petitioners did with much unanimitie make choyse of Dr John Owen to serve in Parliament as their Burgesse and doe now understand that there is some question made about his capacity of sittinge as a Member.

Tis humbly prayed that before any thing bee determined in the present case this Honorable Committee would bee pleased to heare what the University shall offer concerning it.

And they shall ever pray etc.

November 21st 1654.

2. The introductory words, 'To all Christian people to whom these presents shall come, the Chancellor, Masters and Schollars of the University . . . do send greeting', appear at the head of four documents.
   a. 20 January 1653. Nicholas Greaves of Welwyn is authorised to collect and receive rents for property bequeathed by Sir Henry Savile to pay for two Lecturers and two Professors of Mathematics. p.180.
   b. 8 March 1653. Thomas Berke of Morton Henmarsh is released from rent arrears. p.191.
   c. 18 March 1654. Arthur Blaney is authorised to collect rents at Bexley. pp.239–40.
   d. 26 February 1657. John Hopkins and John Shippard are authorised to seize the goods of felons, outlaws, fugitives etc. p.297.

3. The following indentures were also contracted.
   a. 22 September 1652. With William Powell of Bray for lease of land at Medmenham in Buckinghamshire. pp. 102ff.
   b. 8 March 1653. With John Blincow for lease of land at Purston in Northamptonshire. pp.108ff.
   c. 20 March 1653. With George Waylor for lease of land at Rettendon in Essex. pp.192ff.
   d. 18 August 1653. With William Markland for lease of land in the parish of St. Lawrence, Old Jury, London. pp.213ff.
   e. 1 September 1653. With Thomas Westley for lease of land near Mayden Street in the Parish of St. Augustine, London. pp.218ff.
   f. 17 March 1656. With Amy Benskyn for lease of land at Syston in Leicester. p.277.
   g. 26 February 1657. With Simon Winch for lease of land at Bray in Berkshire. p.295.

4. On 20 July, 1657 the Letters Patent of the Office of Chancellor were sent by the University to Richard Cromwell (p.306). He was formally admitted as Chancellor in a service at Westminster Abbey on 29 July, 1657.

67. From the University Archives.

From Unton Croke.

Sir,
It is beelieved that although consent bee growne very common that . . . is possible, a rape may be committed and that lately hath happened upon the body of this poore man's daughter.[2] It is probable (that it) may pass unpunished in this world. It is informed that two Gentlemen of a Colledge[3] have rabished the child and some . . . suit made and examinations taken but upon pretence of want of power in those Justicers[4] the matter is laid aside and now presented before me. I shall be very tender yet cannot refuse to do my office being required thereto. It should seem the schollers are made knowne unto you and as yet are at libertie; it is fitt they should bee secured or committed. The father and mother are praying for justice yet confess they have been tampered withall for compositions. Sir, Bee pleased the schollers may bee secured or otherwise justice will fail to the great scandall of the government and if you please upon Saturday morning before all the Justicers that you bee attended I shall be ready to give my assistance hoping it will prove but a dutie to gain a composition whereas Justicers can bee no instruments.
    Sir, I take leave and remaine yours assured to command,
                                                    UNTON CROKE.
11 August 1653.

[1] This letter is found amongst papers relating to the Chancellor's Court in the University Archives, Oxford, reference W.P.a.23 (12), and it was probably addressed to John Owen. According to the *Register*, p. 361, the matter was discussed by the Visitors on 22 August. Unton Croke was a personal friend of Owen and a Serjeant-at-law.

[2] The man was employed by New College but I cannot make out his name as the writing is very faded.

[3] According to the *Register*, the men were William Dennys, who went to sea in 1654 and died in Jamaica in 1655, and Obadiah How.

[4] Probably J.P.s in Oxford city.

PART III
Patriarch of Independency
1660-1683

CHAPTER VI

Introductory

FROM 1660 to 1662 John Owen held services of worship each Sunday in his home at Stadhampton. To these small gatherings came such students and teachers as William Penn, then a student at Christ Church, Francis Howell, the ejected Principal of Jesus College, and Thankfull Owen, the ejected President of St John's College. The royalists looked upon these meetings with suspicion and raided the house on several occasions, on one of which they found and took away six cases of pistols. Either just before or just after black Bartholomew's Day 1662, when many of his friends were ejected from their livings, he moved with his wife to the home of Lady Abney near Theobalds in Hertfordshire, and sent the children to stay with friends in Buckinghamshire. In 1662 and on several occasions in the next five years, during the period when the lot of Nonconformists was very difficult, he thought of leaving England to settle in Massachusetts and even got so far as to have his belongings packed and taken to a boat after the plague of London. He seems to have stayed with Lady Abney either at her country or London homes for at least a year and then to have taken his wife to the home of the Fleetwood and Hartopp families in Stoke Newington. The parish registers of that village (which is now part of Greater London) record the burials of two children, Judith and Matthew Owen. They must have died whilst the family was living in the large 'Fleetwood House'. Also before the Fire of London he seems to have spent some time living at the house of a Mrs Holmes in Moorgate in the company of Thomas Goodwin and there to have held services. Thus it would appear that to avoid persecution of his family and himself he found it necessary or expedient to move from place to place. Happily he had rich and influential friends who were very willing to offer help.

In 1667 when the time seemed ripe for indulgence to be granted to the Nonconformists because of the belief that God's judgement was evident in the plague and fire of London, John Owen's pen was active in seeking to persuade the government to grant religious freedom to churches of the Congregational way outside the parish system of the Established Church. But his efforts failed. Unlike some leading Presbyterians, Thomas Manton for example, he did not desire comprehension within the State Church. The presence of diocesan bishops and liturgies with the lack of spiritual discipline over communicants made any such move impossible for him. It was basically the same factors that stood in the way when he discussed the possibility of some form of Church unity with Richard Baxter in 1669. A large group of Presbyterians favoured the parish system and were willing to compromise on other matters in order to achieve a unified Church of England, but Owen stood firm in his belief that each church must be composed only of true believers and not be subject to any external control save that of Jesus Christ. Yet he was willing to join Presbyterians in various regular preaching services. At Clapton in the home of Alderman Ashhurst he preached with such men as Thomas Watson and William Bates, at Cripplegate he took part in the Morning Exercises on casuistry, and at Pinners' Hall he preached at the Merchants' Lecture.

John Owen was regarded by his contemporaries as the leading theologian amongst the Congregationalists. As such his advice and help was often sought by men in both Old and New England. Some of this correspondence has survived and is printed in the next chapter. Apart from the time-consuming task of replying to letters, he was also pastor of a small church in the City of London (which was the continuation of the church which met in 1659 at Wallingford House), a writer of theological and devotional books, and one who was wholly involved in the task of defending the principles of Nonconformity and seeking to persuade the king and Parliament that religious freedom for orthodox Nonconformists was in the best interests of the nation. When the king eventually granted an Indulgence in 1672 Owen personally thanked him on behalf of his brethren in the following words:

May it please your Majesty,
We humbly thank you for the favour of this opportunity wherein we may acknowledge that deep sense which we have of your gracious clemency, the effects whereof we every day enjoy. It is that alone which has interposed between the severity of some laws, and some men's principles and us, which otherwise would have effected our ruin; though we are persuaded that neither the one nor the other could countervail your Majesty's damage thereby.

It is this principally wherein the kings of the earth may render themselves like to the King of heaven, when by their power, wisdom, and goodness, they relieve the minds of their peaceable subjects from fear, distress, and distracting anxieties, and trials on their persons, (rendering their lives burdensome to themselves, and useless to others), which your Majesty has done towards multitudes of your subjects in this nation: And we do rejoice in this advantage to declare to your Majesty that as we have as conscientious respect to all those obligations to loyalty which lie on the commonality of your subjects, so being capable of a *peculiar one* in the greatest of our concerns, the liberty of our consciences and assemblies, which others are not, (as desiring no more, but what they esteem their right by law), we hold it our duty which we engage into before you, not only to be partakers with them, but to preserve in our minds a peculiar readiness to serve on your Majesty's commands, and occasions, as we shall be required or advantaged for it.

And we humbly pray the continuance of your gracious favour, and we shall pray that God would continue his presence with you in all your affairs, and continue your royal heart in these counsels and thoughts of *indulgence,* whose beginnings have restored quietness to neighbours, peace to counties, emptied prisons, and filled houses with industrious workers, and engaged the hands of multitudes into the resolved and endeavoured readiness for your Majesty's service, as not knowing any thing in this world desirable to them, beyond what, under your government, and by your favour, they may enjoy.[1]

Then he proceeded to use his influence and his new home in Charterhouse Yard to obtain and keep safely, until collected, the licences for buildings and preachers which the Congregationalists throughout the country sought. Strangely he does not seem to have obtained one for himself.

From his pen between 1667 and 1683 came many solid books which have often been reprinted. Amongst these were a four-volume folio edition of his 'Commentary on the Epistle to the Hebrews', a detailed study of the doctrine of the 'Gospel' Church, several books outlining the doctrine of the Holy Spirit and many others dealing with the Christian life and the growth in grace. Not a few of these volumes had their origin in sermons preached to his congregation which in June 1673 was greatly enlarged when it joined with that to which Joseph Caryl had preached until his death. The unified congregation worshipped in a meeting-house in Leadenhall Street. Included in its membership were such people as Sir John and Lady Hartopp, the former Colonels Desborough, Berry and Ellistone and their families, Sir Thomas Overbury, the Countess of Anglesea and Lady Abney.

From time to time between 1672 and 1683 he went to convalesce in Stadhampton and whilst there preached in his own house to a congregation drawn from the village and even perhaps from Oxford. On one occasion when in Oxfordshire he helped Philip Lord Wharton by making inquiries about a suitable wife for his son, Thomas Wharton. He also maintained friendly contacts with the D'Oyley family who,

[1] This was printed for the first time in *The Gentleman's Magazine,* Vol. XXXI, p. 253.

as we saw in the first chapter, owned the manor house in the village, and after the death of his wife, Mary, he married Dorothy D'Oyley, neice of John D'Oyley of Stadhampton, in June 1676. At this time only one of his eleven children born to his first wife was alive and she died before 1683. During the last three or four years of his life when he was often chronically ill with liver and kidney complaints he lived first in Kensington and then in Ealing, which was, in those days, a delightful country village.

Despite ill health he entered into controversy in 1680 with Edward Stillingfleet, Dean of St Paul's Cathedral, who published a sermon entitled, *The Mischief of Separation*. This called upon the Nonconformists to join the National Church and raise a Protestant bulwark which Popery could not overcome. In reply Owen argued that the government and worship of the Church of England were not scriptural and thus Nonconformists had no alternative but to follow the path in which they walked. Ten years earlier he had defended the principles of the Congregational way and of Nonconformity by similar argumentation in controversy with a less charitable opponent than Stillingfleet, namely Samuel Parker, who was notorious for his violent language against those with whom he disagreed.

Whilst Oliver Cromwell died on the anniversary of his great military victories, John Owen died on the anniversary of one of the blackest days in English religion, for 24 August 1683 was the twenty-first anniversary of the Great Ejection of St Bartholomew's Day 1662. From Ealing, where he died, his body was conveyed to a house in St James's where it lay for several days. On 4 September it was taken to Bunhill Fields attended by the carriages of sixty-seven noblemen and gentlemen; 'devout men carried him to his burial'. Today as his books continue to be reprinted his name and influence live on and thus he is justly regarded as one of the greatest Protestant theologians which England has ever produced.

CHAPTER VII

Correspondence 1660-1683

THE following letters, which comprise the extant correspondence of John Owen for the years 1660 to 1683, reveal the varied activities, concerns and friendships of Owen in a period of history when there was little material joy in being a Nonconformist. In the first three, written to John Thornton, we catch a glimpse of the way in which Owen talked and wrote to his friends and we note that he was able to use both wit and sarcasm. On the other hand, the letters preserved in New College, London, reflect the spiritual and pastoral concern of Owen and his close relationship with certain members of his London church, notably the Hartopp and Fleetwood families. Although the letters represent only a small proportion of his total correspondence, they do supply evidence to support the belief that he was regarded by both his brethren and enemies as the acknowledged leader of the English Congregationalists in the dark days of the rule of Charles II.

68. TO JOHN THORNTON[1]

For my much esteemed friend Mr John Thornton, These etc.

Good Sir,

I could hardly find time for this scrible, by reason of Dr Manton[2] to whose company I cannot but elevate my selfe whiles hee is here. Newes we have none but whats evill. The Diurnall[3] gives you a true (though malicious) account of the late petition, But conceiles the occasion, because it reflects much on the honor of the Lord Chancellor and another great person. For the Chancellor sent to Dr Manton etc. and asks them why they did not petition, telling them that the king thought they were sullen and had some designe in hand, assuring them also that the king would give an indulgence to Dr Manton, Dr

---

[1] Bodleian Rawlinson Letters 109, f. 87. John Thornton was the chaplain to the Duke of Bedford at Woburn Abbey. See *C.R.*

[2] For Thomas Manton, the well-known Presbyterian, see *C.R.* and *D.N.B.*

[3] The *Diurnall* was a news-journal. The petition described in this journal was delivered to the king three days after St Bartholomew's Day 1662, but Lord Clarendon's advice proved hasty and the indulgence was not granted. The matter is discussed by R. S. Bosher, *The Making of the Restoration Settlement*, 1951, p. 144.

Bates,⁴ and some few more; wherefore they petitioned in that forme that you read and yet were put off with a flay of a fox taile. So that the younkers in the house of commons are like to call them to barre for petitioning against an act of parliament, and then they must name the persons that encouraged and invited them thereto, and that will cause something to doe at court. Yet Mr Edward Russell⁵ says the next session of parliament will relieve us all. Credat Judius Apella. The tumults in London are nothing so bad as common fame represents them, though some disturbances the new preachers had by the boyes and by none else in three or four churches. I am somewhat troubled to heare that Mr Gurnall, Mr Ford, Dr Horton, Dr Lightfoot⁶ should conforme. But by his owne strength shall no man be strong. Mr Jeanes⁷ is reported to have conformed and presently to dye sadly and desperately. The Lord Booth⁸ is ragingly distracted; the Lord remember him for good. I hope the cryes of many 1000 soules in England for the bread of life will pierce the heavens (there being neere 2000 ejected ministers) and that God who hath now hid his face, will repent him of the evill. To which end the Lord purge away the iniquity of the daughter of Sion. The Duke of York would have had . . .⁹

⁴ For William Bates see *C.R.*
⁵ Edward Russell was the son of Francis Russell (1593–1641), the fourth Earl of Bedford. See *D.N.B.*
⁶ William Gurnall, Thomas Horton and John Lightfoot all conformed (see *D.N.B.* for details) but Stephen Ford was ejected from Chipping Norton, Oxfordshire, for whom see *C.R.*
⁷ Henry Jeanes died at Wells in August 1662 and was buried in the Cathedral. See *D.N.B.*
⁸ This is George Booth, the first Lord Delamere, who led the insurrection in 1659. See *D.N.B.*
⁹ Unfortunately the letter was torn at this point and the ending is lost. The contents of the letter suggest that it was written in September 1662.

69. TO JOHN THORNTON¹

For my much esteemed friend Mr John Thornton at Woburn Abbey, these

Good Sir,

You see our journey into Northamptonshire is layd aside and Mr Sherbury² layes the fault upon you, saying that you sent him word that we could not goe. Which if you did you committed a very great mistake. But I rather looke upon it as an excuse of his framing. Now my wife would be infinitely beholding to you, if you could find time

¹ Bodleian Rawlinson Letters 109, f. 88.
² Mr Sherbury was presumably a coachman.

to step to Hanslope³ and see the children, seeing we are not like to see them God knowes when. Our Lady is newly gone to London; she is indifferently healthy.⁴ Wee are all now preparing for the remoove. I must it seems preach in the house every Lords Day forenoone while we are there. Which if I doe will be some helpe towards my recovering what I have lost. I have been a while under physick for my eye and tis now I blesse God very welle. I have found I think the certaine and proper remedy at last, viz the millegides.⁵ Newes we have none, but talk of a great plot againe in the North which you may believe when you see it. All discourse is about the Turke who is reported to have underhand dealing not onely with the French but with the Suede and the confident princes of the empire. I yet hope that some good will come of his conquest upon the empire. Pray present my humble service to your two young ladyes⁶ and the two Stacyes and Mrs Roberts.⁷ And lets hear a word or two from you. Dr Pierce⁸ his sermon is so answered by one that hath discovered his false quotations and by an other who hath answer at large his reasons, with so much strength and gallantry that he cannot possibly stand, but will in sight of all be ashamed. I wish you had them. As you could not but laugh to see how unfortunate the poor Doctor is in his attempts to

But I take leave and remaine, yours as ever

My service to Mrs Sparke⁹

My wife remembers you all there,

J.O.

³Hanslope is actually in Buckinghamshire but near the Northamptonshire border. The children were probably staying with the Tyrell family; cf. D.N.B. s.v. Sir Thomas Tyrell.
rise to great preferment by his sermon.

⁴The lady was probably Lady Abney, who had a house at Theobalds on the edge of Epping Forest. Later she became a prominent member of the London Congregational Church of which John Owen was pastor. See D.N.B. s.v. Sir Thomas Abney for brief details of Sir Edward, husband of Lady Abney.

⁵Presumably this medicine is connected with melicrate, a mixture of honey and water. Meliceris seems to have been a disease (cysts containing matter resembling honey) often found in eyelids.

⁶These were the daughters of the Duke of Bedford.

⁷Presumably these people were workers on the Woburn Estate.

⁸For Thomas Pierce see D.N.B. The famous sermon was preached at Whitehall on 1 February 1663. As various replies to it were published quickly we may date this letter in the Spring of 1663.

⁹Mrs Sparke was an employee of the Duke.

70. TO JOHN THORNTON[1]

Good Sir,

And so at length you have written in short. However wee shall lay it up among the records of your kindnes and also returne you such animadversions as our scantling of leisure and intelligence will afford. As for your complementall conscript of my being taken up with the letters of etc: So that your question whither I can stoop to peruse the impertinent scriblings of meere private wights &c. Let me tell you that if that wight hath either wit or weight in his scriblings they are not to be impertinent no more than hee is impersonall. Your Baker[2] I have and when I can have accesse to Pernassus will petition Apollo to obliterate him forever from the catalogue of the virtuosi, for his terrible violating the lawes of history. 1. He is partiall all along to the worst of churchmen. 2. Hee is tedious in the narrative of some trifles, defective and short in some things of moment. 3. Especially in the life of Queene Elizabeth and King James. In both which hee mentions some things ignorantly, uncertainly and at randome, and with a wretched partiality, more specially in the latter, wherein he committed a manifold absurdity. (1) In treading too neare on the heels of truth, (2) which is one cause why hee is so shamefully briefe in his life, and wholly omits some of the most considerable momentous passages in that kings life. 4. His stile (especially in his characters) is an affected rhime or cadency, to which both the truth, seriousness and fulness of matter are forced to give place. And so let him go. My papers are as you said with Mr Oldeburgh[3] who pretends his relation to the virtuosi to increase so much worke upon his hands, that he must leave my papers untoucht. I hope they are upon some serious consultations for the benefit of mankind, how a hen may sit on her eggs and addle none, how oysters may be so geometrically layd that in stead of 200 or 300, and oyster wench may lay 8 or 900 in her basket at once and sell them all without tearing her throat or tyring her head, how his majestys bears may be taught to bite none but fanatickes and that without hurting their teeth, besides many other devices for the promoting of trade, the preventing the Dutch, and the ruine of Gayland and all which are under deliberation, and when their designes are compleated then ad Graecas Calendas or a little before, they are to bee exposed to publique view. As for reliquia Cartropenses, they doe now trouble mee to speake after the manner of the scholar for 1. Alienativè, my genig and busines being theological tu opus alienum. 2. Elaborativè,

[1] Bodleian MS. Rawlinson Letters, 109, ff. 85–6.
[2] Sir Richard Baker, author of *Chronicle of the Kings of England*, 1643.
[3] Henry Oldenburg (1615–1677), a member of the Royal Society.

for the right composing, transcribing etc. require multum olii. 3. Sumptibiliter, unless (which I cannot expect) sint Macenates. So let them lye a while nonumque premantur in annum. Now for newes. You serve me a neat trick of bidding me aske my. . . . Like the plagiary annetator that send me with a vide to another place and author and he with a vide back againe to the former. But I shall use you more honestly and give you twenty newes. 1. My Lady hath a coatch horse not well yet. 2. The ship of Algier bearing 40 guns carrying 400 men, of five years old, having taken (at times) 80 Christian ships, and lately taken by Sir Ch. Berkleys son[4] is in the Thames preparing for the strict observation of his . . . . & the shipwrights, as a great rarity. 3. The wings of my Ladyes little parrot are growne out againe and hee can fly. 4. Count Lerini hath laid downe his commission & articles against Montrimuli. 5. The . . . is at Vienna, hearkens yet to no counsell but of Jesuits and the Turk is marching towards him again demolishing as he passes all popish churches and sparing the churches of the protestants. 6. Peace with the Hollanders. 7. They say here that by a letter to the King out of France it is certifyed that Col. Russell hath there killd the Ld Sunderland.[5] 8. We are sending 10 ships to Guinea to worme out the Hollanders there. 9. The plague increases terribly in Holland. 10. Dr Manton was warned friendly by Sir Wm Morrice[6] to forebeare his meeting, telling him that search had been made already for some country ministers that were in Towne. 11. The Anabaptists here at Theobalds and the quakers in London more numerous than ever.[7] 12. The Lord Fanshaw[8] apprehending the conventiclers fined them 5s a piece which they refused to pay, then 12s which they refused likewise and so were sent to prison where they remained 2 or 3 days and then hee let them out desiring them that they would meet no more. But now what shall I doe to make it up to 20. Ile try. 13. Our learned Dr Reeve[9] preached one sermon without railing. 14. A troope (viz: the county troope) came to Theobalds last Lords day thinking to catch the Anabaptists at their meeting, but you would not thinke how many

---

[4] This was Sir William Berkeley, a vice-admiral, for whom see *D.N.B.* There are references to Berkeley and Algerian ships in Samuel Pepys' diary for 9 and 18 November 1663.

[5] The reason for this rumour was that Robert Spencer, the second Earl of Sunderland, was due to marry Anne Rigby, a niece of Edward Russell, in July 1663, and he failed to turn up for the wedding.

[6] For Sir William Morice see *D.N.B.* John Owen dedicated the first volume of his monumental commentary on the Epistle to the Hebrews to Sir William.

[7] For the Baptists at Theobalds see *Transactions* of the Congregational Historical Society, Vol. V, pp. 252ff., and *C.R.* s.v. Joseph Maisters.

[8] This was Sir Thomas Fanshaw of Ware in Hertfordshire.

[9] Dr. Thomas Reeve was the incumbent of Waltham Abbey.

came to warne them of it, so they dispersed and though the troopers stood gazing 3 or 4 hours on high ground to watch their rendezvous, yet they escaped their sight and met in a wood undiscovered. 15. The Lord Carburyesson Sir John Vaughan Kt of the Bath[10] is said to be taken at a conventicle in Stepney, and being a parliament man, answered, that as hee had testifyed against it in the house by speeches, so now by practise. Thereupon he was carryed to Newgate, if not since released. 16. The Tartars in vast numbers demande of the K. of Poland passage into Silesia, which he dares not deny least they force their passage. 17. They say the Hollanders wives mutinyed against the state crying out of the hand of God upon them by the pest, & desyred peace, and that thereupon. Sir Geo. Downing[11] being arrived among them, they acceded to all our kings demands about the Prince of Orange, Amsterdam excepted. 18. A friend of mine did preach in Publique at London a fortnight since and tells me of many others of the same predicament that still doe the like. 19. There are strange robberyes dayly committed at our forrest, the particulars are strangely burlesque and tedious to relate. Mr Manning[12] late minister of Enfield, being in great want, having with much disquiet of mind told me his condition, went into Huntingdonshire to his wives rich friends to seek some reliefe, & at Royston was robbed of his watch (worth £5) 40s in money, a beaver hat, onley his tobacco box of silver, having his arms on it, was rendred to him; His companion likewise of 20s. Their tackling cut in pieces, their horses turned loose, so that their curriers came up to them presently after the fact, yet by that time they had assisted in catching their horses, mending their tackling, the blades were gone. This was done at eleven in the forenoone. 20. The Lady Castlemaine[13] hath a strange coach presented her by him—of the rarest make that was ever seen, 'tis all the talke in the city. Now my number is up, with much adoe. My Wife hath been her journey into Northamptonshire in Mr Sherburys coatch, but I went not with her. Wee both remember our most heart respects to Mrs Roberts, the 2 sisters, your selfe, to whom

I am,

Votre tres humble tres affectione serviteur,

J.O.

My very humble service to your 2 young Ladyes.

[10] For Sir John Vaughan (K.B. 1661) see *D.N.B.* and *Transactions of the Cymmrodorion Society*, 1963, pp. 129–136.

[11] For Sir George Downing, the ambassador to Holland, see *D.N.B.*

[12] For Daniel Manning, ejected minister of Enfield, see *C.R.*

[13] Lady Castlemaine was the wife of Roger Palmer whom Charles II created Earl of Castlemaine. She was the mistress of the king.

Our musk melons are ripe, witnes that I have sent you, I would have sent more but you know Mathew.[14] Is your Venison ripe, if it bee, pray speake to Mrs Roberts to speake to my Lady, to speake to my Lord for a piece to bee sent for Mr Sherbury to Mrs Harvey at the greene crosse in Thomes Street for him (i.e.) if you can with conveniencey, for so my deare wife bides mee say.

[14] Matthew died in April 1665 and was buried at Stoke Newington.

71. FROM THE GENERAL COURT OF MASSACHUSETTS[1]

Reverend Sir,

It hath pleased the Most High God, possessor of Heaven and Earth, who giveth no account of his matters, to take unto himself, that pious and eminent minister of the gospel, Mr John Norton,[2] late teacher of the Church of Christ in Boston, whose praise is in all the Churches; the suitable and happy repair of which breach is of great concernment, not only to that church, but to the whole country. Now, although most of us are strangers to you, yet having seen your labours and heard of the grace and wisdom communicated to you from the Father of lights, we thought meet to write these, to second the call and invitation of that church unto yourself, to come over and help us; assuring you it will be very acceptable to this Court, and we hope to the whole country, if the Lord shall direct your way hither, and make your journey prosperous to us.[3] We confess the condition of this wilderness doth present little that is attractive, as to outward things; neither are we unmindful, that the undertaking is great, and trials many that accompany it; the persons that call you, are unworthy sinful men, of much infirmity, and may possibly fall short of your expectation (considering the long and liberal day of grace afforded us);—yet, as Abraham and Moses being called of God, by faith forsook their country and the pleasures thereof, and followed the Lord, the one not knowing whither he went, the other to suffer affliction with, and bear the manners of the people of God in the wilderness: and God was with them and honoured them: so we desire that the Lord would clear your call, and give you his presence. You may please to consider those that give you this call, as your brethren and companions in tribulation; and are in this wilderness for the faith and testimony of Jesus; and that we enjoy, through the

[1] The *Collections* of the Massachusetts Historical Society, 2nd Series, Vol. II, pp. 265–7.

[2] For John Norton see *D.N.B.*

[3] *The Records of the First Church in Boston, 1630–1868*, were published in 1961 by the Colonial Society of Massachusetts and at p. 59 there are several entries relating to the call of Owen.

distinguishing favour of God, the pleasant things of Zion in peace and liberty. And while the Lord shall see meet to entrust us with this mercy, we hope no due care will be found wanting in the government here established, to encourage and cherish the churches of Christ and the Lords faithful labourers in his vineyard. Thus praying to the God of the spirits of all flesh, to set a man over this congregation of the Lord, they may go in and out before them, and make your call clear, and voyage successful to us; that if the Lord shall vouchsafe to us such a favour, you may come to us in the fulness of the blessing of the gospel of Christ; with our very kind love and respect,

We remain, your very loving friends,

JOHN ENDECOTT,[4]

In the name, and by appointment of the General Court, sitting at Boston in New England.

Dated the 20th October, 1663.

[4] For John Endecott see D.N.B. He was the governor of the Colony.

72. TO RICHARD BAXTER[1]

Sir,

The continuance of my Cold, which yet holds me, with the severity of the Weather, have hitherto hindred me from answering my purpose of coming unto you at Acton but yet I hope ere long to obtain the advantage of enjoying your Company there for a Season. In the mean time I return you my Thanks for the Communication of your Papers[2]; and shall on every occasion manifest, that you have no occasion to question whether I were in earnest in what I proposed, in

[1] *Reliquiae Baxterianae* (1696), Bk. III, D. W. L. Baxter Lrs. 59.5.18, pp. 63ff. The original of this letter is in Dr. Williams's Library, London.

[2] These papers are no longer extant. Early in January, 1669, hearing that Owen was talking freely of a possible agreement between men of the Presbyterian and Congregational ways, Baxter decided to visit him. 'I told him', wrote Baxter, 'that I must deal freely with him; that when I thought of what he had done formerly, I was much afraid lest one that had been so great a breaker, would not be made an Instrument of healing. But in other respects I thought him the fittest man in England for this work; partly because he could understand the case, and partly because his experience of the humours of men, and of the mischiefs of dividing principles and practices had been so very great, that if experience should make any man wise, and fit for a healing work, it should be him; and that a book which he had lately printed (*Brief Instruction in the Worship of God, a Catechism*, 1667) . . . was my chief motive to make this notion to him; because he there giveth up two of the worst of the principles of popularity; acknowledging, 1. That the people have not the power of the keys. 2. That they give not the power of the keys or their office-power to the pastors.' Then Baxter drew up some proposals and sent them to Owen. *Reliquiae*, op. cit., Bk. III, p. 61.

reference to the Concord you design. For the desire of it is continually upon my heart, and to express that desire on all occasion, I esteem one part of that Profession of the Gospel which I am called unto. Could I contribute any thing towards the Accomplishment of so holy, so necessary a Work, I should willingly spend my self, and be spent in it. For what you design concerning your present Essay, I like it very well, both upon the reasons you mention in your Letter, as also that all those who may be willing and desirous to promote so blessed a work, may have Copies by them to prepare their Thoughts in reference to the whole.

For the present, upon the Liberty granted in your Letter (if I remember it aright) I shall tender you a few Quaeries; which if they are useless or needless, deal with them accordingly.

As 1. Are not the Severals proposed or insisted on, too many for this first Attempt? The general Heads I conceive are not; but under them, very many Particulars are not only included, which is unavoidable, but expressed also, which may too much dilate the original Consideration of the whole.

2. You expressly exclude the Papists, who will also sure enough exclude themselves, and do, from any such Agreement: But have you done the same as to the Socinians, who are numerous, and ready to include themselves upon our Communion? The Creed, as expounded in the Four first Councils will do it.

3. Whether some Expressions suited to prevent future Divisions and Separations, after a Concord is obtained, may not at present, to avoid all exasperation, be omitted, as seeming reflective on former Actings, when there was no such Agreement among us, as is now aimed at?

4. Whether insisting in particular, on the power of the Magistrate, especially as under civil Coercition and Punishment, in cases of Error or Heresie, be necessary in this first Attempt? These Generals occurred to my Thoughts, upon my first reading of your Proposals. I will now read them again, and set down, as I pass on, such apprehensions in particular, as I have of the Severals of them.

To the first Answer, under the first Question, I assent; so also to the first proposal, and the explanation: Likewise to the second and third. I thought to have proceeded thus throughout; but I fore-see my so doing would be tedious and useless; I shall therefore mention only what at present may seem to require second Thoughts. As,

1. To Propos. 9. by those instances (what words to use in Preaching, in what Words to pray, in what decent Habit) do you intend Homilies, prescribed Forms of Prayer, and Habits superadded to those of vulgar decent use? Present Controversies will suggest an especial sense under general Expressions.

2. Under Propos. 13. Do you think a Man may not leave a Church, and joyn himself to another, unless it be for such a cause or Reason, as he supposeth sufficient to destroy the Being of the Church? I meet with this now answered in your 18th. Propos. and so shall forbear further particular remarks, and pass on.

In your answer to the Second Qu. Your 10th. Position hath in it some-what that will admit of further consideration, as I think. In your Answer to the 3d Qu. have you sufficiently expressed the accountableness of Churches mutually in case of Offence from Male-Administration and Church Censures? This also I now see in part answered, Prop. 5th. I shall forbear to add any thing as under your Answer to the last Question, about the power of the Magistrate, because I fear, that in that matter of punishing, I shall somewhat dissent from you; though as to meer Coercion I shall in some cases agree.

Upon the whole Matter, I judge your Proposals worthy of great Consideration, and the most probable medium for the attaining of the End aimed at, that yet I have perused. If God give not an Heart and Mind to desire Peace and Union, every Expression will be disputed, under pretence of Truth and Accuracy: But if these things have a place in us answerable to that which they enjoy in the Gospel, I see no reason why all the true Disciples of Christ might not upon these, and the like principles, condescend in Love unto the Practical Concord and Agreement, which not one of them dare deny to be their Duty to Aim at. Sir, I shall Pray that the Lord would guide and prosper you in all Studies and Endeavours, for the Service of Christ in the World, especially in this your Desire and Study for the introducing of the Peace and Love promised among them that Believe, and do beg your Prayers.

Your truly and affectionate Brother,
And unworthy Fellow-Servant,
JOHN OWEN

Jan.25.1669

73. FROM RICHARD BAXTER[1]

Sir,

Upon the perusal of Yours when I came home, I find your Exceptions to be mostly the same which you speak; and therefore shall be briefer in my Answer upon Supposition of what was said.

To your First Qu. I answer, I am as much for Brevity as you can possibly wish: so be it our Agreement be not thereby frustrated, and made insufficient to its ends. I would desire you to look over all the Particulars, and name me not only every one that you think unsound, but every one which you judge unprofitable or needless.

---

[1] *Reliquiae Baxterianae*, Bk. III, pp. 64ff.

But if we leave out that which most, or many will require, and none have any thing against, it will but stop our Work, and make Men judge of it, as you did of the want of a longer Profession than the Scriptures against Socinianism: And it will contradict the Title, The Just Terms of Agreement: For our Terms will be insufficient.

And as to your Words [the first attempt] my business is to discover the sufficient Terms at first, that so it may facilitate Consent: For if we purposely leave out any needful part as for [a second attempt] we bring contempt upon our first Essay; and before the second, third, and perhaps twentieth Attempt have been used to bring us to Agreement, by Alterations, and cross Humours, and Apprehensions, things will go as they have done, and all be pulled in pieces. Therefore we must, if possible, find out the sufficient Terms before too many hands be ingaged in it. Your own Exceptions here say, That if too many Explications had not afterward occurred, you had been unsatisfied in that which went before. And you know what Mr. Nye is wont to say against drawing a Hose over our differences (though for my part I know no other way where we agree not in particulars, but to take up with an Agreement in Generals). But where indeed we do agree in Particulars, I know no Reason why we should hide it, to make our Difference to seem greater than it is.

2. The Reasons, why I make no larger a Profession necessary than the Creed and Scriptures, are, because if we depart from this old sufficient Catholick Rule, we narrow the Church, and depart from the old Catholicism: And we shall never know where to rest: From the same Reasons as you will take in Four Councils, another will take in Six, and another Eight, and the Papists will say, Why not the rest, as well as these?

3. Because we should Sin against the Churches 1200 Years Experience, which hath been torn by this Conceit, That our Rule or Profession must be altered to obviate every new Heresie. As if you could ever make a Creed or Law which no Offender shall misinterpret, nor hypocritically profess. By this means the Devil may drive us to make a new Creed every Year, by Sowing the Tares of a new Heresie every year. Hilary[2] hath said so much against this, not sparing even the Nicene Creed itself, that I need say no more than he hath done upon that Argument of Experience, but only that if 30 or 40 Years Experience so much moved him against new Creedmaking, what should 1200 Years do by us?

4. And the Means will be certainly Fruitless, seeing that Hereticks are usually Men of wide Consciences, and if their Interest require it, they will Equivocate, as Men do now with Oaths and Subscriptions, and take any Words in their own sense.

[2] i.e. Hilary, the early Church Father.

5. And the Means is needless, seeing there is another and fitter Remedy against Heresie provided, and that it is not making a new Rule or Law, but judging Hereticks by the Law of God already made. Either they are Hereticks only in Heart, or in Tongue also, and Expression: If in Heart only, we have nothing to do to Judge them. Heart-Infidels are and will be in the Churches. If they be proved to be Hereticks in Tongue, then it is either before they are taken into the Communion of the Church, or after. If before, you are to use them as in case of proved Wickedness; that is, call them to publick Repentance before they be admitted: If it be after, they must be admonished, and Rejected after the first and second contemned Admonition: And is not this enough? And is not this the certain regular way? Is it not confusion to put Law for Judgment, and say there wants a new Law or Rule, when there wants but a due Judgment by the Rule in being.

6. Lastly, We shall never have done with the Papists, if we let go the Scripture-Sufficiency. And it is a double Crime in us to do it, who Dispute with them so vehemently for it. And we harden and justifie Church-Tyranny and Impositions when we will do the like our selves.

If there be nothing against Socinianism in the Scripture, it is no Heresie: If there be (as sure there is enough, and plain enough) Judge them by that Rule, and make not new ones.

But if any will not hold to this truly Catholick Course, I shall next like your Motion very well, to take up with the Creed, as Expounded in the four First Councils, called General: which I can readily subscribe my self, but it is better let them all alone, and not to be so fond of one onely Engine, which hath torn the Church for about 1200 Years. I mean departing from the Ancient Rule, and making new Creeds and Forms of Communion.

To your Third Qu. I. I suppose you observe that what I say about Separation is not under the third Head (of the Concord of Neighbour Churches; but under the second Head of the Concord of Members in the same particular Churches) and were you not heretofore at Agreement in your own Churches? And is it not the Duty and Interest of your own Churches to keep Unity, and that the Members separate not unjustly whether you agree with other Churches or not?

2. Either what I say about Separation is that which we are all (now Uniting) agreed in, or not: If it be, it honoureth our Brethren to profess it, and can be no Reproach or Offence to them to declare it: If any have sinned against their own present Judgment, I hope they are not so impenitent, as to desire us to forbear agreeing with their own Judgments, because it is against their former sins. And here is no word said Historically to upbraid any with these Sins at

all. But if we are not all agreed thus far against Separation, I desire you to name the Terms which we agree not in, and then we shall see whether we may leave them out, or whether it render our Concord desperate and impossible (of which anon).

To your Fourth Qu. The Jealousies and Errors of these Times do make it necessary to our Peace, to make some Profession of our Judgment about Magistracy; and I think there is nothing questionable in this. I am sure there is nothing but what many of the Congregational-Party do allow; but if you come to Particulars, I shall consider of them again.

The particular Exceptions which you Obliterate not your selves are but these.

1. To Qu. Prop. 9. Whether I mean prescribed Forms, and Homilies, and Habits by the Terms (what Words to use in Preaching and Prayer, &c.) Answ. That which I say as plain as I can is, 1. That a determination of such Circumstances is not a sinful Addition to God's Word, nor will allow the People therefore to avoid the Churches Communion. 2. That it belongs to the Pastor's Office to determine them (what Words he shall Preach and Pray in, &c.). Therefore you have no cause to ask my meaning about imposing upon him, but only whether he may so far impose upon the Flock, as to use his own Words in Preaching, Prayer, &c. 3. That yet if the Pastor determine these Circumstances destructively, the People have their Remedy. And is not this enough? Why must I tell you whether you may read a Sermon (or Homily) of your own Writing, or another Man's unto the People? Or if you do, whether they must separate? Or else if you read a Prayer, &c. Either you determine these things to the Churches hurt, or not? If not, why should they blame you, or Separate? If you do, they have their Remedy. But whether you do or not. I now decide not. If we meddle with all such particulars, we shall never agree: more than those must be left to liberty. You think our Particulars are too many already, and would you have more? And if the Controversies of the Times will tempt any to Expound our General Terms of Agreement amiss, we must not go from Generals for that.

To the Tenth Prop. You say there is something that will admit of a farther Consideration: Whereupon I considered it, and have added [Supposing it be a publick Profession of Christianity which is made]: Because, though the People are not bound to try the Persons beforehand, that are so to be received to Communion, yet they may ordinarily expect, that when they are admitted, their Profession be publick, or made known to the Church, which I imply'd before.

And now, Sir, I pray give me leave to speak some-what freely to the Cause itself, (assuring you I shall patiently, if not thankfully receive as free Language from you or others). I shall 1. mention what it is that we have to do; and 2. what Reasons we have for doing it.

Our Business is to heal Church-Divisions, and Heart-Divisions; therefore you must give us leave to say much against Divisions or Separations which are unjust, because this is our end, and all the rest is but the means; and if you would have us leave out that, it is all one as to say [Let us agree to have no Agreement or Unity]; or [we will be healed, so we may continue to be unhealed]; or, [do excuse us from Concord, and we will agree with you]. The Reason why we would bear with other Differences, is because we cannot bear with the absence of Unity, Love and Peace, else we may let go to Divisions, without any more ado.

And the great things which hinder the Presbyterians and Moderate Episcopal Men from closing with you are principally these.

1. Because they think that your way tends to destroy the Kingdom of Christ, by dividing it, while all Excommunicate Persons, or Hereticks, or humorous Persons, may at any time gather a Church of such as Separate from the Church which they belonged to, though it be on the account of Ungodliness, or Impatience of Discipline, &c. and then may stand on equal Terms with you; especially when you are not for the constant Correspondency of Churches in Synods, by which they may strengthen themselves against them.

2. They think, while you seem to be for a stricter Discipline than others, that your way (or usual Practice) tendeth to extirpate Godliness out of the Land; by taking a very few that can talk more than the rest, and making them the Church, and shutting out more that are as worthy, and by neglecting the Souls of all the Parish else, except as to some Publick Preaching; against which also you prejudice them by unjust Rejections; and then think that you may warrantably account them unworthy: because you know no unworthiness by them, when you estrange your selves from them, and drive them away from you. They think that Parish-Reformation tendeth to the making Godliness universal, and that your Separation tendeth to dwindle it to nothing. I know that some of you have spoken for endeavouring the good of all; but (pardon my plainness) I knew scarce any of you that did not by an unjust espousing of your few, do the People a double Injury, one by denying them their Church-Rights, without any regular Church-Justice, and the other by lazily omitting most that should have been done for their Salvation. In our Countrey almost all the rest of the Ministers agreed to deal seriously and orderly with all the Families of their Parishes (which some did to their wonderful benefit) except your Party, and the highly Episcopal, and they stood off. The doubt was when I came to Kidderminster, Whether it were better to take twenty Professors for the Church, and leave a Reader to head and gratifie the rest? Or, to attempt the just Reformation of

the Parish? The Professors would have been best pleased with the first, and I was for the latter, which after full tryal, hath done that which hath satisfied all the Professors: so that professed Piety, and Family-Worship (in a way of Humility and Unity) was so common, that the few that differ among some Thousands are mostly ashamed of their Difference on the account of Singularity, and would seem to be Godly with the rest.

The last Week I had with me an honest Scotchman, and one of my Acton Neighbours, and I asked him how their Nation came to be so unanimous in the approbation of Godliness without any Sect. And he told me that usually they had twelve Elders in a Parish, and every one took their Division and observed the manners of the People, and if any Family prayed not, &c. They admonished them, and told the Pastor; and that the Pastor then went to them (though many Miles off) and taught them to Pray, and led them in it, and set them upon other means as we teach Children to read: And that once a Week they had a meeting of the Elders, to consult about the good of the Parish, and once a week a meeting of the People to pray and confer, and receive resolution of Doubts, before the Pastor, and every Lord's Day after Sermon, they stayed to discourse of the things Preached of, that Objections might be answered, and those urged to their duties that had nothing to say against it. This, and more, the Scotchman averred to me. My Acton Neighbour told me, that there is now but one Person (a Woman) in all this Town and Parish that was here admitted to the Sacrament, and that the rest were partly by this course (and other reasons) distasted, and their dislike encreased, and partly neglected and left to themselves: That of rich Families (Mr Rous, Major Skippons, Collonel Sely, and Mr Humphreys) were admitted while the rest were refused or neglected: And that one surviving Person who was admitted, is but a Sojourner here. Whereas upon a little Tryal, I am able to say, that there are comparatively few openly scandalous Persons in the Town; that there are many who, I have reason to believe do seriously fear God, and are fit for Church-Communion: That almost the whole Town and Parish (even those that seemed most averse) are desirous and diligent to hear, even in private; and seem to be desirous of Family-helps, and desire good Books to read in their Families. And I hear not of one Person (or hardly any if one) that speak against the strictest Godliness, but commonly rather take part with those that are judged to fear God. Even the very Inns and Ale-houses themselves do signifie no Opposition or ill-will: In a word, the willingness seemeth so great and common, that if I were their Pastor, and had time to go to them in private, and try, and promote their knowledge (which comes not at once) I see no reason to doubt but Godliness might become the common

Complexion of the Parish. I speak this to shew you (if Experience signifie anything with you) that your separating way tendeth to Laziness, and the grievous hinderance of that Godliness which you seem to be more zealous for than others, and that the way of Reforming Parish-Churches, is not so hopeless as you make your selves believe it is, Some one wrote lately Exceptions to Mr Eliot,[3] upon his Proposals, in which he asketh him [What shall one, or two or three in a parish do, who usually are as many in most, or many Parishes as are fit for Communion &c.]. Men first estrange themselves from the poor People whom they should teach with tenderness, and diligence, and then they think their ignorance of the People ground enough to Judge them ignorant, and talk of one or two in a Parish. But Christ will find many more, I am past doubt, even Members of his Mystical Church, than these Men can do of the visible, which is much larger. And you cannot say, if there be any difference of Successes, that it is only from the difference of Persons, and not of the several ways: For here where I live were two of the worthiest Persons of your way (Mr Nye, and Mr Elford[4]) whose ability and Piety were beyond all question, and so was their great advantage then. But your way is your disadvantage, and Christ's Friends should suspect that way of honouring Godliness, which tendeth to diminish it, or suppress it.

I tell you some few of the things offensive to your Brethren, that you may see wherein our Agreement must give Satisfaction. The rest I now omit.

I had thought to have said more of the Reasons why you should heartily promote it. But I will now say but these two things. 1. That he that can consider what the effects of our Divisions have been upon Church and State, and the Lives of some, and the Souls of Thousands, both of the openly ungodly, and Professors, and that knows how great a reproach they are now to our Profession, and hardening of the Wicked, and hinderance to that good, even of the best, and yet doth not thirst to see them healed, hath small sense of the interest of Christ, and Souls.

2. That he, that considereth what it was to continue such Divisions unheal'd for twenty Years, under such Warnings and Calls to Unity; and to do what we have done against ourselves and others, after such smart, and in such manner to the least, is most dreadfully impenitent, if Repentance do not now make him zealous for a Cure. And in particular, if you, and Mr Nye, and I, be not extraordinary zealous for this work, there are scarce three Men to be found in the World, that will be more hainously guilty, and without excuse: (I need not

---

[3] John Eliot, apostle to the American Indians. See below p. 153.
[4] Thomas Elford, who until 1660 was Rector of Acton. See *C.R.*

tell you why). And truly if we have zeal, and yet not skill for such a Cure, (when all say that the People are willinger than the Pastors) it will be a shame for us to cry out on them, that Silence us: as if such Shepherds were necessary to the Flock, that have skill to Wound, and none to Cure. Therefore, as I am heartily glad of your forwardness and willingness to this Work, pardon me for telling you, I will Judge of it by the Effects. I address my self to you alone, because I know that Understanding and Experience are great Assistants (to lead on Charity) in this Work; and there is no dealing with them that understand not the Case. And I will hope that the Effect will show, that no Humours of others (Men of narrow Minds, and Interests, and injudicious Passions) shall prevail with you against so great a work of Repentance, and Love to God and Godliness, and the Souls of Men. Again, pardon this Freedom used by,

Your much Honouring and Unworthy Brother,

Feb.16.1669   RICH. BAXTER[5]

[5] These two letters reveal the basic difference in attitude of two leaders of seventeenth-century nonconformity towards the problems of the maintenance of orthodoxy and the reform of the Church. Their letters and discussions produced no definite result.

74. TO THE GOVERNOR OF THE COLONY OF MASSACHUSETTS[1]

We shall not here undertake (in the least) to make any apology for the persons, opinions and practices of those who are censured among you.[2] You know our judgement and practice to be contrary unto theirs, even as yours; wherein (God assisting) we shall continue to the end. Neither shall we return any answer to the reason of the reverend elders, for the justification of your proceedings, as not being willing to engage in the management of any the least difference with persons whom we so much love and honour in the Lord. But the sum of all which at present we shall offer to you is, that though the court might apprehend that they had good grounds in general warranting their procedure (in such cases) in the way wherein they have proceeded, yet that they have any rule or command rendring their so proceeding indispensably necessary, under all circumstances of fines or places,

[1] C. Mather, *Magnalia Christi Americana*, Hartford, 1853, Vol. II, p. 534.
[2] On 28 May 1665 a Baptist Church was formed at Boston which admitted into membership people excommunicated by the State (Congregational) Church. The General Court became afraid that matters might grow from small beginnings into a new 'Münster tragedy' and so they passed various laws for the restraint of the Baptists. These proved to be an embarrassment to the Nonconformists in Old England and so the letter came to be written, but it produced no immediate relaxation of the laws.

L

we are altogether unsatisfied; and we need not represent unto you how the case stands with ourselves and all your brethren and companions in the services of these latter days in these nations. We are sure you would be unwilling to put an advantage into the hands of some who seek pretences and occasions against our liberty, and to reinforce the former rigour. Now we cannot deny but this hath already in some measure been done, in that it hath been vogued that persons of our way, principles and spirit, cannot bear with dissenters from them. And as this greatly reflects on us, so some of us have observed how already it has turned unto your own disadvantage.

We leave it to your wisdom to determine whether, under all these circumstances, and sundry others of the like nature that might be added, it be not advisable at present to put an end unto the sufferings and confinements of the persons censured, and to restore them to their former liberty. You have the advantage of truth and order; you have the gifts and learning of an able ministry to manage and defend them; you have the care and vigilancy of a very worthy magistracy to countenance and protect them, and to preserve the peace; and (above all) you have a blessed Lord and Master, who hath the keys of David, who openeth and no man shutteth, living for ever to take care of his own concernments among his saints; and assuredly you need not be disquieted, though some few persons (through their own infirmity and weakness, or through their ignorance, darkness and prejudices) should to their disadvantage turn out of the way, in some lesser matters, into by-paths of their own. We only make it our hearty request to you, that you would trust God with his truth and ways so far, as to suspend all rigorous proceedings in corporal restraints or punishments, on persons that dissent from you and practise the principles of their dissent without danger, or disturbance to the civil peace of the place.

London,
March 25th 1669

DR OWEN, DR GOODWYN, MR NYE,
MR CARYL and nine others

75. TO THE INDEPENDENT CHURCH AT HITCHIN[1]

Brethren beloved in the Lord,

Grace and Peace be unto you from God our Father and our Lord Jesus Christ. We give thanks unto God for you all, understanding

[1] The original is lost but this copy is from J. Ivimey, *History of the English Baptists* (1814), Vol. II, pp. 189–191. A very similar copy is in S. Palmer, *Nonconformist's Memorial* (1802), Vol. I, pp. 170–2, and in the 'First Church Book' of Hitchin Baptist Church. The present Baptist Church in Hitchin dates its origin to this letter and celebrated its 300th anniversary in 1969.

that the word of the kingdom is come unto you, not in word only, but in power and the Holy Ghost, and that ye are become followers of the Lord in this day of affliction, and of the patience of Jesus Christ, and we trust your faith shall grow, and the love of every one of you towards each other shall abound more and more. As for the persons (Mr Beare and Mr Waite[2]) whom you write about we are willing at your desire to let you know, that upon hearing what the Brethren (sent up to us from that church whereof Mr Holcroft is Pastor[3]) had to produce from the records they kept of their proceedings to cast out Mr Beare first, and Mr Waite afterwards, we did unanimously judge, that the church (for ought appeared to us) had not sufficient ground for their proceedings against them as they did. And our advice to them was, that they would again receive them into fellowship; nor do we therefore know any rule of the gospel that will be infringed by your continuing to honour Mr Waite for his work's sake, or by your encouraging him in his labour in the Lord. We rejoice in that blessed success that the Lord hath crowned his ministry withall amongst you (some of you being it seems the seals thereof) and we heartily therefore pray that he may yet be more and more of use unto you, for your building up. We are sorry to hear that any brother or brethren of that church in Cambridgeshire, before spoken of, should go about to weaken his hands, or to work a prejudice to his ministry, by giving an unjust, and wrong, and untrue, account of our judgment in Mr Beare's and his case. That letter of ours[4] they have in their hands, does plainly shew what our sentiments were, and what we judge (and we humbly believe we have the mind of Christ in that we did judge) was regular and meet for them to do for the repairing the honour of Christ, and for the obtaining of a blessing to themselves, as also for the healing of that scandal, that hath come upon the way of the gospel, by the precipitant and undue casting out of persons out of the visible kingdom of our Lord Jesus Christ, and we are not without our hopes, but that the God of the Spirits of all flesh will keep them to look upon the counsel we have given them, as upon an ordinance of Christ which they ought to have reverence for.

As touching those five of your number that dissent and separate themselves from you body, our present advice is that you would be much in prayer for them, carry it in all love, with tenderness towards them, and patiently wait, if peradventure God will give them

---

[2] Waite and Beare were preachers who assisted Francis Holcroft (see *C.R.*). Cf. *Original Records of Early Nonconformity* (ed. G. L. Turner, 1911-14), Vol. III, pp. 294-8. Holcroft founded the Hitchin Independent Church.

[3] The Church met in Bridge Street, Cambridge.

[4] I cannot trace this letter.

repentance to the acknowledging of the truth. We account that they are overtaken in a fault, in this present continued separation of theirs, but we also desire you would (and we hope you will) shew yourselves so spiritual, as to seek the restoring of them in no other way than the spirit of meekness, considering yourselves lest ye also be tempted, and remembering that ye must bear the burdens of one another, and so fulfil the law of Christ. Finally, brethren, be perfect, be of good comfort, be of one mind, live in peace, and the God of love and peace be with you all, according to the prayer of your brethren and companions in tribulation, and in the kingdom and patience of our Lord Jesus Christ.

Signed in the name and by the appointment of several Elders of churches walking in and about London.

London,
the 18th of the third month, 1669.

JOHN OWEN
GEORGE GRIFFITH

76. TO [CHARLES?] NICHOLS[1]

My Good Friend,

I was very glad to heare of your life and welfare especially by your wife who surely is a good soule and one that God owned. I would be very glad to see you that we might converse together once more in this world. But I see little hopes thereof considering how infirme I heare you are and that I my selfe am going apace towards my rest. I am in the patience of God yet alive labouring in the vineyard of the Lord according to my weak measure; but I have daily warnings from my age, being now about fifty four and many infirmities to be preparing for my dissolution. Let us endeavour to be faithfull to the death and we shall not come short of a crowne of life. I thank you kindly for your remembrance of me now and shall always be ready, to the utmost of my ability, to approve my selfe to be,

Your reall friend in our Lord Jesus Christ,
JOHN OWEN

London, Nov. 10.
[1670?][2]

[1] 'Owen MS. Letters' in New College Library, London. The Rev. Dr G. F. Nuttall kindly allowed me to consult them. Since I copied the letters the Hist. MSS. Comm. has listed them. The MS. just has 'Mr Nicholls'. A member of Owen's church was called Nichols and he may have been the recipient (see MS. List of Members in the Congregational Library). Or it may have been Charles Nichols of Kent (see C.R.).

[2] No year is given in the MS. but Owen's age given as fifty-four supplies the year 1670.

77. FROM THE MAGISTRATES AND MINISTERS OF MASSACHUSETTS[1]

To the Reverend & much honoured Doctor Goodwin, Dr Owen, Mr Nye, Mr Carrill, Mr Greenhill, Mr Lockier, Mr Knowles, Mr Hooke, Mr Griffith, Mr Brooke, Mr Barker, Mr Cockin, Mr Palmer, Mr Venning, Mr Loather, Mr Mead, Mr Lee, Mr Collins, & Dr Hoare[2], these present

Honoured, reverend, and beloved in our Lord Jesus,

When we recount the singular favour of God to his people in these utmost ends of the earth and wherein he hath, by a line of his admirable loving kindnesse distinguished us from the rest of the plantations in this Western world, this is not the last in the Catalogue thereof, that he hath planted such a nursery of learning amongst us, we mean the Colledge in Cambridge, whence have sprung up so many choice plants as by whose pleasant fruits (we hope we may say it without carnall boasting, but) through grace, the heart of God and men hath been cheared. Whence both this land hath been in a great measure provided for as to a supply in the ministry and whence also have issued forth those streams into remoter parts, that have made glad the citty of God. And although it hath been partly through the poverty of the country, or what other cause, at times, languishing and is so still, yet we have found the Lord tenderly affected for it, and stirring up the hearts of divers in England and elsewhere, to afford no small contribution of encouragement for its reviving (for all which we desire to bless the Father of lights and to be duely thankfull unto those worthy persons who have not yeilded to any temptation of despising the day of small things with us). And we still find that your care of us is flourishing again for this School of the prophets with us as in part we have been informed by a Letter directed to the Governor & other persons of note among us wherein it is advised that the Overseers of the Colledge might be consulted with and that the present state of the Colledge, in order to some assistance from such as are nobly disposed may be represented to persons of speciall interest, zeal, largnesse of heart, and singular affection to this weighty concernment of the glory of God who may have a leading and successful influence thereinto; The fullness of our persuasion that your selves are persons of that character hath occasioned this our Application to your selves in particular.

[1] Massachusetts Archives, Boston, MS. lviii, ff. 72-3., and printed in *Publications* of the Colonial Society of Massachusetts, Vol. XI, pp. 388 ff.

[2] All these ministers are in *C.R.* 'Loather' = 'Loder'.

There are three things (much honoured in the Lord) which we shall therefore take the boldnesse to acquaint you with, which have matter of affliction and fear accompanying them to our hearts. 1st. The ruinous and almost irreparable state of the edifices, in conjunction with our inability to erect some other more capacious and accommodate; this notwithstanding upon serious and late debate, a new structure of stone, or brick, is resolved upon,[3] and that speedy preparations shall be made towards the same: The Country (we hope) may be enabled to contribute about a thousand pounds, which added unto by the favour and beneficience of such our worthy friends as have set their affection to this so seasonable and important designe of supporting and advancing the interest of learning and religion in this wildernesse will (we trust) in some good measure attaine the end proposed and desired. 2. The danger of our loasing the aged and reverend president of the Colledge. As we cannot but acknowledge it to the praise of God that he hath continued him, with a rich blessing, hitherunto in the service of his generation, so neither can it be expected by himself, or us, that (in an ordinary course of providence) it should be long before he must sleep with his fathers and receive his reward; now to have none in view that might, as Eliazar be invested with the dignity of succession to dying Aaron (to be left destitute of one to whom in that noble race the lamp might be delivered when the other hath finished his course, and is to receive his crown) your selves cannot but understand how great an exercise of afflictive thoughts of heart it doth occasion; In which respect we begg that we may be so happy as to prevail with your selves to make it your joynt interest with us to advise and assist toward our supply as there may be need in this case. 3. The paucity of scholars in the Colledge: the number of whom falls now far short of what hath been in former dates. It is well known to your selves what advantage to learning accrues by the multitude of persons cohabiting for scholasticall communion, whereby to actuate the minds one of another, and other waies to promote the ends of a Colledge-Society; We have experienced no small blessing from heaven upon the studies of those who have been hitherto trained up therein (and in that respect dare not complain) but yet were the number of scholars much more multiplyed, we think it would render the same much more desirable and add an higher reputation thereunto; in which case we shall account it a smile of providence if any of those in whose hearts are the waies of God, may be inclined to look this way for the education of their children.

[3] This allusion is to the second Harvard College, erected between 1672 and 1682, and burned in 1864. Charles Chauny, the president, died on 19 Feb. 1672.

But as to the premises and what else we might suggest, we may give a further account, by word of mouth, from our worthy friend Mr Richard Saltonstall,[4] than our present straits of time will permit us to commit unto this paper. The good Lord influence all hearts by his holy Spirit, and guide and lead in the way that is pleasing before him. We pray that the Lord may direct your and our hearts, more and more, into the love of God and into the patient wayting for Christ and that the good will of him that dwelt in the bush may abide with your selves and us. In whom we are,

Your servants[5] in the Lord and for the Gospell,

CHARLES CHAUNCY	RICHARD BELLINGHAM
JOHN ELLIOTT	JOHN LEVERETT
JOHN OXENBRIDGE	DANIEL GOOKIN
THOMAS THACKER (Senior)	RICHARD RUSSELL
JOHN MAYO	EDWARD TYNG
JAMES ALLEN	THOMAS DANFORTH
SAMUELL DANFORTH	WILLIAM STOUGHTON
THOMAS SHEPPARD	
INCREASE MATHER	

Boston,
21 Aug. 1671

[4] For Richard Saltonstall see *Dictionary of American Biography*, 1931.
[5] The names in the first column are those of ministers and in the second column those of magistrates for all of whom see *Dict. Amer. Biog.*

78. TO THE MAGISTRATES AND MINISTERS OF MASSACHUSETTS[1]

Right Worshipfull, Reverend and Beloved,

We received yours dated from Boston Aug.21.1671, directed to many of us which also we have severall times considered, as the providence of God hath permitted to us opportunities of meeting together. The importance of the contents thereof, together with the honor and respect we owe you all, obligeth us to return you such answer as we are at present capable of, according to that disposall which it hath pleased the infinitely wise God to make of us in our stations, and also of the conditions which he hath measured out to his people amongst whom he hath placed us, from whom, as well as ourselves, you cannot expect (as things stand with us) to receive that fruit that either your need calls for or our love would produce, were we not ourselves, together with the churches of Christ in these nations, intangled in many straits, and thereby call'd to a more universall designment of what God hath graciously left his poor people to the

[1] T. Hutchinson, *Collection of Papers*, 1769, pp. 429 ff.

supportation of the interest of his gospell and the ministers and professors thereof, whose daily relief depends, as to many counties, principally upon this citty, from whom also we must promise ourselves the greatest part if not all of that little we can hope to attain to, to express the value we have for the interest of our dear Lord Jesus amongst you, and more especially the promoting of the continuance of it in our assistence to the education of such as may by the blessing of his grace and spirit be usefull in their generation for the running and glorifying of his gospell in and by your numerous growing posterity.

As to the three branches of your letter, which comprize the whole of it, we doe according to the best of our judgments represent our thoughts to you, which we hope will be acceptable to you, as you may find in it any labor of love towards you.

First, We join with you in that humble thankfullnesse which is due to the God and Father of our Lord Jesus Christ, that he hath for so long a time planted and continued amongst you a school of the prophets, from whence have issued such instruments as God hath used for service to himselfe, even in both Englands, and heartily condole, that not only the dead stones, but also the living ones in that foundation are so much crumbled and diminished, and gladly would we contribute our helping hand to the repairing of the one and the reviving of the other, were our power suited to our wills. But upon consideration of the straits and troubles the ministers and churches of Christ are here wrestling with, and after consultation had with some wise and godly gentlemen, sincere lovers of you, we find in ourselves and them the concentring of the same thoughts, that the exhausted purses of those that are most able to contribute, cannot reach any summe considerable towards the repair of the edifice, so many of Gods servants here calling for daily relief, even of necessaries to them and their impoverished families, yet have we advised about sending you what assistance God shall enable us unto for the maintenance of Fellows and Tutors for the instruction and education of youths, who may be bred up in good literature and fear of the Lord, for future imployment in church and commonwealth, in which we can say there is a reall zeale for you and them in this great concerne. Several wayes have been proposed and debated, we cannot yet acquaint you with any fully determinate meanes for effecting, yet this we were willing to advise you of, that you are in our hearts, and that we are fully purposed (if the present liberty we have to meet be not interrupted by those presaged hurryes which seeme to be in the womb of Providence coming upon us) to use all our indeavour to collect such summes of money (and so to dispose them by the best advice we can take) as may in time amount to some comfortable help towards the end which we specified before, in the service whereof we judge that which is most necessary for you (at least that we are capable of) may be attended.

2dly, As we desire to bless God with and for you, that so reverend and judicious a person as your president hath for so long a time been continued with you, and that so usefully, so it is a grief of heart to us that there appears none amongst yourselves to succeed him in that employment, and more that we cannot find persons whose hearts God hath touched to goe over to you, in order to a supply of that expected losse which you mention; yet, if our advice herein be worth attending to, we would suggest, that it having pleased God to stirre up the heart of our beloved friend Dr Hoare[2] to intend a voyage towards you by this shipping, we do suppose a speaking providence in it, and doe judge that God hath so farr furnished him with the gifts of learning and the grace of his spirit, as that if your judgements concurre with ours and his inclinations (if God shall bring him to you) he may in some measure supply that want and help to make up this breach, and we shall hope and pray that it may be to some good fruit to you and yours.

3dly, For what concerns our promoting the sending of youths over to you for their education, wee can say no more but this, that where we find any inclined so to dispose of their children, we shall not be wanting to incourage it as farre as we hear there shall be reason for it, by the Lords provision of such help amongst you as shall be continued yet unto you or further added by him in whose hands is the residue of the spirit, to be poured out on you and on your seed according to his covenant. So commending you to the Lord and to the word of his grace, we remaine

Your servants in the Lord and for the gospel.

JOHN OWEN	PH. NYE
MATT. BARKER	JOHN KNOWLES
ARTH. PALMER	JOSEPH CARYL
JOHN ROWE	WILLIAM HOOK
THO. BROOKS	GEORGE GRIFFITH
JO. LODER	GEO. COCKAYN
JOHN COLLINS	

London.
Feb.5.1672

[2] For Leonard Hoare and Harvard see S. E. Morison, *Harvard College in the Seventeenth Century*, Cambridge, Mass., 1936, chapter 19.

79. TO JOHN ELIOT[1]

Sir,

... As to what concerns the natural strength of man, either I was

[1] Mather, *Magnalia*, Vol. I, pp. 536–7.

under some mistake in my *expression*, or you seem to be so in your *apprehension*.² I never thought, and I hope I have not said (for I cannot find it), that the continuance of the Sabbath is to be commensurate unto the natural strength of man, but only that it is an *allowable mean* of men's continuance in Sabbath duties; which I suppose you will not deny, lest you should cast the consciences of professors into inextricable difficulties.

When first I engaged in that work, I intended not to have spoken one word about the *practical* observation of the day; but only to have endeavoured the revival of a truth, which at present is despised and contemned among us, and strenuously opposed by sundry divines of the United Provinces, who call the doctrine of the Sabbath, *Figmentum Anglicanum*. Upon the desire of some learned men in these parts it was that I undertook the vindication of it. Having now discharged the debt, which in this matter I owed unto the *truth* and *church* of God, though not as I ought, yet with such composition as I hope through the interposition of our Lord Jesus Christ might find acceptance with God and his saints, I suppose I shall not again engage on that subject.

I suppose there is scarce any one alive in the world who hath more *reproaches* cast upon him than I have; though hitherto God has been pleased in some measure to support my spirit under them. I still relieved myself by this, that my poor endeavours have found acceptance with the churches of Christ: but my holy, wise, and gracious Father sees it needful to try me in this matter also; and what I have received from you (which it may be contains not your sense alone) hath printed deeper, and left a greater impression upon my mind, then all the virulent revilings and false accusations I have met withal from my professed adversaries. I do acknowledge unto you that I have a dry and barren spirit, and I do heartily beg your prayers that the Holy One would, notwithstanding all my sinful provocations, water me from above; but that I should now be apprehended to have given a wound unto *holiness* in the churches, it is one of the saddest frowns in the cloudy brows of Divine Providence.

The doctrine of the Sabbath I have asserted, though not as it should be done, yet as well as I could; the *observation* of it in holy duties unto the utmost of the strength for them which God shall be pleased to give us, I have pleaded for; the necessity also of a serious *preparation* for it in sundry previous duties, I have declared. But now to meet with severe expressions—it may be it is the will of God that

---

² According to Mather the short passage in Owen's *The Divine Institution of the Lord's Day*, 1671, went as follows: 'I judge that the observation of the Lord's day is to be commensurate unto the use of our natural strength on any other day, from morning to night.'

vigour should hereby be given to my former discouragements, and that there is a call in it to surcease from these kinds of labours.

JOHN OWEN

[1672?]

80. TO LORD WHARTON[1]

My Lord,

By the best enquiry I can make use of, I find that the lady is not yet twenty years of age[2]; her portion in present is but £3000. Expectation is good and sure. I cannot learne but that her parents have always lived in good reputation—from time immemorial with all my friends, which is all the present haste of the messenger will allow him to say who is,

My Lord,
Your most faithful and most humble servant,

JOHN OWEN

If I have any thing further brought unto me in this matter I will send it unto you by the way you have prescribed.[3]

[1] Bodleian Rawlinson MS. Lett. 52. f. 64. For Philip Lord Wharton see *D.N.B.* For a recent study of Wharton see G. F. Trevallyn Jones, *Saw-Pit Wharton*, Sydney, 1967. For the religious and philanthropic work of Wharton see B. Dale, *The Good Lord Wharton*, 1906.

[2] The young lady was probably Anne Lee, the second daughter and co-heiress of Sir Henry Lee, third baronet of Ditchley, for whom see *D.N.B.*

[3] It would seem that he was staying at his Stadhampton home when he wrote this and the subsequent letter.

81. TO LORD WHARTON[1]

My Lord,

Mr Gilbert[2] who gave me the favour of your Lordships letter desired me to meet him this morning at Abingdon where we now are and upon considering our thoughts I make bold to give you the trouble of this returne unto you. I should very gladly embrace the opportunity of waiting on you at Wooburne or anywhere else that you should command my attendance; but at present do not for a sufficient occasion of puting you to so much trouble: I was satisfyed as you must perceive by my last that there was no great reason for persisting in your first thoughts and proposall and there is to me a consideration that

[1] Bodleian Rawlinson MS. Lett. 52. f. 110.

[2] Thomas Gilbert did many services for Lord Wharton and many of his letters to his patron and benefactor are contained in the Rawlinson Letters, Vols. 49 ff., in the Bodleian Library. See Letter No. 41 above.

makes the latter a little unseasonable. There are at present some offers made unto the person intended which on the first way fixed on would immediately (as I suppose) have sank underwater so they will greatly prejudice the latter; we having to doe with persons, who though I believe they would be content to ingage into a religious family, yet I fear they will not lay such weight upon it as to outballence other considerations of this world; and although I know that all which is in present agitation with them will come to nothinge without our appearance in it and I cannot but feare that if we whould do so now whilst their thoughts are exercised with things of greater advantage, as they will suppose unto them, it might render it rejected which hereafter may be very kindly accepted of; but I referre all things unto your Lordships wisdome and shall waite for your further direction, hopinge that you will upon these reasons excuse me for not proceeding any farther until I hear from you again; my other neighbour was from home when last I saw you and hath been so until this last night, I will, God willinge waite on him tomorrow and give you a speedy account of my thoughts in that business also; I have no need at present to trouble you withall but only to assure you that I shall indeavour in all things to show how much you are sincerely honoured and esteemed by,[3]

My Lord,
Your Lordships very humble and most faithful friend,
J.O.

May 11th (1673?)

[3] This letter probably refers to the same subject as the previous one. Thomas Wharton did in fact marry Anne Lee at Adderbury Church in Oxfordshire in September 1673.

82. TO LORD WHARTON[1]

My Lord,
I know not well how to excuse my selfe for not writinge this last week; that which I have to plead is my expectation of your speedy cominge to towne, and my owne occasion in the death and buriall of my deare friend Major Robinson[2]; and that I submit to your Lordships consideration for my pardon.

About my journey into Warwickshire, this is the account; I set out from hence according to my purpose about the end of August;

[1] Bodleian Rawlinson MS. 63.f. 19. (62.)

[2] Major Robinson lived in Middlesex and served on various commissions in the Protectorate. Cf. Firth and Rait, *Acts and Ordinances*, Vol. II, pp. 619, 1073. I have been unable to ascertain the date of his death and thus cannot put a date to this letter.

and having some businesse in Oxfordshire, I went that way and stayd one night at my owne house. At the end of my next days journey (about thirty miles) it pleased God, in whose hands are my life and all my ways, to visit me with a relapse into my fluxe with such violence that I had the sentence of death in my selfe. It so fell out by his providence that I was not farr from a good friends house (Sir Thomas Overburys[3]) who hearinge of me carried me to his house, where I had all needfull accomodation and assistance, without which I suppose I had not escaped with my life. There I lay four days in much weaknesse, and despairing to make my journey when I had got a little strength, I returned unto this place in a coach to be present with my there-dying friend in his last triall. I was troubled at your disappointment more than my owne, but satisfyed that you know how to rest in the will of God; that affaire I know will suffer nothinge by this delay.

It is a sore trouble unto me to heare of your illnesse. The surgeons are honest men and well experienced, and I hope God will mind me to pray for a blessinge on their indeavour, for I will assure you I esteeme my concernment in your welfare to be very great. At present I am my selfe in a course of physick; and have no hope speedily to see you unless God bringe you hither, which I must longe for: His presence be with your ways and occasions,

My Lord,
Your most humble and obliged servant
JOHN OWEN

[3] Sir Thomas Overbury had a house at Bourton-on-the-Hill in Gloucestershire and he became a member of Owen's London church. See *D.N.B.*

83. TO LADY ELIZABETH HARTOPP[1]

Deare Madam,

Every worke of God is good; the Holy One in the middest of us will do no iniquity. And all things shall work together for good unto them that love him, even those things which at present are not joyous, but grievous. Only his time is to be waited for, and his way submitted unto, that we seem not to be disappointed in our hearts that he is Lord over us. Your dear infante is in the eternal enjoyment of the fruits of all our prayers[2]; for the covenant of God is ordered

[1] This and letters 84–87 are from the 'Owen MS. Letters' in New College, London. Elizabeth was the wife of Sir John Hartopp and the daughter of Charles Fleetwood. Sir John's mother, who was widowed in 1658, married Charles Fleetwood in 1664 and both families lived in the village of Stoke Newington, near London. Cf. A. J. Shirren, *The Chronicles of the Fleetwood House*, 1951.

[2] This child was probably Anne who died in May 1674.

in all things, and sure. We shall goe to her; she shall not returne to us. Happy she was in this above us, that she had so speedy an issue of sin and misery, being born only to exercise your faith and patience, and to glorify Gods grace in her eternal blessedness. My trouble would be great on the account of my absence at this time from you both, but that this also is the Lords doing; and I know my own uselessness wherever I am. But I will beg of God for you both, that you may not faint in this day of trial; that you may have a cleare view of those spirituall and temporall mercyes wherewith you are yet intrusted all undeserved, that sorrow of the world may not so overtake your hearts as to disenable to any duties, to grieve the Spirit, to prejudice your lives; for it tends to death. God in Christ will be better to you than ten children, and will so preserve your remnant, and so adde to them as shall be for his glory and your comfort. Only consider that sorrow in this case is no duty; it is an effect of sin, whose cure by grace we should endeavour. Shall I say, Be cheerfull? I know I may. God help you to honour grace and mercy in a compliance therewith. My heart is with you; my prayers shall be for you; and I would have seene you this day could I have borrowed a coach.

Deare Madam,
Your most affectionate and unworthy pastor,
JOHN OWEN

[May 1674?]

84. TO SIR JOHN HARTOPP

Deare Sir,

I am much refreshed to heare God hath answered my earnest desires and prayers in bringing you and your deare lady safely and in peace to your habitation. I hope I shall be able in some weake measure to acknowledge the mercy and my interest in it. That you and she are pleased to overlooke all the inconveniences of your poore entertainment and to fix a value on the sincere love and entire affection from whence it proceeded is an obligation next unto that of your company which I shall ever highly esteem. I hope the Lord was graciously pleased to make our mutuall society very usefull, as it was to me pleasant and refreshing. I bless the Lord my distressing pains have not returned on me though I feel the relicks of them in some discompossure and weakness. I suppose that if God will, and I live, about ten days hence I shall be providing for my returne, for I must needs say that you have carried away so much of the satisfaction of the country from me that the thought of it being added to the remembrance of my duty and love of my worke, I doe but endure the place where I am. I have not anything which is worth your further trouble in the perusal of my scribling. I hope all with you are in good health and desire you would make my excuse for not writing at present unto your Father and Brother F.[1] for besides that, I have nothing to communicate to them. I am at present a little intent upon another occasion. My affectionate service unto them all and particularly to your deare Lady, whom I love in the truth.

Sir, I am,
Your most affectionate friend,

Stadham, July 3rd [1674?]   JOHN OWEN

[1] He refers to Charles Fleetwood and his son Smith Fleetwood.

85. TO CHARLES FLEETWOOD

Deare Sir,

I received yours, and am glad to heare of your welfare. There is more than ordinary mercy in every days preservation. My wife, I bless God, is much revived, soe that I do not despair of her recovery; but for my selfe I have been under the power of various distempers for fourteen days past, and do yet soe continue. God is fastening his instruction concerning the approach of that season wherein I must lay downe this tabernacle. I think my mind has been too much intent upon some things, which I looked on as services for the church; but God will have us know that he has no need of me nor them, and is therefore calling me off from them. Help me with your prayers, that I may, through the riches of his grace in Christ, be in some measure ready for my account. The truth is, if we cannot see the latter rain in its season as we have seen the former, and a latter spring thereon, death, that will turne in the streams of glory unto our poor withering souls, is the best relief. I begin to feare that we shall die in the wilderness; yet ought we to labour and pray continually that the heavens would drop downe from above, and the skies poure downe righteousness—that the earth may open and bring forth salvation, and that righteousness may spring up together. If ever I return to you in this world, I beseech you to contend yet more earnestly than ever I have done, with God, with my own heart, with the church, to labour after spiritual revivalls. Our affectionate services unto your Lady, and to all your family that are of the household of God. My wife received a letter from your daughter M[1] and much acknowledges her kindness therein. Soe soon as she is able she will returne her thanks with her owne hand.

> I am, dearest Sir,
> Yours most affectionately whilst I live,
> J. OWEN

Stadham,
July 8th. [1674?]²

¹This was either his own daughter Mary or his daughter-in-law, Mary Hartopp, who was married to his son, Smith Fleetwood.

²Owen was preaching at Stadhampton in the summer of 1674. Cf. *Works*, Vol. IX, p. 484.

86. TO SIR JOHN HARTOPP

Deare Sir,

The reason why I write so seldom unto any of my friends is because I have nothing to write; at least nothing that is worth reading in my scribling. And as for you I am sure I have noe need to tender you any new assurance of my cordiall respects and love unto your selfe and your Lady. My duty, my obligations and my inclination do all concurr in the esteeme I have for you both and I doe make mention of you daily in my poore supplications (which is all I am) and that with particular respect unto the present condition of your Lady, that God who hath revealed himselfe unto us as the God that hears our prayers will yet glorify his name and be a present help unto her in the time of trouble. In the meane time, let her and you and me strive to love Christ more, to abide more with him, and to be less in our selves: He is our best friend and ere long will be our only friend. I pray God with all my heart that I may be weary of every thing else but converse and communion with him; yea, of the best of my mercyes so farr as at any time they may be hindrances thereof. I hope you are all in health and shall now begin to have thoughts about my return having mett with some disappointment in the weather. My wife presents her humble service unto your Lady, so doth also,

> Sir,
> Your most affectionate friend and servant in our deare Lord.
> JOHN OWEN

Stadham,
Aug.21. [1674?]

87. TO SIR JOHN HARTOPP

Deare Sir,

Although I have nothing to write yet I cannot but give you this remembrance of my selfe who yet believes that I am not in the least forgotten by you and I can assure you that both your selfe, my deare friend your Lady, with all the hopefull branches of your family, are continually in my heart both in a way of duty and the way of entire affection. I hope God is pleased to continue his presence with you and them all. I cannot at present give you such an account of my selfe as I would desire. I can say in all sincerity, more on the account of the church than mine owne. The great change of the weather in this moist place hath stirred up my old distemper with some additions of now so that I am thinking of a returne soe soone as I can conveniently and am able soe to do. God, I hope, is teaching me his mind in and by all these things. I doe crave a remembrance in your prayers as you are mentioned in mine always with respect unto your particular condition and circumstances soe farr as known to me, your Ladys present state and your little child especially.[1] I wrote a second to my Lord which I know not whither he hath received or noe. My hearty service to your Brother F. and his Lady. I would have written unto him but that I had nothing to write and my letters are not worth reading for nothing. I have spoken with Mr Cole[2] and find him sufficiently inclinable to come unto us. He is a person of great worth; but I shall doe nothing until my returne. My service with my wifes unto my dearest Landlady. I long to be with you and beg your excuse for this trouble.

                      Deare Sir,
                      I am,

Stadham,   Your affectionate friend and brother,
Sept. 2nd [1674?]   JOHN OWEN

[1] This may refer to Edward who died in 1676, or if the letter was written in 1672 then it would refer to Charles who died in that year.

[2] This is Thomas Cole, the Independent minister, whom presumably Owen desired as his assistant.

21. TO ROBERT ASTY[1]

Deare Sir,

I received yours by Mr B.,[2] unto whom I shall commit this returne, and hope it will come safely to your hands. For although I can acknowledge nothing of what you were pleased out of your love to ascribe unto me, yet I shall be always ready to give my thoughts

[1] 'Owen MS. Letters' in New College, London. The next two letters are from the same source also. Robert Asty was a member of the Cong. Church in Coggeshall in the 1660s and married the daughter of John Sams, Owen's successor in the church at Coggeshall. After the death of Thomas Allen, minister of the Norwich church, Asty often preached to the society. Cf. J. Browne, *History of Congregationalism in Norfolk and Suffolk*, 1877, pp. 252ff. John, a son of Robert Asty, wrote the *Memoir* of Owen in 1721.

[2] This was presumably Mr Balderstone, an elder at the church at Norwich from which society Asty received the call.

in the way of brotherly advice, whenever you shall stand in need of it. And at present, as things are circumstanced, I do not see how you can waive or decline the call of the church, either in conscience or reputation. For, to begin with the latter; should you doe so upon the most Christian and cogent grounds in your owne apprehensions, yet wrong interpretations will be put upon it; and as farr as it is possible we ought to keep ourselves, not only *extra noxam* but *suspicionem* also. But the point of conscience is of more moment. All things concurring, the providence of God in bringing you to that place the judgement of the church on your gifts and grace for their edification and example, the joynt consent of the body of the congregation in your call, with present circumstances of a singular opportunity for preaching the Word, I confess at this distance (I see not) how you can discharge that duty you owe to Jesus Christ (whose you are, and not your owne, and must rejoyce to be what he will have you be, be it more or less) in refusing a compliance unto these manifest indications of his pleasure. Only remember that you sit downe and count what it will cost you, which I know you will not be discouraged by. For the daily exercise of grace and learning of wisdom should not be grievous unto us, though some of their occasions may be irksome. For the latter part of your letter, I know no difference between a pastor and teacher but what follows their different gifts.³ The office is absolutely the same in both; the power the same, the right to the administration of all ordinances every way the same: and at that great church at Boston in New England, the teacher was always the principal person; so was Mr Cotton and Mr Norton. Where gifts make a difference, there is a difference; otherwise there is none. I pray God guide you in this great affaire; and I beg your prayers for my selfe in my weak, infirme condition.

Your affectionate friend and brother,

March 16 [1675?] J. OWEN

³Many seventeenth-century Congregational churches had both a pastor and teacher as well as elders and deacons. Cf. the two letters to Asty written by Thomas Goodwin in *Works* (1687) IV, pp. 49ff.

89. TO ROBERT ASTY

Sir,

I am very sorry to find that there is a difference arisen between Mr C.¹ and your selfe. Since the receipt of yours I received one from him with an account of the difference and his thoughts upon it at

¹John Cromwell for whom see *C.R.* Asty became the teacher and Cromwell the pastor of the Norwich church after the death of Thomas Allen.

large. I doe not therefore judge it meet to write any thing at present about it untill I am ready to give unto you both an account of my thoughts which by reason of many avocations I cannot now doe. All that I shall therefore say at present is that without mutual love and condescension no interposition of advise will issue this business to the glory of Christ and the Gospel. I pray God guide you both by that Spirit which is promised to lead us into all truth. Upon the first opportunity you will have a further account of his sense who is,

Your affectionate brother,
J. Owen

2 Jan. 1679

90. TO ROBERT ASTY

Deare Sir,

Before I could have leasure to answer your first I received a second letter from you by Mr B. Soe I would entreat you to take heed that such apprehensions of things as may prove mistaken may not make too deep impression on your mind. I never heard of any desire that Mr C. and your selfe should come to me; only I once said and wrote, that if his occasions and yours brought you to London you might here take advice. I never heard that Mr C. intimated any such thing unto you. I never heard that ever any such thing was proposed in the church or unto any member of the church; soe that there was no need of any testimony unto the contrary. Nor did Mr B., as he tells me, write any such thing unto you, but only that one private brother did once (I know not when) offer such a thing unto your selfe alone. Nor do I think it was so well done, as is necessary in such cases, to write unto you a word spoken in private. Believe me, Sir! This earnestness of spirit and aggravation of things in our owne concerns will not lead unto the encrease of love and peace. On all such occasions I would labour for nothing more then not to know the author of such mistakes, whereby they quickly come to nothing. And if this should prove to be none, you will not be pleased when you have concerned your selfe in it. To beare and forbeare, to heare and be deafe, to be father yet to carry it as a mother, as a nurse, is our duty and our crowne. Excuse this confidence in,

Deare Sir,
Your affectionate friend and servant,
John Owen

London
April 25, 1679

91. TO AN UNKNOWN RECIPIENT

Sir,

I have received your letter, and that not without great trouble, that a person who makes profession of religion should so behave himselfe as you have done therein. For to be briefe with you, I desire to know, who made you a bishop over another's church and its elders to reprove and confirm them as you doe. And if you would make your selfe a Bishop, Why doe you judge of a matter before you have heard it and determine upon it as you doe? Why doe you take up false reports and throw about your censures upon them? It is a false report that I am now endeavouring to bring in ruling elders into the church; it is a most false report that this church hath been broken by ruling elders. It hath had ruling elders though all of them are now dead, but one, about five and twenty years and noe difference in the least about them; it is a false report that Mr Goddard[2] should say any such thing to me as you pretend. All those things are contrary to express rules of the Word; and I cannot wonder that such as you should oppose ruling elders. And pray consider with what confidence you sett up your owne wisdome and judgement against the churches of Christ, and reprove them and censure them at your pleasure. Doe you not know that all the Churches of Christ in New England are for ruling elders; and all the Congregational in Old England that mett at the Savoy doe declare their judgement for them; and that all churches in the world but the Papal and Episcopall have them. I say not this, that you must therefore be of the same mind, seeing you suppose your selfe to be wiser and more knowing in this matter than they all; yet certainly it will be looked on as noe part of your humility that you soe boldly condemne them all; especially considering that you can touch upon nothing but you leave some impression of your weakness and want of understanding upon it. Who told you that the Papists have Lay-Priests; or that Constantine the Great set up an universal bishop? It is well that you talk at this rate unto him who will never expose you. But what I can gather from your letter I doe judge that you are no way able to answer the Scripture evidence which I can produce for ruling elders. And therefore I doe heartily advise you as you tender your owne peace in walking attending unto rule and the reputation of the Gospel especially if you be a member of any Congregational church: (1) That without order, rule or call you make not your selfe a judge of other churches and elders and what is done in them having never heard the Matter as stated among

---

[1] 'Owen MS. Letters' in New College, London.

[2] Perhaps this was Jonathan Goddard, Warden of Merton College, Oxford, in the 1650s. Cf. *D.N.B.*

them. (2) That you would attend unto an humble and holy walk according unto your owne light and not meddle too much with things that are too hard for you. This is the present advice of him who perhaps for some reasons you do not do well to put unto any unnecessary trouble.

JOHN OWEN

[1679?]

92. TO MONSIEUR PETER DU MOULIN[1]

Sir,

I have received your strictures upon our Confession, wherein you charge it with palpable contradiction, nonsense, enthusiasm and false doctrine; that is, all the evills that can be crowded into such a writing; and I understand, by another letter since, that you have sent the same paper unto others, which is the sole cause of the returne which I now make to you. And I beg your pardon in telling of you, that all your instances are your owne mistakes, or the mistakes of your friend, as I shall briefly manifest to you.

First, you say there is a plaine contradiction betweene chapter the third, article the sixth,[2] and chapter the thirtyeth, article the second.[3] In the first place it is said that None but the elect are redeemed; but in the thirtyeth chapter article the second it is said, The sacrament is a memorial of the one offering of Christ upon the cross for all. I do admire to find this charged by you as a contradiction. For you know full well that all our divines who maintaine that the elect only were redeemed effectually by Christ do yet grant that Christ dyed for all, in the Scripture sense of the word; that is, some of all sorts; and never dreamt of any contradiction in their assertions. But your mistake is worse; for in chapter the thirtyeth, article the second, which you refer unto, there is not one word mentioned of Christs dying for all; but that the sacrifice which he offered was offered once for all, which is the expression of the apostle, to intimate that it was but once offered, in opposition to the frequent repetition of the sacrifices

---

[1] 'Owen MS. Letters'. For Peter Du Moulin see *D.N.B.* He was the brother of Lewis Du Moulin, the Camden Professor of History at Oxford when Owen was Vice-Chancellor. Peter intended to translate the Savoy *Declaration* (1658) into French.

[2] Part of this reads, 'Neither are any other redeemed by Christ, or effectually called, justified, adopted, sanctified and saved, but the Elect onely'.

[3] This reads, 'In this Sacrament Christ is not offered up to his Father, nor any real Sacrifice made at all for remission of sin of the quick or dead, but onely a memorial of that one offering up of himself upon the Cross once for all, and a spiritual Oblation of all possible praise unto God for the same'.

of the Jews. And pray, if you go on in your translation, do not fall into a mistake upon it; for in the very close of the article it is said, That Christs only sacrifice was a propitiation for the sins of the elect. The words you urge out of Peter the second epistle, chapter the second, verse one, are not in the text: they are by your quotation, Denyed him that had redeemed them; but only Denyed the soveraign Lord which had bought them; which words have quite another sense.

Something you quote out of chapter the sixth, article six,[4] where I think you suppose we do not distinguish betweene the *reatus* and *macula* of sin; and so think that we grant the defilement of Adam's person and consequently of all intermediate propagations, to be imputed unto us. Pray, Sir, give me leave to say, that I cannot but think your mind was employed about other things when you dreamt of our being guilty of such a folly of madness; neither is there any one word in the Confession which gives countenance unto it. If you would throw away so much time as to read any part of my late discourse about Justification,[5] it is not unlikely but that you would see something of the nature of the guilt of sin, and the imputation of it, which may give you satisfaction.

In your next instance, which you refer unto chapter the nineteenth, article the sixth,[6] by some mistake there being nothing to the purpose in that place you say, It is presupposed that some who have attained age may be elected, and yet have not the knowledge of Jesus Christ; which is pure enthusiasm, and is contrary to chapter the twentyeth, article the second. Why, Sir! that many who are eternally elected, and yet for some season, some less, some long, doe live without the knowledge of Christ, untill they are converted by the Word and Spirit, is not an enthusiasm; but your exception is contrary to the whole Scripture, contrary to the experience of all days and ages, overthrows the work of the ministry, and is so absurd to sense, and reason, and daily experience that I know not what to say of it. Only, I confess that if, with some of the Arminians, you do not believe that any are elected from eternity, or before they do actually believe, something may be spoken to countenance your exception: but that we cannot regard, for it was our design to oppose all their errors.

---

[4] This reads, 'Every sin, both original and actual, being a transgression of the righteous Law of God, and contrary thereunto, doth in his own nature bring guilt upon the sinner whereby he is bound over to the wrath of God, and cause of the Law, and so made subject to death with all miseries, spiritual, temporal and eternal'.

[5] *On the Doctrine of Justification* (1678).

[6] This is a long article and explains the relationship of the true believer to the Law of God and to the Covenant of Works.

Your next instance is a plain charge of false doctrine, taken out of chapter the eleventh, article the first,[7] speaking as you say, of the active obedience of Christ imputed to us, which is contrary to article the third, where it is said that Christ acquits by his obedience in death, and not by fulfilling of the law.[8] Sir, you still give me cause of some new admiration in all these objections, and I feare you make use of some corrupt coppy of our Confession. For we say not, as you alledge, that Christ by his obedience in death did acquitt us, and not by his fulfilling of the law. But we say that Christ, by his obedience and death, did fully discharge the debt of all those who are justifyed, which comprehends both his active and passive righteousness. But you adde a reason, whereby you designe to disprove this doctrine of ours concerning the imputation of the active righteousness of Christ unto our justification. Why, you say, it is contrary to reason; for that we are freed from satisfying God's justice by being punished by death but not from the fulfilling of the law. Therefore the fulfilling of the law by Christ is no satisfaction for us; we are not freed from active obedience, but from passive obedience. Pray, Sir! Do not imagine that such mistaken reasonings can give us any occasion to change our judgements in an article of truth of this importance. When you shall have been pleased to read my book on Justification, and have answered solidly what I have written upon this subject, I will tell you more of my mind. In the meane time I tell you, we are by the death of Christ freed from all sufferings as they are purely penal and the effects of the curse, though they spring out of that root. Only, Sir! you and I know full well that we are not freed from pain, afflictions, and death itselfe, which had never beene, had they not proceeded from the curse of the law. And so, Sir! By the obedience of Christ we are freed from obedience to the law, as to justification by the works thereof. We are no more obliged to obey the law in order to justification than we are obliged to undergo the penaltyes of the law to answer its curse. But these things have been fully debated elsewhere.

In the last place, your friend wishes it could be avoided and declined to speak any thing about universal grace, for that it would raise some or most divines against it. I judge my selfe beholden to your friend for the advice, which I presume he judges to be good and wholesome; but I beg your pardon that I cannot comply with it, although I shall

[7] This states that God justifies the elect 'by imputing Christ's active obedience unto the whole Law, and passive obedience in his death for their whole and sole righteousness'.

[8] This begins 'Christ by his Obedience and Death did fully discharge the Debt of all those that are justified, and did by the sacrifice of himself, in the blood of his Cross, undergoing in their stead the penalty due unto them, make a proper, real, and full Satisfaction to God's Justice in their behalf'.

not reflect with any severity upon them who are of another judgement. And, to tell you the truth, the immethodical new method[9] introduced to give countenance to universal grace, is, in my judgement, suited to draw us off from all due conceptions concerning the grace of God in Jesus Christ; which I shall not now stay to demonstrate, though I will not decline the undertaking of it, if God gives me strength at any time. And I do wonder to hear you say that many, if not most divines, will rise against it, who have published in print that were but two in England that were of that opinion, and have strenuously opposed it your selfe. How things are in France, I know not; but at Geneva, in Holland, in Switzerland, in all the Protestant churches of Germany, I do know that this universal grace is excluded and exploded. Sir! I shall trouble you no farther. I pray be pleased to accept of my desire to undeceive you in those things, wherein either a corrupt coppy of our Confession, or the reasoning of other men, have given you so many mistaken conceptions about our Confession.[10]

JOHN OWEN

[9] The 'new method', taught at the Academy of Saumur, and often called Amyraldianism after Amyraldus, one of its leading expositors, gave a different logical order to God's eternal decrees from that found in orthodox Calvinism. It put the decree to redeem before the decree to elect—this was the new method.
[10] As far as I can ascertain the French translation of the Savoy *Declaration* proposed by Moulin was never published.

93. TO MRS POLHILL[1]

Deare Madam,

The trouble expressed in yours is a great addition to mine; the sovereignty of divine wisdome and grace is that on many accounts I have this day to retreat unto; God direct you thereunto also, and you will find rest and peace. It adds to my trouble that I cannot possibly come downe to you this week. Nothing but engaged duty could keep me from you one houre; yet I am conscious how little I can contribute to your guidance in this storme, or your satisfaction. Christ is your Pilott; and however the vessel is tossed whilst he seemes to sleepe, he will arise and rebuke these winds and waves in his owne time. I have done it, and shall farther wrestle with God for you according to the strength he is pleased to communicate. Little it is which at this distance I can mind you of; yet some few things are necessary. Sorrow not too much for the dead; she is entered into rest,

[1] 'Owen MS. Letters'. Mrs Polhill was the wife of Edward Polhill who lived in Sussex and for whom see *D.N.B.* Owen wrote a preface for Edward Polhill's book, *The Divine Will Considered in its Eternal Decrees.*

and is taken away from the evill to come.² Take heed lest, by too much griefe, you too much grieve that Holy Spirit, who is infinitely more to us than all natural relations. I blame you not that you so farr attend to the call of God in this dispensation as to search your selfe, to judge your selfe and to condemne your selfe: grace can make it an evidence unto you that you shall not be judged nor condemned of the Lord. I dare not say that this chastisement was not needful. We are not in heaviness unless need bee; but if God be pleased to give you a discovery of the wisdome and care that is in it, and how needfull it was to awaken and restore your soule in any thing, perhaps in many things, in due time you will see grace and love in it also. I verily believe God expects, in this dealing with you, that you should judge your selfe, judge your sins, and judge your decays; but he would not have you misjudge your condition. But we are like froward children, who, when they are rebuked and corrected, neglect other things, and only cry that their parents reject them and hate them. You are apt to feare, to thinke, to say, that you are one whom God regards not, who are none of his; and that for sundry reasons which you suppose you can plead. But, saith God, this is not the business; this is a part of your frowardness. I call you to quicken your own grace, to amend your owne wayes; and you think you have nothing to doe but to question my love. Pray, Madam, my deare sister, child and care, between you lose not the advantage of this dispensation: you will do so, if you use it only to afflictive sorrows, or questioning of the love of God, or your interest in Christ. The time will be spent in these things which should be taken up in earnest endeavours after a compliance with Gods will, quickenings of grace, returns after backslidings, mortification of sin and love of the world, untill the sense of it do pass away. Labour vigorously to bring your soul to this twofold resolution: (1) That the will of God is the best rule for all things, and their circumstances; And (2) That you will bring your selfe into a fresh engagement to live more to him: and you will find the remainder of your work easy; for it is part of the yoke of Christ. I shall trouble you no farther, but only to give you the assurance that you are in my heart continually, which is nothing; but it helps to persuade me that you are in the heart of Christ, which is all.

JOHN OWEN

²The person who had died was her sister, Loyd.

94. TO THE CHURCH MEETING IN LEADENHALL STREET, LONDON[1]

Beloved in the Lord,

Mercy, grace and peace be multiplied to you from God our Father and from our Lord Jesus Christ, by the communication of the Holy Ghost. I thought and hoped that by this time I might have been present with you, according unto my desire and resolution; but it hath pleased our holy and gracious Father otherwise to dispose of me, at least for a season. The continuance of my painfull infirmities and the increase of my weaknesses will not allow me at present to hope that I should be able to bear the journey. How great an exercise this is to me, considering the season, he knows, to whose will I would in all things cheerfully submit my selfe.

But although I am absent from you in body, I am in mind, affection and spirit present with you, and in your assemblies; for I hope you will be found my crown and rejoicing in the day of the Lord: and my prayer for you night and day is, that you may stand fast in the whole will of God, and maintain the beginning of your confidence without wavering, firm unto the end. I know it is needless for me at this distance to write to you about what concerns you in point of duty at this season, that work being well supplied by my brother in the ministry; yet give me leave, out of my abundant affections towards you, to bring some few things to your remembrance as my weakness will permitt.

And in the first place, I pray God it may be fixed and rooted in our minds, that the shame and loss we may undergo for the sake of Christ and the profession of the Gospel, is the greatest honour which, in this life, we can be made partakers of. Hence it is reckoned to the Philippians in a peculiar manner, that it was given unto them, not only to believe in Christ, but also to suffer for him; That it is far more honourable to suffer with Christ than to reigne with the greatest of his enemies. If this be fixed by faith in our minds, it will tend greatly to our encouragement. I mention these things only, as knowing that they are more at large pressed on you.

And secondly, the next thing I would recommend unto you at this season is the increase of mutual love among your selves. For every trial of our faith towards our Lord Jesus Christ is also a trial of our love towards the brethren. This is that which the Lord Christ expects from us, namely, that when the hatred of the world doth openly manifest and act it selfe against us all, we should evidence an active love among ourselves. If there have been any decays, any coldness herein, if they are not recovered and healed in such a season, it can

---

[1] 'Owen MS. Letters'. This was the church of which he was pastor. In the later part of his life he was helped by several assistant ministers.

never be expected. I pray God therefore that your mutual love may abound more and more in all the effects and fruits of it towards the whole society and every member thereof. You may justly measure the fruit of your present trial by the increase of this grace amongst you: in particular have a due regard to the weak and tempted that 'that which is lame may not be turned out of the way, but rather let it be healed'.

Furthermore, brethren, I beseech you to heare a word of advice in case the persecution increases, which it is like to do for a season. I could wish that because you have no ruling elders, and your teachers cannot walk about publickly with safety, that you would appoint some among your selves, who may continually as their occasions will admit, goe up and down from house to house and apply themselves peculiarly unto the weake, the tempted, the fearful, those who are ready to despond, or to halt, and to encourage them in the Lord. Choose out those unto this end who are endued with a spirit of courage and fortitude; and let them know that they are happy whom Christ will honour with his blessed work. And I desire the persons may be of this number who are faithfull men, and know the state of the church; by this means you will know what is the frame of the members of the church, which will be a great direction to you, even in your prayers.

Watch now, brethren, that if it be the will of God, not one soul may be lost from under your care. Let not one be overlooked or neglected. Consider all their conditions, and apply your selves to all their circumstances.

Finally brethren that I be not at present further troublesome to you, examine your selves, as to your spirituall benefit which you have received or do receive, by your present fears and dangers, which will alone give you the true measure of your condition. For if this tends to the exercise of your faith and love and holiness, if this increases your valuation of the privileges of the gospel, it will be an undoubted token of the blessed issue which the Lord Christ will give unto your troubles.

Pray for me as you do, and do it the rather, that if it be the will of God, I may be restored to you. And if not, that a blessed entrance may be given to me into the kingdome of God and glory. Salute all the church in my name. I take the boldness in the Lord to subscribe my selfe,

Your unworthy pastor and your servant for Jesus sake,

J. OWEN

Postscript.

I humbly desire you would remember in your prayers the family where I am[2]; from whom I have received and do receive great Christian kindness. I may say as the Apostle of Onesiphorus: the Lord give unto them that they may find mercy of the Lord in that day; for they have often refreshed me in my great distress.

[2] He was staying at Wooburn as a guest of Philip Lord Wharton.

95. TO THOMAS WHITAKER[1]

Sir,

I received yours by the bearer, who has done me the favour to call for an answer: and although, at present, I have scarce leisure to write a line yet I was not willing to omit the opportunity of saluting you with one word. I am glad to heare of your welfare, and of the peace of the church with you, which I pray God to continue. I hope it is well also with you as to spiritual thrift and growth; and I earnestly desire it may be so. For indeed amongst all the tokens of Gods displeasure that abound in the world, and especially in this nation, there are none so sad as the open evidences which we have of His withdrawing his presence from His Churches and other professors of the gospel, which appear in the fruits and effects of it. But I cannot at present give you my dreadful apprehensions of the present state of things in the world; I may possibly have another opportunity for it. My second part of Evangelical Churches is finished[2]; but when it will be published, as yet I know not. It doth comprise, not only that which you want, but all the cases wherein the practice of our way is concerned. I pray excuse my haste, and remember him in your prayers who is labouring with age, infirmities, temptations, and troubles, being,

Your affectionate brother in our dearest Lord,

London,   J. OWEN
Oct. 29 (1681?)

[1] A transcript is printed in *The Works of John Owen* (ed. T. Russell), 1826, Vol I, p. 423, but the source is not given. Thomas Whitaker was a Nonconformist minister in Leeds.

[2] *The True Nature of the Gospel Church* was not in fact published until 1689. An abridged edition of this famous book was published as recently as 1947, edited by John Huxtable, and it is still in print.

96. TO CHARLES FLEETWOOD[1]

Deare Sir,

The bearer hath stayed long enough with us to save you the trouble of reading an account of me in my owne scribling: a longer stay I could not prevail with him for, though his company was a

[1] This and the following letter are from the 'Owen MS. Letters'.

great refreshment to me. Both you and your whole family, in all their occasions and circumstances, are daily in my thoughts; and when I am enabled to pray, I make mention of you all without ceasing. You and I, I find, are much in complainings. For my part I must say, And is there not a cause? Soe much deadness, soe much unspirituality, soe much weakness in faith, coldness of love, instability in holy meditations, as I find in my selfe, is cause sufficient of complaints. But is there not cause also of thanksgiving and joy in the Lord? Are there not reasons for them? When I begin to think of them I am overwhelmed; they are great, they are glorious, they are inexpressible. Shall I now invite you to this great duty of rejoicing more in the Lord? Pray for me that I may do soe, for the near approach of my dissolution calls for it earnestly. My heart has done with this world even in the best and most desirable of its refreshments. If the joy of the Lord be not now strength unto it, it will fail. But I must have done.

I have the same thoughts of Mr C.[2] that you have and I did formerly acquaint you with them. But what shall I say! Shall I speake without offense? Wisdome and ability in preaching (Oh how rare to be found) will not do the Work of that Church. Unless God be pleased to affect some person or persons with a deep sense of our declining condition, of the temptations and dangers of the day, filling them with compassion for the souls of men, making them fervent in spirit in their work, it will go but ill with us. It may be these thoughts spring from causeless fears—it may be none amongst us has an evill, a barren heart but my selfe: but beare with me in this my folly: I cannot lay downe these thoughts until I die; nor doe I mention them at present as though I should not esteeme it a great mercy to have so able a supply as Mr C., But I am groaning after deliverance; and being neare the centre, doe hope I feele the drawing of the love of Christ with more earnestness than formerly: but my naughty heart is backward in these compliances. My affectionate service with my wifes to Sir John Hartopp, and his Lady, and to the rest of your family, when God shall returne them unto you.

I am, deare Sir,
Yours most affectionately in everlasting bonds,

Aug. 6. 1682.   J. OWEN

[2] David Clarkson who succeeded John Owen in 1683.

97. FROM DR EDMUND KING[1]

Honoured Sir,

have received your viol tach that came in it, and I doe believe you have a stone too bigg to pass which galls the internal superficies of your kidney, but has been kept hitherto from an ulcer which I am glad of. This kidney being in this condition will be subject to injuries: and therefore it concerns you to take all things that may be convenient for its preservation for fear you should be of less use; if you have one good one, which we may hope for, which will speed never the worse for care of this: But because we can not be sure, its the safest way to suspect the worst. I have sent you such things as I hope will doe you good service if you please to follow the advice of

Sir,

Your faithful servant

Jan. 26th 1683. E. KING

[1] Bodleian Rawlinson Letters 51:127. Edmund King was a doctor of medicine who attended Owen. This letter was conveyed by Lord Wharton who wrote on it: 'The letter I brought from Mr King to Dr Owen'. It has been preserved amongst Lord Wharton's papers.

98. TO CHARLES FLEETWOOD

Deare Sir,

Although I am not able to write one worde my selfe; yet I am very desirous to speak one word to you more in this world, and do it by the hand of my wife. The continuance of your entire kindness knowing what it is accompanied withall is not only greatly valued by me but will be a refreshment to me, as it is, even in my dying houre. I am going to him whom my soul hath loved, or rather who hath loved me with an everlasting love; which is the whole ground of all my consolation. The passage is very irksome and wearysome through strong pains of various sorts which are all issued in an intermitting fever. All things were provided to carry me to London today attending to the advice of my physician, but we were all disappointed by my utter disability to undertake the journey. I am leaving the ship of the church in a storm, but whilst the great Pilot is in it the loss of a poore under-rower will be inconsiderable. Live and pray and hope and waite patiently and doe not despair; the promise stands invincible that he will never leave thee nor forsake thee. I am greatly afflicted at the distemper of your deare Lady; the good Lord stand by her and support and deliver her. My affectionate respects to her and the rest of your relations who are soe deare unto me in the Lord. Remember your dying friend with all (forbounty).[1] I rest upon it that you doe soe, and am,

Yours sincerely

J. OWEN

Aug. 22. 1683

[1] John Owen died on the 24th.

APPENDIX I

The Works of Dr John Owen

1. Θεομαχια Αυτεξουσιαστικη, or a Display of Arminianism (1643)
2. The Duty of Pastors and People Distinguished (1643)
3. Two Short Catechisms, wherein the Doctrines of Christ are explained (1645)
4. A Vision of Unchangeable Free Mercy, a Sermon (1646)
5. Eshcol; or Rules of Direction for the Walking of the Saints (1647)
6. Salus Electorum, Sanguis Jesu; or the Death of Death (1647)
7. Ebenezer; a Memorial of the deliverance in Essex: two sermons (1648)
8. Righteous Zeal: a sermon with an Essay on Toleration (1649)
9. Ουρανων Ουρανια: a sermon (1649)
10. Of the Death of Christ, the Price He Paid (1650)
11. The steadfastness of the Promises: a sermon (1650)
12. The Branch of the Lord: two sermons (1650)
13. The Advantage of the Kingdom of Christ: a sermon (1651)
14. The Labouring Saint's Dismission to Rest: a sermon (1652)
15. Christ's Kingdom and the Magistrate's Power: a sermon (1652)
16. Humble Proposals for the Propagation of the Gospel [with others] (1652)
17. Proposals for the Propagation of the Gospel . . . also some principles of Christian religion [with others] (1653)
18. De Divina Justitia Diatriba (1653)
19. The Doctrine of the Saints' Perseverance (1654)
20. Vindicae Evangelicae: or the Mystery of the Gospel Vindicated (1655)
21. Of the Mortification of Sin in Believers (1656)
22. A Review of the Annotations of Grotius (1656)
23. God's Work in Founding Zion: a sermon (1656)
24. God's Presence with His People: a sermon (1656)
25. Of Communion with God the Father, Son and Holy Ghost (1657)
26. Of Schism (1657)
27. A Review of the True Nature of Schism (1657)
28. An Answer to a later Treatise of Daniel Cawdry about . . . Schism (1658) in *A Defence of Mr John Cotton* (1658)
29. Of Temptation: the Nature and Power of it (1658)
30. Pro Sacris Scripturis Exercitationes adversus Fanaticos (1658)

31. Of the Divine Original . . . of the Scriptures (1659)
32. A Vindication of the Hebrew and Greek Texts (1659)
33. The Glory and Interest of Nations: a sermon (1659)
34. Two Questions concerning the Power of the Supreme Magistrate about Religion (1659)
35. Θεολογουμενα Παντοδαπα (1661)
36. Animadversions on a Treatise entitled Fiat Lux (1662)
37. A Discourse concerning Liturgies (1662)
38. A Vindication of the Animadversions on Fiat Lux (1664)
39. Indulgence and Toleration Considered (1667)
40. A Peace-Offering, in an Apology and Humble Plea for Indulgence (1667)
41. A Brief Instruction in the Worship of God (1667)
42. The Nature, Power, Deceit and Prevalency of Indwelling Sin (1667)
43. A Practical Exposition of Psalm cxxx. (1668)
44. Exercitations on the Epistle to the Hebrews, I (1668)
45. Truth and Innocence Vindicated (1669)
46. A Brief Declaration and Vindication of the Doctrine of the Trinity (1669)
47. An Account of the Grounds and Reasons on which Protestant Dissenters desire Liberty (1670)
48. Reflections on a Slanderous Libel (1670)
49. Exercitations concerning the . . . Day of Sacred Rest (1671)
50. A Discourse concerning Evangelical Love, Church-Peace and Unity (1672)
51. A Vindication of some passages in a Discourse concerning Communion with God (1674)
52. Πνευματολογια, or a Discourse on the Holy Spirit (1674)
53. An Exposition of the Epistle to the Hebrews, II (1674)
54. The Testimony of the Church is not the chief reason for our believing the Scripture to be the Word of God (printed in N. Vincent, *The Morning-Exercises against Popery*) (1675)
55. How we may bring our hearts to bear reproofs (printed in S. Annesley, *A Supplement to the Morning-Exercises*) (1676)
56. The Nature of Apostasy from the Profession of the Gospel (1676)
57. The Reason of Faith (1677)
58. The Doctrine of Justification by Faith (1677)
59. Συνεσις Πνευματικη, or the Causes, Ways and Means of understanding the Mind of God (1678)
60. Χριστολογια, or a Declaration of the Glorious Mystery of the Person of Christ (1678)
61. The Church of Rome no Safe Guide (1679)
62. Some Considerations of Union among Protestants (1680)

63. A Brief Vindication of the Nonconformists from the charge of Schism (1680)
64. A Continuation of the Exposition of the Epistle to the Hebrews, III (1680)
65. An Inquiry into the Original, Nature . . . and Communion of Evangelical Churches (1681)
66. An Humble Testimony unto the Goodness and Severity of God (1681)
67. Φρονημα του Πνευματος, or the Grace and Duty of being Spiritually-minded (1681)
68. A Discourse of the Work of the Holy Spirit in Prayer (1682)
69. A Brief and Impartial Account of the Protestant Religion (1682)
70. The Chamber of Imagery in the Church of Rome Laid Open (in *The Morning Exercises against Popery*) (1683)
71. A Letter concerning the Matter of the Present Excommunications (1683)
72. Meditations and Discourses on the Glory of Christ (1684)
73. A Continuation of the Exposition of the Epistle to the Hebrews, IV (1684)
74. Of the Dominion of Sin and Grace (1688)
75. True Nature of the Gospel Church (1689)
76. Seasonable Words for English Protestants: a sermon (1690)
77. Meditations and Discourses on the Glory of Christ Applied (1691)
78. A Guide to Church-Fellowship and Order (1692)
79. Two Discourses, of the Holy Spirit as Comforter . . . and Author of Spiritual Gifts (1693)
80. Gospel Grounds and Evidences of the Faith of God's Elect (1695)
81. An Answer unto Two Questions . . . with Twelve Arguments against any Conformity to Worship not of Divine Institution (1720)
82. A Complete Collection of the Sermons of . . . J. Owen . . . also several tracts . . . to which are added his Latin Orations (1721)
83. Three Discourses delivered at the Lord's Table (1750)
84. Thirteen Sermons preached on various occasions (1756)
85. Twenty-five Discourses suitable to the Lord's Supper (1760)
86. Posthumous Sermons (in Goold, *Works*, Vol. XVI) (1854)

APPENDIX II

Books which contain 'Prefaces', 'Epistles to the Reader' or 'Commendations' by Dr John Owen

1. Henry Whitfield, *Strengthe out of Weaknesse* (1652)
2. Thomas Taylor, *A Collection of the Works of T. Taylor* (1653)
3. William Twisse, *The Riches of God's Love* (1653)
6. William Eyre, *Vindiciae Justificationis Gratuitae* (1654)
5. George Kendall, *Sancti Sanctiti* (1656)
6. Lewis Du Moulin, *Paraenesis ad Aedificatores imperii in imperio* (1656)
7. Philolaeclerus (pseud.), *The Private Christian's Non Ultra* (1656)
8. ——, *Banners of Grace and Love* (1657)
9. John Cotton, *A Defence of Mr. John Cotton* (1658)
10. William Guild, *The Throne of David* (1659)
11. Patrick Gillespie (?), *Ark of the Testament Opened* (1661)
12. James Durham, *Clavis Cantici* (1669)
13. Theophilus Gale, *The True Idea of Jansenisme* (1669)
14. Henry Lukin, *An Introduction to the Holy Scripture* (1669)
15. Mrs. Alleine, *The Life and Death of . . . Joseph Alleine* (1672)
16. Jean Daillé, *Sermons on the Epistle . . . to the Colossians* (1672)
17. Joseph Caryl, *The Nature and Principles of Love* (1673)
18. ——, *Scottish Metrical Version of Psalms* (1673)
19. Edward Polhill, *The Divine Will Considered in the eternal decrees* (1673)
20. Vavasor Powell, *A New and Useful Concordance* (1673)
21. Thomas Gouge, *The Surest and Safest Way of Thriving* (1674)
22. Henry Scudder, *The Christian's Daily Walk* (1674)
23. Samuel Petto, *The Difference between the Old and New Covenant* (1674)
24. James Durham, *The Law Unsealed* (1676)
25. Patrick Gillespie, *The Ark of the Covenant Opened* (1677)

26. Samuel Corbyn, *An Awakening Call* (in later editions entitled *The Necessity, Seriousness and Sweetness of Practical Religion*) (1677) (2nd ed)
27. Elisha Coles, *A Practical Discourse of Gods Sovereignty* (1678)
28. Stephen Lobb, *The Glory of Free Grace* (1680)
29. Bartholomew Ashwood, *The Best Treasure* (1681)
30. Samuel Clark, *The Holy Bible with Annotations* (1690)

Notes

1. In 1671 a preface signed 'J.O.' appeared in *The Freeness of the Grace and Love of God* by William Bridge. Owen denied that he wrote this in his 'epistle' in Caryl's *Nature of Love* (1673) after Dr John Echard had launched an attack upon him for writing it.

2. In The *Life and Death of Mr Henry Jessey* (1671) there is a poem attributed to 'J.O.' but this is not Dr John Owen.

3. *Banners of Grace and Love* (1657) seems to be a revised edition of Whitfield, *Strengthe out of Weaknesse* (1652).

APPENDIX III

Proposal for Indulgence

IN 1667 John Owen composed a proposal for Indulgence to be granted to Congregationalists and Baptists who were not covered by the proposed Comprehension Bill drawn up by John Wilkins. The text of Owen's proposals were preserved in the papers of Thomas Barlow and printed in *The Theological Works of Herbert Thorndike*, Oxford, 1854, Vol. V., p.308.

> The Indulgence desired for those who cannot come within the Comprehensive Bill is as follows—that those who professe faith in God the Father, and Jesus Christ His Eternall Sonne, the true God; and in the Holy Ghost God co-equal with the Father and the Sonne, God blessed for ever; and doe acknowledge the Holy Scriptures of the Old and New Testaments to be the revealed word and will of God; though in other things they differ in doctrine, worship, and discipline from the publique profession of the State, may not be compelled thereto by penalties, nor restrained from their profession, but protected from all injuries and molestation in their assembleinge for the exercise of religion in the profession and practice of their faith. Provided that this shall not extend to the liberty or exercise of those who shall disturb the publique peace in those assemblies; nor to Popery; or to the countenancing such who publish horrible blasphemies, or hold forth or practise licentiousness or profaneness under the profession of Christ. Care to be taken that their meeting-places be publique and open, and authorized by the justices of the Quarter-Sessions, who are to be authorized and required hereunto.

APPENDIX IV

The Will of Dr John Owen

I, JOHN OWEN of London, Doctor of Divinity, being weake in body but of perfect and disposeing mind and memory, blessed be God. Revoking all former and other my Wills and Testaments declare my last Will and Testament to be in manner following, that is to say, Whereas the said John Owen by my deed of grant and release bearinge date the Nine and Twentieth day of June in the Nine and Twentieth Yeare of the Raigne of his now Majesty king Charles the second, betweene me of the first part, John Disbrow[1] of Eltisley in the County of Cambridge Esq since deceased and Richard King[2] of the Citty of London Merchant of the second Part, and Dorothy Doyley of London, Widdow, of the Third Part, for the considerations therein mentioned, did grant and release all the Farmes, Messuages, lands, tenements and hereditaments in Stadham and Soulderne in the County of Oxon and Eaton in the County of Berks therein mentioned (Except as is therein excepted) to the said John Disbrowe and Richard King and theire Heires to the severall uses therein mentioned (that is to say) amongst other uses the said Farms and Lands in Stadham and Soulderne with their appurtenances after the determination of the Estates lymitted to or for the severall uses of me and the said Dorothy then my intended and now my wife and the issue begotten between us. To the use of Mary Kynaston my late daughter and wife of Roger Kynaston[3] gent. for her life and after to the said John Disbrowe and Richard King and their Heires for the life of the said Mary Kynaston for preserving the contingent remainders therein lymitted. And after the death of the said Mary to the use of her sons and daughters successively in tayle and for want of such issue to the use of Henry Owen my brother and his Heires forever. And the said lands in Eaton from and after the deaths of me the said John Owen and Dorothy my wife without any issue begotten between us to the use

[1] John Disbrow=John Desborough, for whom see *D.N.B.* He was a major-general under Oliver Cromwell.
[2] Richard King was perhaps the Richard King of Llanbister, Rads., a supporter of Vavasor Powell, and on the Commission for the Propagation of the Gospel in Wales. For more details about him see the works on Welsh Puritanism by T. Richards and A. H. Dodd.
[3] Roger Kynaston was from Plas Kynaston, Ruabon. Cf. A. N. Palmer, *History of the Older Nonconformity of Wrexham*, p. 48, and G. L. Turner, *Original Records*, Vol. II, p. 1199.

of the said Henry Owen and his Heires forever. And whereas in the said indenture of release thereto conteyned a provisoe in these words or to the effect following, viz. provided also and it is declared and agreed by and between the parties to these presents, That it shall and may be lawfull to and for me at anytime or times by any deed or deeds in my life time or by my last Will and Testament in writing, or by any Codicill thereunto in the presence of Three or more sufficient Witnesses, to alter revoke or make void any the uses and estates before herein lymited and appointed which are to take effect after the deathes of me, the said John Owen, and Dorothy Doyley and either of us without any issue to be begotten between us of the same premisses or any part thereof as aforesaid. And by the same Deed and Will or otherwise to limitt the same or other uses so as such power extends not nor be construed to extend to make any revocation alteration or the making void of any of the uses and estates therein before lymitted to the use of the same Dorothy Doyley or any other issue to be begotten by me the said John Owen upon the body of the said Dorothy my wife as aforesaid. And by the said indenture colacion being thereunto had may appeare. Now my mind and will is, And I, the said John Owen, for divers good causes and considerations me thereunto moveing, I do by this my last Will and Testament in writing in the presence of Three or more Sufficient Witnesses revoke and make void all the said uses and estates lymited by the said recited dead, to take effect after my death and the death of my said wife Dorothy Owen without any issues of our body begotten or to the use and uses of the said John Disbrowe, Richard King, Mary Kynaston, the sons and daughters of her body begotten and of the said Henry Owen and his Heires or any of them, and whereas I, the said John Owen, and Dorothy, my wife, have for valuable considerations by sufficient conveyance in the Law sold the said lands in Soulderne unto Ursula Cartwright, Spinster, which said lands were settled upon the said Dorothy my wife for her Joynture, in lieu whereof I do hereby settle the said lands in Eaton upon the said Dorothy my wife. Now my will and mind is, and I, the said John Owen, do give devise and limit unto the said Dorothy Owen my wife all that my Farms, Messuages, Lands, Tenements and Hereditaments in Eaton aforesaid in the said county of Berks with the Appurtenances for her Joynture, in case she shall happen to survive me, To have and hold the Lands Messuages and Premises with the Appurtenances unto the said Dorothy Owen my wife and to her Assignes for and dureinge the terms of her naturall life in case she shall happen to survive me the said John Owen. And I do hereby in consideration of the natural love and affection which I have and bare to the said Henry Owen, my only brother, and his issue, and to Mary Hall, my

Heire, wife of Bartholomew Hall[4] of Henley in the county of Oxon Gent. and for other the considerations herein after mentioned give, devise and limit all the said Farms, Messuages, Lands, Tenements, Hereditaments and Premisses aforementioned in Stadham and Eaton aforesaid from and after the respective estates lymitted by the said deed, and through my will or either of them to me, the said John Owen, and Dorothy my wife or either of us without any issue begotten between us, To the uses intents and purposes and under the provisoes, limitations, declarations following and to noe-other use intent or purpose whatsoever (that is to say) as to the said Farme, Messuages, Lands, Tenements, and Hereditaments with the Appurtenances in Stadham aforesaid in the said county of Oxon from and after the determination of the Estates lymitted by the said verified indenture to me the said John Owen and to the issue begotten by me on the body of the said Dorothy my wife, I give and devise the same to my said brother Henry Owen for and during the terme of his naturall life, and from and after his decease, I give and devise the same to Henry Owen son of the said Henry Owen for and during the term of his naturall life, and from and after his becease to the Heires of his body lawfully to be begotten, and for want of such issue the remainder to the said Mary Hall and to the Heires of her body lawfully begotten, and for want of such issue the remainder to the right Heires of me the said John Owen forever, provided alwaies and the true intent and meaning so that it shall and may be lawfull to and for the said Henry Owen, my brother, and the said Henry Owen, his son, and the said Mary Hall dureinge their said severall Estates of and in the premisses or any part thereof from time to time to demise and lease the said respective premisses or any part thereof lymitted to their uses respectively as aforesaid for any term not exceeding their lives, or one and twenty years or for any number of years determinable upon three lives or fewer, so as such lease and demise be made in possession and not in reversion or remainder, nor by way of future interest and have the best and improved rent reserved thereupon without any fine or Incombe for the same and be not made dispunishable of waste. And as to and concerning the said Farme, Messuages, Lands, Tenements, and Hereditaments with the Appurtenances in Eaton, in the said County of Berks, from and after the determination of the uses and Estates lymitted in and by the said recited Indenture, and this my Will or either of them to or for me, the said John Owen, and Dorothy my wife or either of us, and the Heires of my body upon the body of the said Dorothy begotten, I

---

[4] Sir Noel Hall and Bishop R. O. Hall are direct descendants of Bartholomew and Mary Hall. Cf. p. 9 above.

give and devise the same, after the decease of my said wife, to my said Brother, Henry Owen, for the terme of his naturall life and from and after his decease to Henry Owen, son of the said Henry Owen, for and dureing the terme of his naturall life, and from and after his decease to the Heires of his body lawfully to be begotten and for want of such issue the Remainder to Heneretta Owen, daughter of the said Henry Owen, and sister of the said Henry Owen, the son, for and dureinge the terme of naturall life and from and after her decease to the Heires of her body lawfully to be begotten, and for want of such issue the remainder to my said Heire, Mary Hall, wife of the said Bartholomew Hall, and to the Heires of her body lawfully to be begotten. And for want of such issue the remainder to the right Heires of me, the said John Owen, for ever. Item, my Will is that such debts as I shall owe at the time of my decease and my funerall charges be paid in the first place. Item, I give devise and bequeath unto Doyley Michell, my said wifes Nephew, the summe of one hundred pounds to remaine in the hands of my said wife untill he shall attaine his age of sixteen yeares, the Interest thereof to be disbursed by my said wife towards his maintenance, and if he shall dye before he attaine the said age of sixteene yeares, then I give and devise the said one hundred pounds to the next child of Barnard Michell, my wifes Brother, to be paid by my said wife for the maintenance of such child. Item, I give and devise unto my said wife the summe of Two Hundred Pounds to the intent and purpose that she pay such debts therewith as my Nephews,[5] John Hartcliffe, Philemon Hartcliffe, Samuel Hartcliffe or any or either of them are bound for my said brother Henry Owen and the said Roger Kinaston deceased or either of them. Item, I give, devise and bequeath unto my said Heire Mary Hall the summe of One hundred pounds. Item, I give and bequeath unto Mr Daniell Fogge of Oxon the summe of forty pounds. Item, I give and bequeath unto Mary Lint my servant the summe of thirty pounds. Item, I give and bequeath to Elizabeth Meech my servant the summe of Twenty pounds. Item, I give and bequeath unto Mr John Collins,[6] Minister of the Gospell, the summe of Twenty pounds. Item, I give and devise unto my said wife the summe of Forty pounds to be distributed by her among such and soe many people as she shall think fitt. Item, I give and bequeath to Mr David Clarkson, Mr Robert Ferguson, and Mr Isaac Loafs[7] the severall summes of five pounds apeice. Item, I give and bequeath to Mr James Bury of Battersey in the County of Surrey, the Summe of

---

[5] These three were the sons of John Hartcliffe (see *C.R.*), the curate of Stadhampton. For the first named see *D.N.B.*

[6] For John Collins see *C.R.*

[7] Clarkson, Ferguson and Loeffs are all in *C.R.*

Tenn pounds. Item, I give and bequeath to Mr Jeffery Eliston[8] the summe of Tenn pounds. All and every which Legacyes and other Summes of money herein by me given devised, or bequeathed, my will and mind is and I doe hereby order and appoynt that the same be paid out of the debt or summe of One Thousand, three hundred, thirty two pounds and ten shillings due by Bonds from Ursula Cartwright, Widdow, Jane Hussey, Spinster, and William Hussey, Merchant, which said Bond was taken in the name of Thomas Owen Esq. in trust for me. And if it shall happen that the said debt or Summe of One Thousand, three hundred, thirty two pounds and tenn shillings or any part thereof shall be lost or cannot be received—yet my will and mind is that noe other part or my personall or reall Estate, Lands Messuages, or Tenements shall be charged with the said Legacies or either of them. And all the rest and residue of my personall Estate herein before by me not bequeathed I wholly devise, give and bequeath to my deare and loveinge wife, Dorothy Owen. And I doe make and ordaine my dear and loveinge wife the said Dorothy Owen full and sole Executrix of this my last Will and Testament. And in Testimony that this is my last Will and Testament I have hereunto sett my hand and seale this Three and Twentieth Day of March in the five and twentieth yeare[9] of the reigne of king Charles the second over England & Anno Domini 1682, JOHN OWEN.

This will containing two Sheets of Paper each sheet signed with the Testators owne hand and the last signed and sealed by him and then published and declared by the said Testator to be his last Will and Testament in the presence of us, JANE KINGDON, ELIZ. KINGDON, THO. OWEN, JOHN KING, ROBERT ROBINSON.[10]

---

[8] Jeffery Eliston was probably related to Matthew Eliston, ejected Rector of Stanford Rivers in Essex (see C.R.) and of the Grange, Little Coggeshall, which was licensed for Presbyterian services in 1672.

[9] This must be a copyist's mistake. 1682 was the 33rd year of Charles II (1649+33=1682).

[10] This copy is taken from the copy in Somerset House, London. Cf. *Index of Wills*, Vol. X (1676–1685), p. 252.

Printed and Manuscript Copies from which Correspondence has been taken

a. Printed.

Baxter R., *Reliquiae Baxterianae* (ed. M. Sylvester), 1696.

Burrows M. (ed.), *The Register of the Visitors of the University of Oxford from A.D. 1647 to A.D. 1658*, 1881.

Calendar of State Papers Domestic (1653–59).

Collections of the Massachusetts Historical Society, 2nd Series, Vol. II.

Dunlop R., *Ireland under the Commonwealth*, 1913.

Firth C. H. (ed.), *The Clarke Papers*, 1901, Vol. IV.

Gilbert T., *Vindiciae Supremi Dei Dominii*, 1655.

Hutchinson T., *Collection of Papers*, 1769.

Ivimey J., *A History of the English Baptists*, 1814, Vol. II.

Kendall G., *Fur Pro Tribunali*, 1657.

Lee M. H. (ed.), *Diaries and Letters of Philip Henry*, 1882.

Mather C., *Magnalia Christi Americana*, 1853.

Maurice M., *Monuments of Mercy*, 1729.

Moulin L. Du., *Oratio Auspicalis*, 1652.

Musarum Oxoniensum, 1654.

Palmer S., *Nonconformist's Memorial*, 1802, Vol. I.

Publications of the Colonial Society of Massachusetts, Vol. XI.

Russell T. (ed.), *The Works of John Owen*, 1826, Vol. I.

Thurloe J., *A Collection of State Papers* (ed. T. Birch), 1742, Vols. III & IV.

Toland J., *Letters of General Monck*, 1714.

Truthsbye T., *A Serious Letter to Dr John Owen*, 1660.

Wallis J., Johanni Wallisii, *Elenchus Geometriae Hobbianae*, 1655.

Whitfield H., *Strengthe out of Weaknesse*, 1652.

Wickens R., *A Compleat & Perfect Concordance*, 1655.

Williams J. B., *The Life of Philip Henry*, 1825.

b. Manuscript.

'Balliol College Register, 1514–1682' (in Balliol College, Oxford).
'Baxter MSS. 59, Vol. 5' (in Dr Williams's Library, London).
'Carte MS. 81' (in Bodleian Library, Oxford).
'Christ Church Chapter Book, 1647–1658' (in Christ Church, Oxford).
'Duraeana MS. EII 457 b, f. I' (in Staatsarchiv, Zurich).
'Lansdowne MS. 833' (in British Museum, London).
'Owen MS. Letters' (in New College, London).
'Rawlinson MSS. Lett. 52, 63, 109, A24, A26' (in Bodleian).
'Register of Convocation, 1647–1659' (in University Archives, Oxford).
'State Papers 18/75, 18/77, 18/179, 25/75, 25/76, 25/98' (Public Record Office, London).
'Tanner MSS. 52 & 69' (in Bodleian).
'MS. W.Pa. 23' (in University Archives, Oxford).
'MS. lviii' (in Massachusetts Archives, Boston).

Index of Correspondents

Allen James, 151
Arrowsmith John, 70, 72
Ashe Simeon, 70
Asty Robert, 161ff
Austin Samuel, 70

Balmford Samuel, 70
Barker Matthew, 114, 149, 153
Barron James, 102
Baxter Richard, 136ff
Bellingham Richard, 151
Beverley John, 96
Bolton Samuel, 70
Bridge William, 58, 114
Brooks Thomas, 106, 109, 153

Calamy Edmund, 70
Carter William, 58, 70
Caryl Joseph, 58, 70, 114, 146, 149, 153
Chandler Thomas, 106
Chauncy Charles, 151
Christ Church, 58, 72, 118
Church (Hitchin Indep.), 146
Church (Leadenhall Street), 170
Churches (Congregational), 66
Churches (European), 68
Clarke Samuel, 70
Cockayne George, 149, 153
Collins John, 149, 153
Commissioners (Irish), 50, 59
Conant John, 102
Cooper William, 70
Cornish Henry, 72
Croke Unton, 121
Cromwell Henry, 100
Cromwell Oliver, 52, 54, 62, 64, 65, 72, 74, 78, 84, 85, 92, 94, 98
Cromwell Richard, 100, 101, 121
Cudworth Ralph, 70

Danforth Samuel, 151
Danforth Thomas, 151
Davye Humphrey, 106
Dillingham William, 70
Down Thomas, 83
Drake Roger, 70

Edwards J., 58
Eliot John, 151, 153
Endicott John, 136

Farrar Edward, 81
Fiennes Nathaniel, 94
Fisher Samuel, 70
Fleetwood Charles, 158, 172ff
French Peter, 70, 72
Fuller John, 70

Gale George, 81
Gataker Thomas, 70
Gilbert Thomas, 91
Goffe William, 114
Goodwin Thomas, 58, 68, 70, 89, 146, 149
Gookin Daniel, 151
Gouge Robert, 106
Greenhill William, 58, 106, 109, 114, 149
Greenwood Daniel, 70
Griffith George, 58, 148, 149, 153

Harris Robert, 70
Hartopp Lady, 157
Hartopp Sir John, 159ff
Henry Philip, 79
Herbert Baron, 61
Hoar Leonard, 149
Holland C., 58
Hooke William, 106, 109, 114, 149, 153
Horton Thomas, 70
Howell Francis, 102

Juxon Nicholas, 106

Kendall George, 98
Knight Isaac, 114
Knowles John, 149, 153

Langbaine Gerard, 70
Langley Henry, 70
Lawrence Henry, 71, 88, 99
Lee Samuel, 149
Leverett John, 151
Litton A. P., 84
Lloyd Jenkin, 59

189

Lockyer Nicholas, 149
Loder John, 149, 153
London (City of), 59
Lowe Edward, 73

Maidstone John, 102
Manton Thomas, 70
Marshall Stephen, 70
Martyn Francis, 93
Massachusetts (Court of), 135, 145, 149
Mather Increase, 151
Mayo John, 151
Mead Matthew, 106, 149
Meriton John, 70
Michell William, 84
Mildmay H., 58
Minshall Richard, 70
Monck George, 105ff
Moulin Lewis Du, 51
Moulin Peter Du, 165

Nalton James, 70
Newman Robert, 106
Nichols Charles, 148
Nye Philip, 58, 68, 70, 106, 114, 146, 153

Onge Thomas, 106
Owen Thankful, 70, 102
Owen Thomas, 114
Oxenbridge John, 151
Oxford (University of), 63, 64, 76, 95, 119ff

Palmer Arthur, 149, 153
Parliament, 56, 58, 75
Petty Charnell, 70
Polhill Mrs, 168
Puleston Lady, 103

Roberts Nicholas, 106
Rogers Christopher, 72, 102, 119
Rowe John, 106, 114, 153
Russell Richard, 151

Salwey Richard, 104
Sangar Richard, 70
Savage Henry, 55
Scobell Henry, 106
Seaman Lazarus, 70
Sheppard Thomas, 151
Simpson Sidrach, 58, 68, 70
Smallwood Thomas, 106
Staunton Edmund, 70
Stone John, 114
Stoughton William, 151
Strong William, 58

Thacker Thomas, 151
Thornton John, 129ff
Thurloe John, 82, 84
Trenchard J., 58
Truthsbye Thomas, 116
Tuckney Anthony, 70
Tyng Edward, 151

Upton Ambrose, 72

Vane Henry, 58
Venning Ralph, 58, 149
Viner William, 106
Vines Richard, 70

Wall John, 72
Wallis John, 86
Westlake T., 84
Whalley Edward, 114
Wharton Lord, 155ff
Whitaker Thomas, 172
Whitfield Henry, 58
Whitelocke Bulstrode, 76
Wickens Robert, 89
Widdrington Sir Thomas, 77
Willer Jacob, 106
Wilkins John, 70
Wilkinson Canon Henry, 70, 72, 74, 102
Wilkinson Henry, 70
Witham Peter, 70
Wood Seth, 106, 114
Worthington John, 70

www.ingramcontent.com/pod-product-compliance
Lightning Source LLC
Chambersburg PA
CBHW050757160426
43192CB00010B/1555